FIRE POWER

CREATED BY **ROBERT KIRKMAN**
AND **CHRIS SAMNEE**

ROBERT KIRKMAN
Creator, Writer

CHRIS SAMNEE
Creator, Artist

FIRE POWER VOLUME 2: HOME FIRE
JANUARY 2021
ISBN: 978-1-5343-1718-5

Published by Image Comics, Inc. Office
of publication: 2701 NW Vaughn St., Ste.
780, Portland, OR 97210. Copyright ©
2021 Robert Kirkman, LLC and Chris
Samnee. Originally published in single
magazine format as FIRE POWER™ #1-6.
FIRE POWER™ (including all prominent
characters featured herein), its logo and
all character likenesses are trademarks of
Robert Kirkman, LLC and Chris Samnee,
unless otherwise noted. Image Comics® and
its logos are registered trademarks and
copyrights of Image Comics, Inc. All rights
reserved. No part of this publication may
be reproduced or transmitted in any form
or by any means (except for short excerpts
for review purposes) without the express
written permission of Image Comics, Inc.
All names, characters, events and locales
in this publication are entirely fictional.
Any resemblance to actual persons (living
or dead), events or places, without satiric
intent, is coincidental. Printed in the U.S.A.

SKYBOUND

FOR SKYBOUND ENTERTAINMENT

ROBERT KIRKMAN Chairman
DAVID ALPERT CEO
SEAN MACKIEWICZ SVP, Editor-in-Chief
SHAWN KIRKHAM SVP, Business Development
BRIAN HUNTINGTON VP, Online Content
SHAUNA WYNNE Publicity Director
ANDRES JUAREZ Art Director
ALEX ANTONE Senior Editor
JON MOISAN Editor
ARIELLE BASICH Associate Editor
CARINA TAYLOR Graphic Designer
PAUL SHIN Business Development Manager
JOHNNY O'DELL Social Media Manager
DAN PETERSEN Sr. Director of Operations & Events

Foreign Rights & Licensing Inquiries:
contact@skybound.com

SKYBOUND.COM

FOR IMAGE COMICS, INC.

TODD MCFARLANE President
JIM VALENTINO Vice President
MARC SILVESTRI Chief Executive Officer
ERIK LARSEN Chief Financial Officer
ROBERT KIRKMAN Chief Operating Officer
ERIC STEPHENSON Publisher / Chief Creative Officer
SHANNA MATUSZAK Editorial Coordinator
MARLA EIZIK Talent Liaison
NICOLE LAPALME Controller
LEANNA CAUNTER Accounting Analyst
SUE KORPELA Accounting & HR Manager
JEFF BOISON Director of Sales & Publishing Planning
DIRK WOOD Director of International Sales & Licensing
ALEX COX Director of Direct Market & Speciality Sales
CHLOE RAMOS-PETERSON Book Market & Library Sales Manager
EMILIO BAUTISTA Digital Sales Coordinator
KAT SALAZAR Director of PR & Marketing
DREW FITZGERALD Marketing Content Associate
HEATHER DOORNINK Production Director
DREW GILL Art Director
HILARY DILORETO Print Manager
TRICIA RAMOS Traffic Manager
ERIKA SCHNATZ Senior Production Artist
RYAN BREWER Production Artist
DEANNA PHELPS Production Artist

IMAGECOMICS.COM

MATT WILSON
Colorist

RUS WOOTON
Letterer

SEAN MACKIEWICZ
Editor

ANDRES JUAREZ
Logo, Collection Design

CARINA TAYLOR
Production

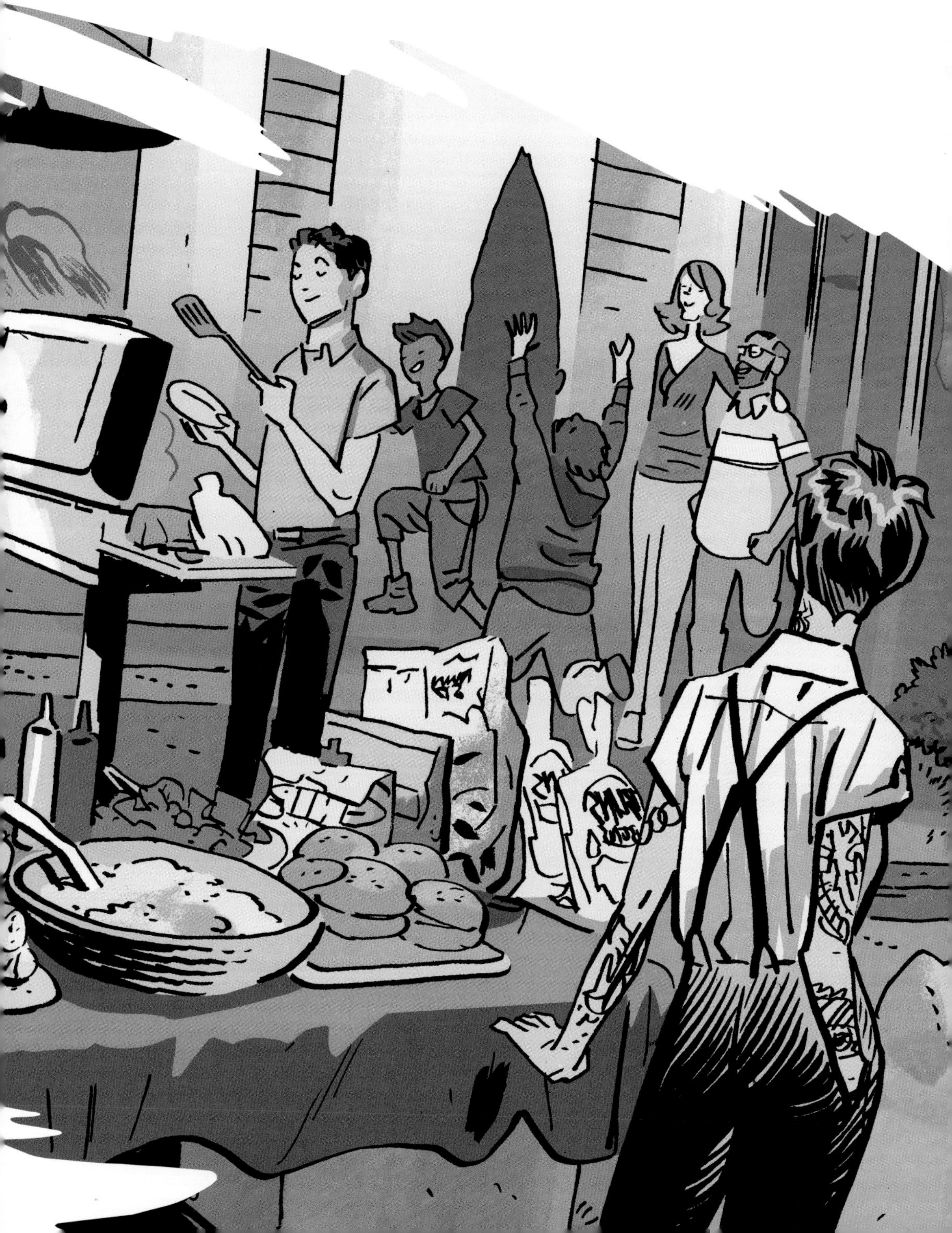

CHAPTER TWO

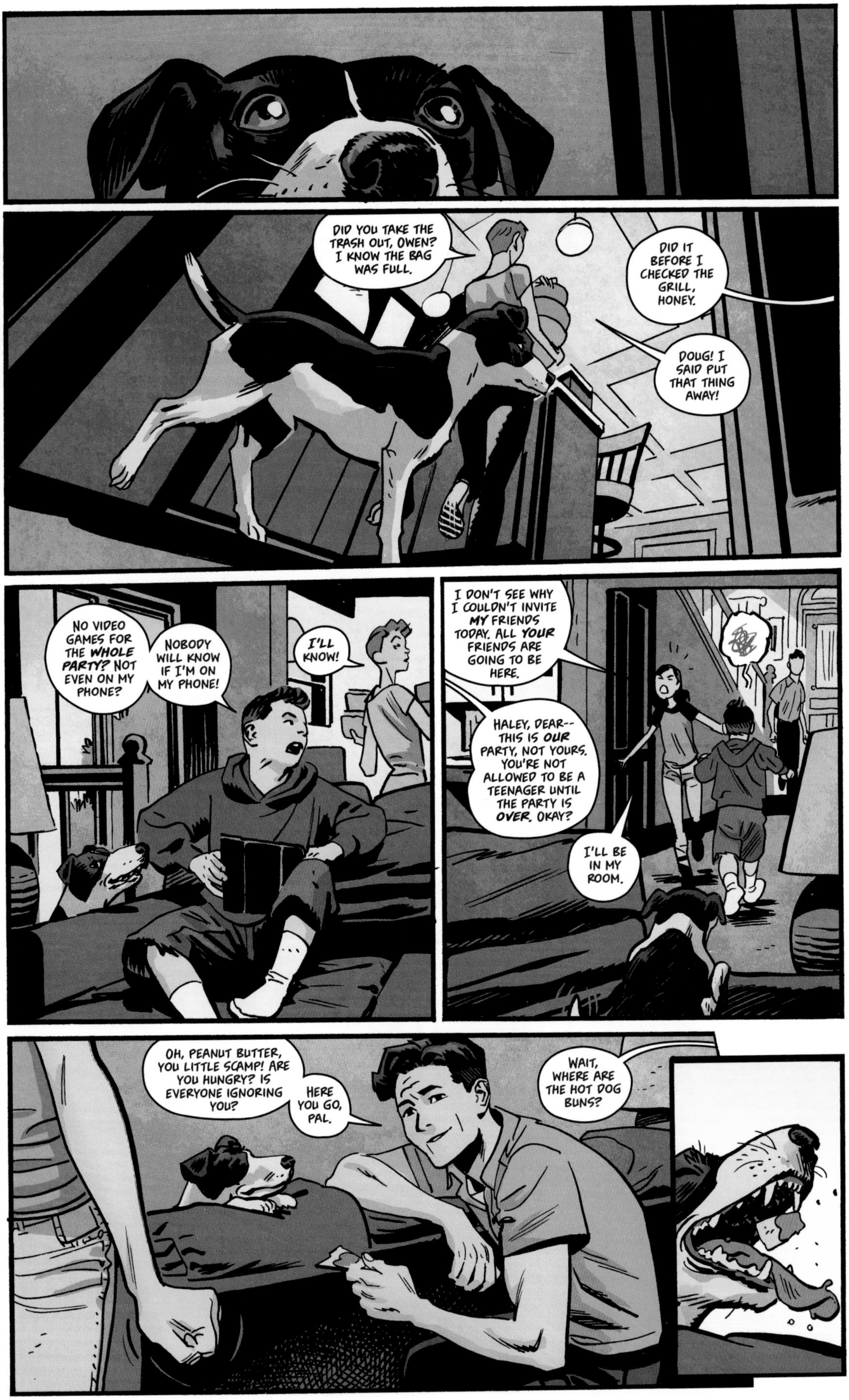
DID YOU TAKE THE TRASH OUT, OWEN? I KNOW THE BAG WAS FULL.
DID IT BEFORE I CHECKED THE GRILL, HONEY.
DOUG! I SAID PUT THAT THING AWAY!
NO VIDEO GAMES FOR THE WHOLE PARTY? NOT EVEN ON MY PHONE?
NOBODY WILL KNOW IF I'M ON MY PHONE!
I'LL KNOW!
I DON'T SEE WHY I COULDN'T INVITE MY FRIENDS TODAY. ALL YOUR FRIENDS ARE GOING TO BE HERE.
HALEY, DEAR-- THIS IS OUR PARTY, NOT YOURS. YOU'RE NOT ALLOWED TO BE A TEENAGER UNTIL THE PARTY IS OVER. OKAY?
I'LL BE IN MY ROOM.
OH, PEANUT BUTTER, YOU LITTLE SCAMP! ARE YOU HUNGRY? IS EVERYONE IGNORING YOU?
HERE YOU GO, PAL.
WAIT, WHERE ARE THE HOT DOG BUNS?

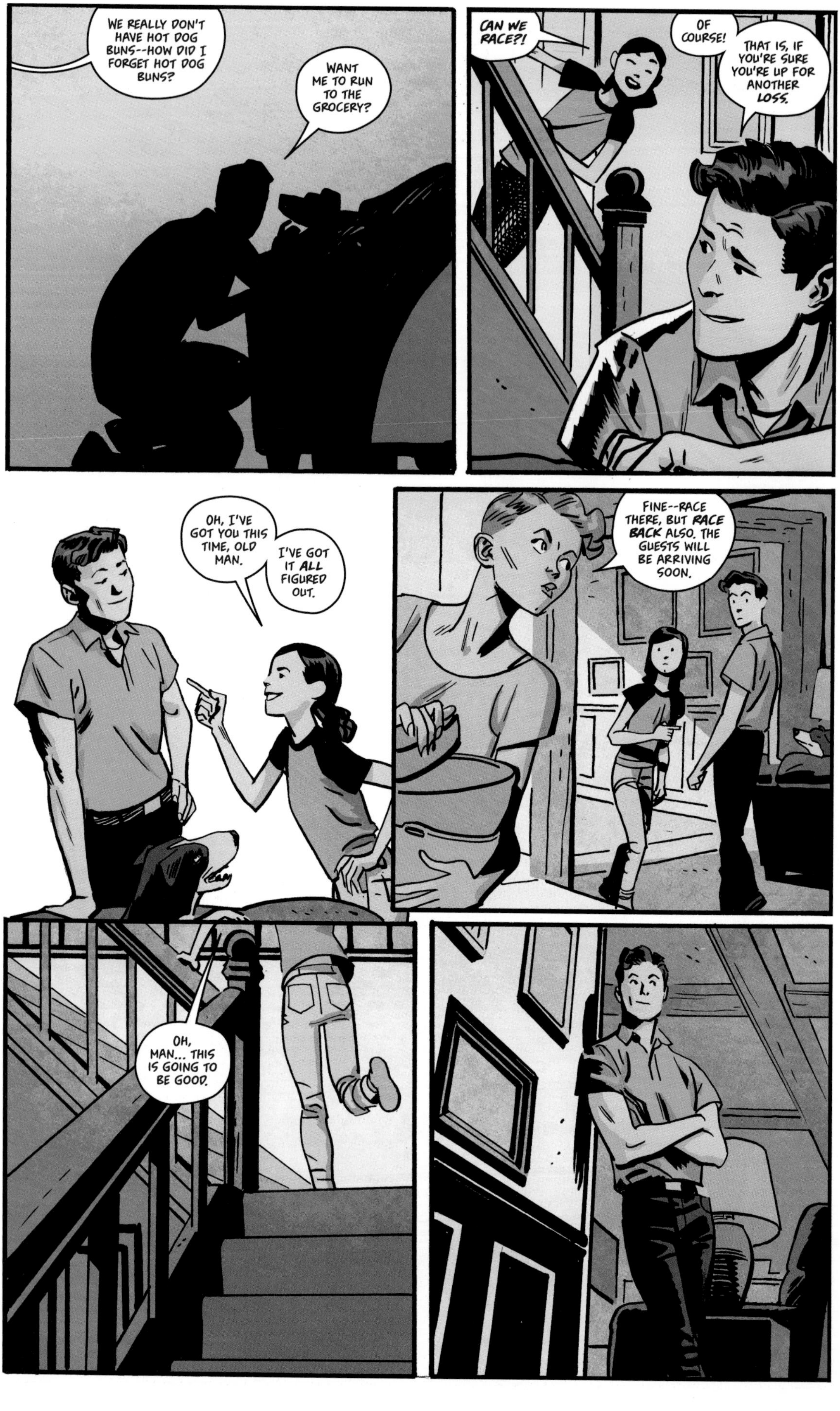

WE REALLY DON'T HAVE HOT DOG BUNS--HOW DID I FORGET HOT DOG BUNS?
WANT ME TO RUN TO THE GROCERY?
CAN WE RACE?!
OF COURSE!
THAT IS, IF YOU'RE SURE YOU'RE UP FOR ANOTHER LOSS.
OH, I'VE GOT YOU THIS TIME, OLD MAN.
I'VE GOT IT ALL FIGURED OUT.
FINE--RACE THERE, BUT RACE BACK ALSO. THE GUESTS WILL BE ARRIVING SOON.
OH, MAN... THIS IS GOING TO BE GOOD.

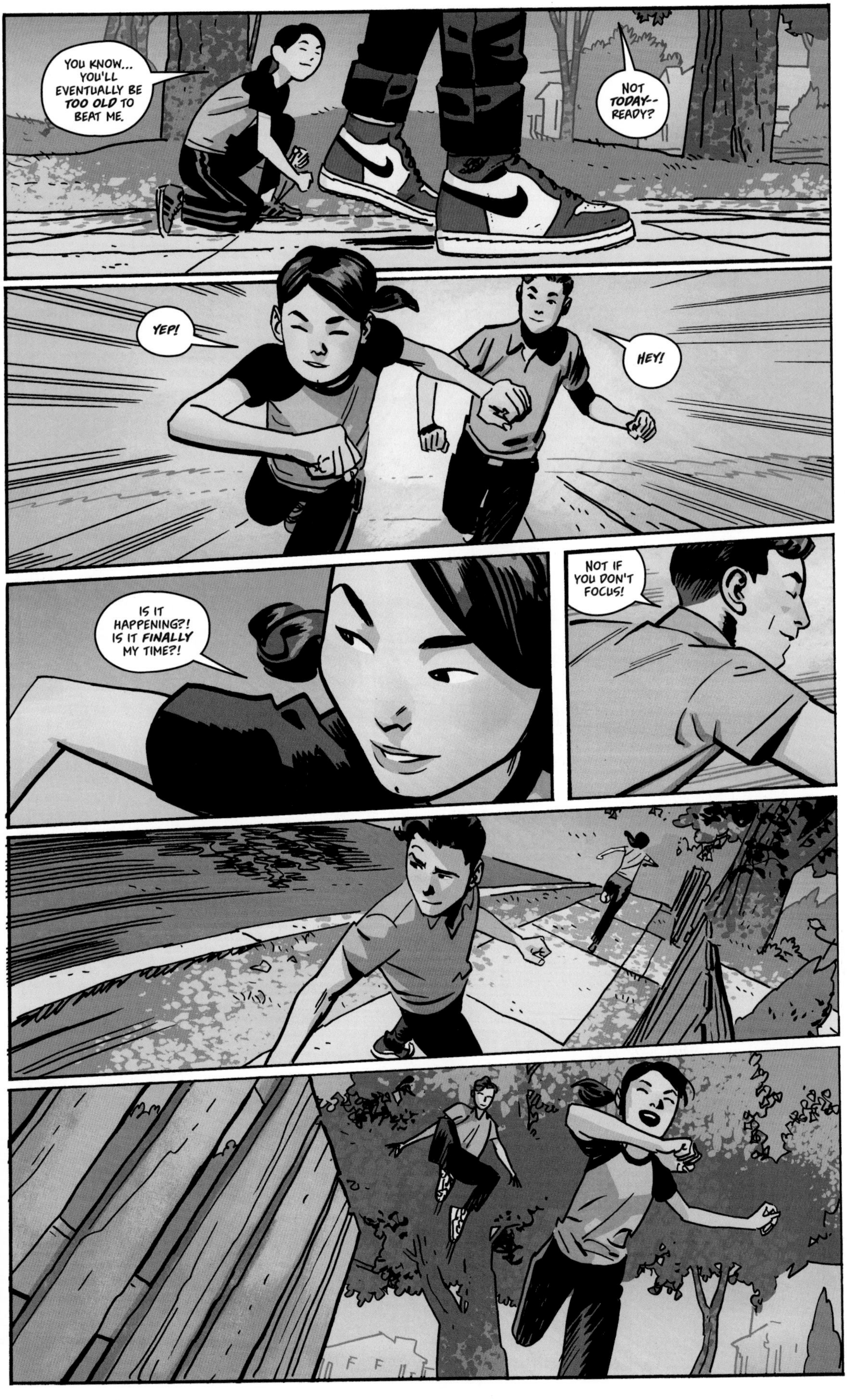
YOU KNOW... YOU'LL EVENTUALLY BE TOO OLD TO BEAT ME.
NOT TODAY-- READY?
YEP!
HEY!
IS IT HAPPENING?! IS IT FINALLY MY TIME?!
NOT IF YOU DON'T FOCUS!

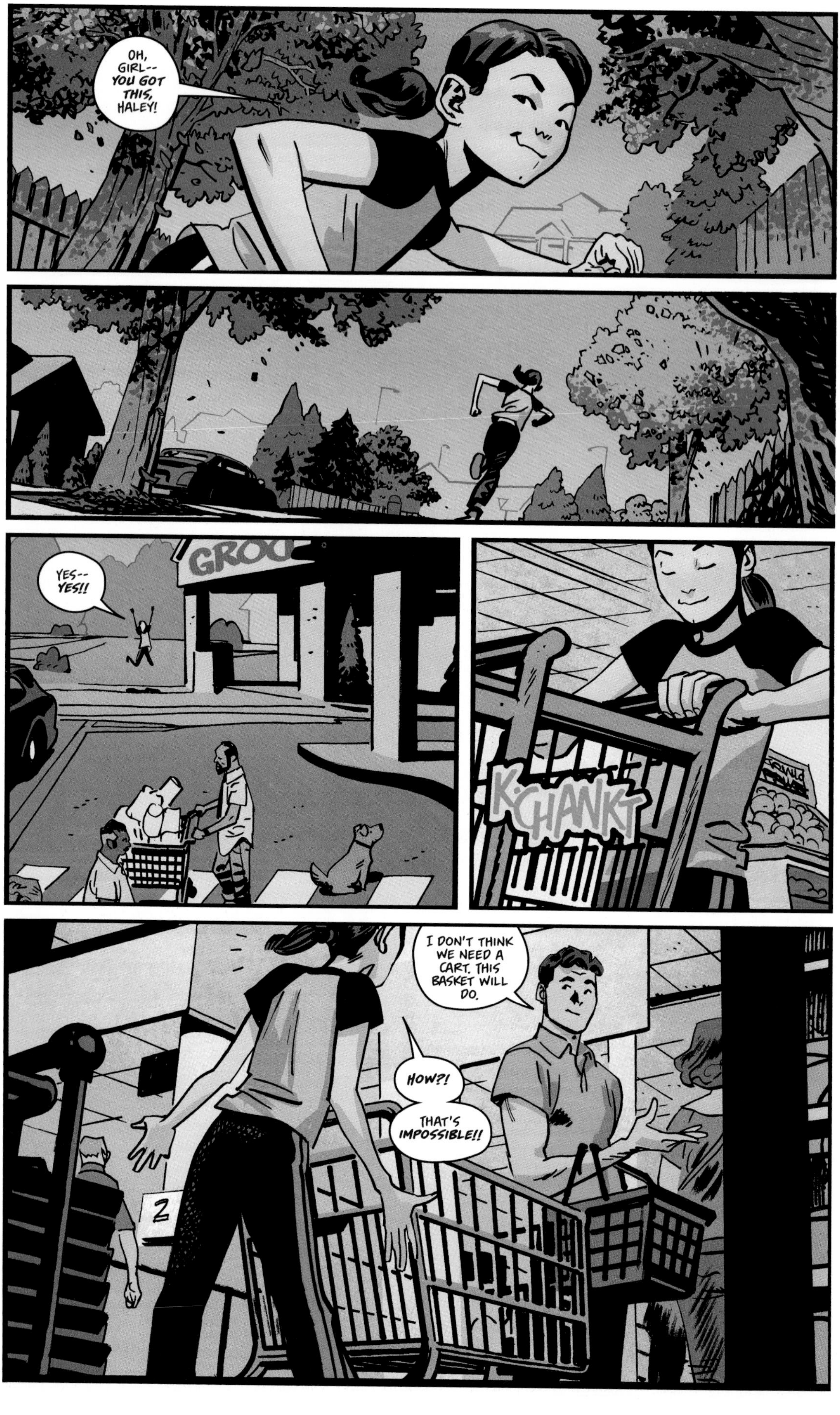
OH, GIRL-- YOU GOT THIS, HALEY!
GROC
YES-- YES!!
K-CHANKT
I DON'T THINK WE NEED A CART. THIS BASKET WILL DO.
HOW?!
THAT'S IMPOSSIBLE!!
2

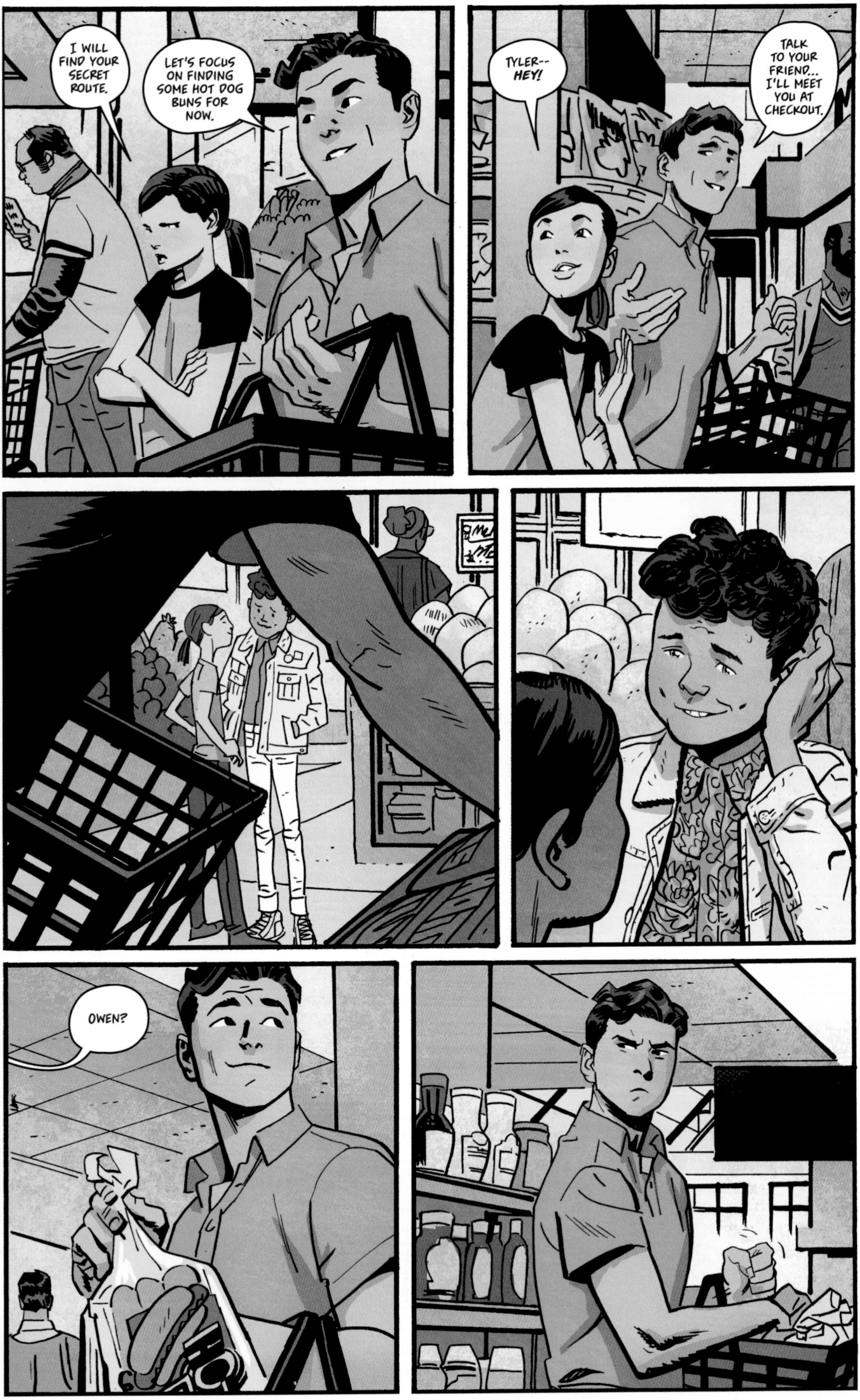
I WILL FIND YOUR SECRET ROUTE.
LET'S FOCUS ON FINDING SOME HOT DOG BUNS FOR NOW.
TYLER-- HEY!
TALK TO YOUR FRIEND... I'LL MEET YOU AT CHECKOUT.
OWEN?

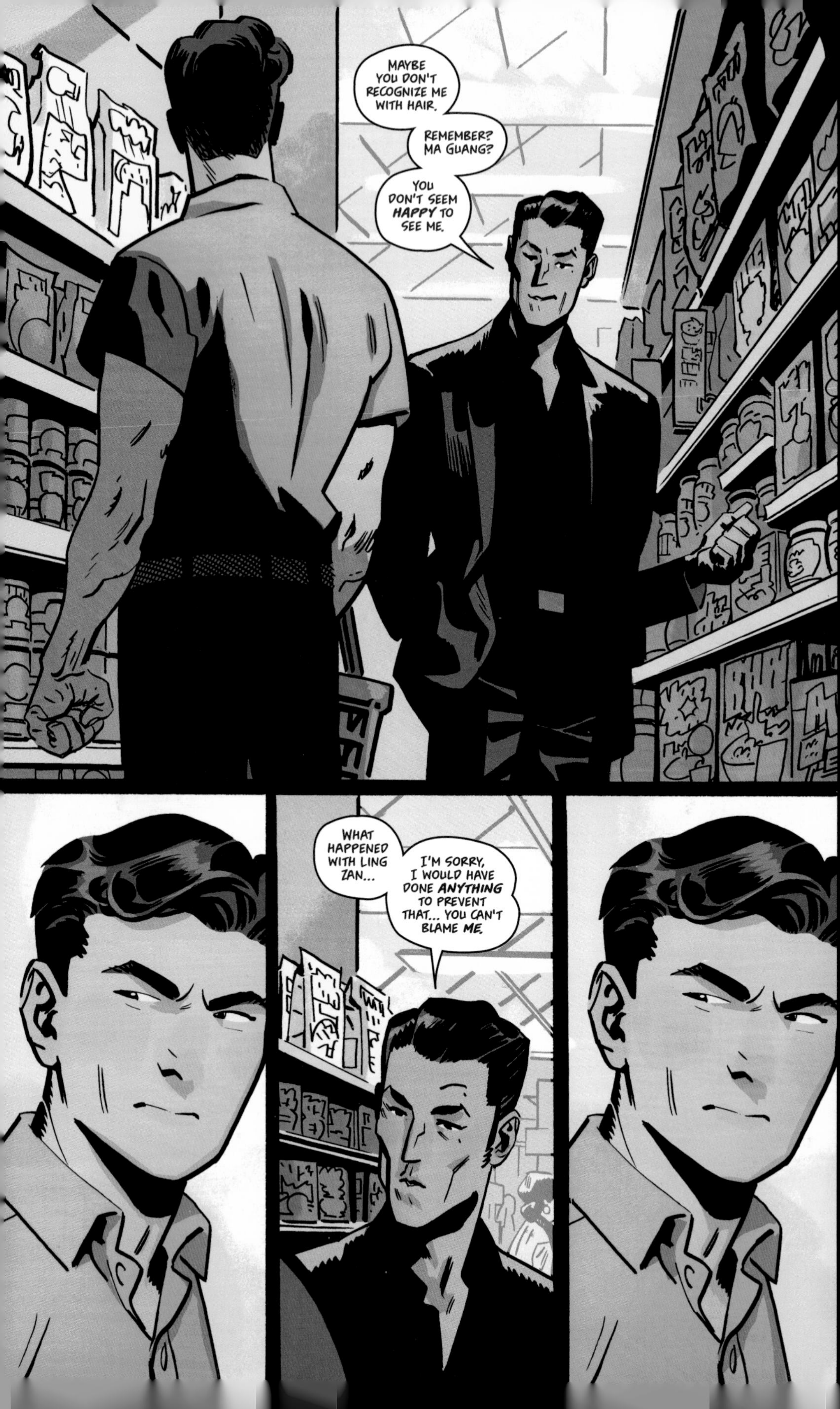
MAYBE YOU DON'T RECOGNIZE ME WITH HAIR.
REMEMBER? MA GUANG?
YOU DON'T SEEM HAPPY TO SEE ME.
WHAT HAPPENED WITH LING ZAN...
I'M SORRY, I WOULD HAVE DONE ANYTHING TO PREVENT THAT... YOU CAN'T BLAME ME.

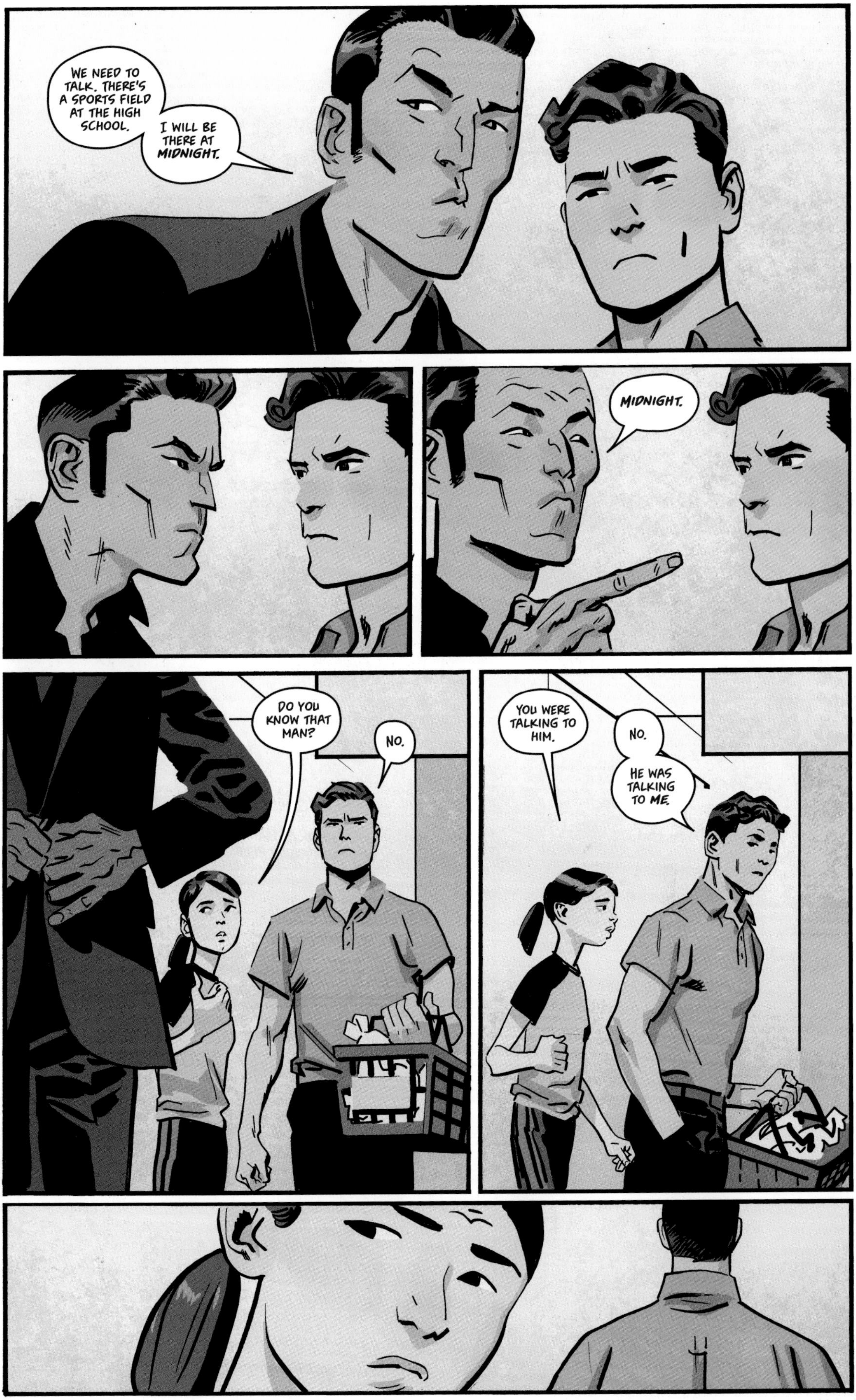
WE NEED TO TALK. THERE'S A SPORTS FIELD AT THE HIGH SCHOOL.
I WILL BE THERE AT MIDNIGHT.
MIDNIGHT.
DO YOU KNOW THAT MAN?
NO.
YOU WERE TALKING TO HIM.
NO.
HE WAS TALKING TO ME.

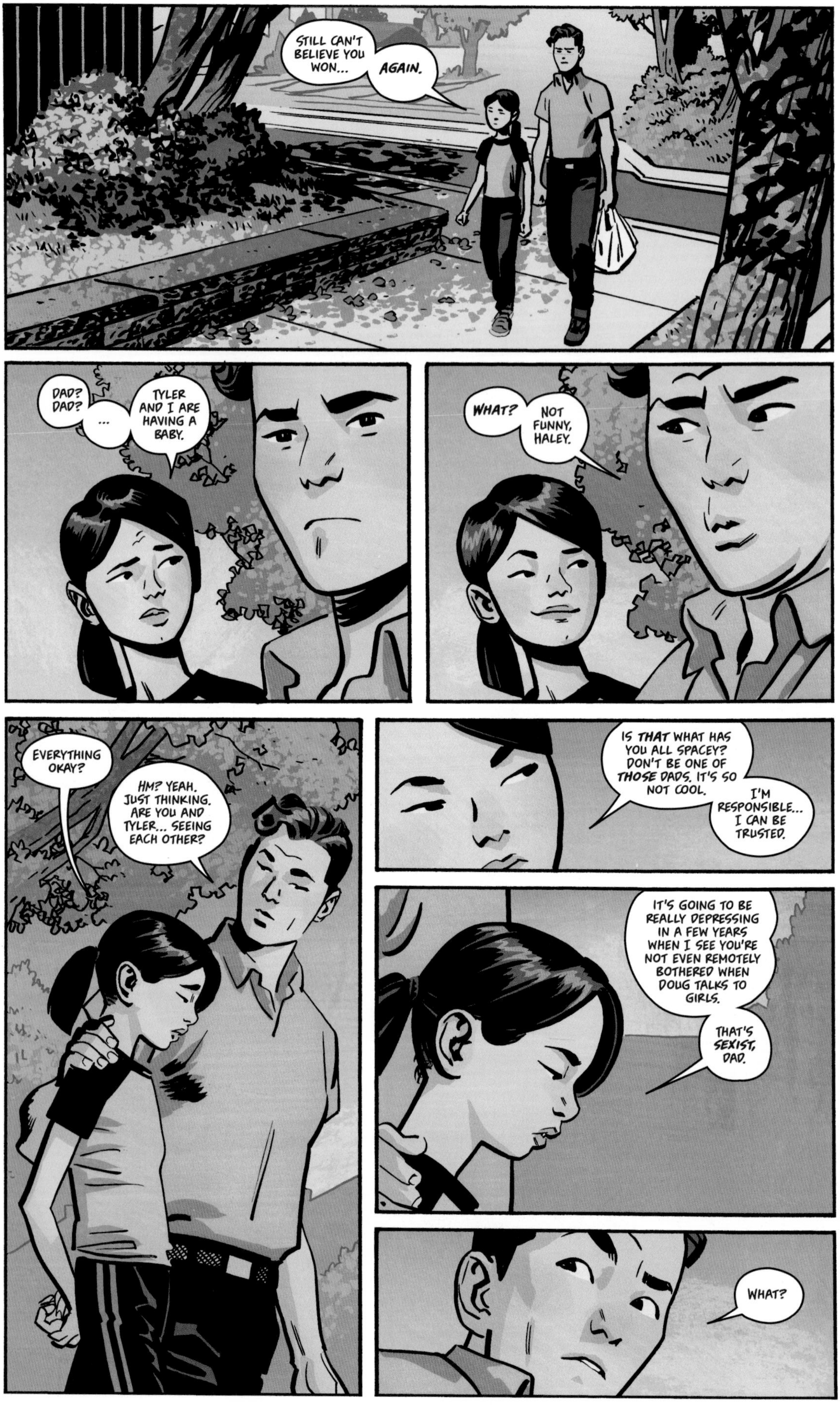
STILL CAN'T BELIEVE YOU WON...
AGAIN.
DAD? DAD?
...
TYLER AND I ARE HAVING A BABY.
WHAT?
NOT FUNNY, HALEY.
EVERYTHING OKAY?
HM? YEAH. JUST THINKING. ARE YOU AND TYLER... SEEING EACH OTHER?
IS THAT WHAT HAS YOU ALL SPACEY? DON'T BE ONE OF THOSE DADS. IT'S SO NOT COOL.
I'M RESPONSIBLE... I CAN BE TRUSTED.
IT'S GOING TO BE REALLY DEPRESSING IN A FEW YEARS WHEN I SEE YOU'RE NOT EVEN REMOTELY BOTHERED WHEN DOUG TALKS TO GIRLS.
THAT'S SEXIST, DAD.
WHAT?

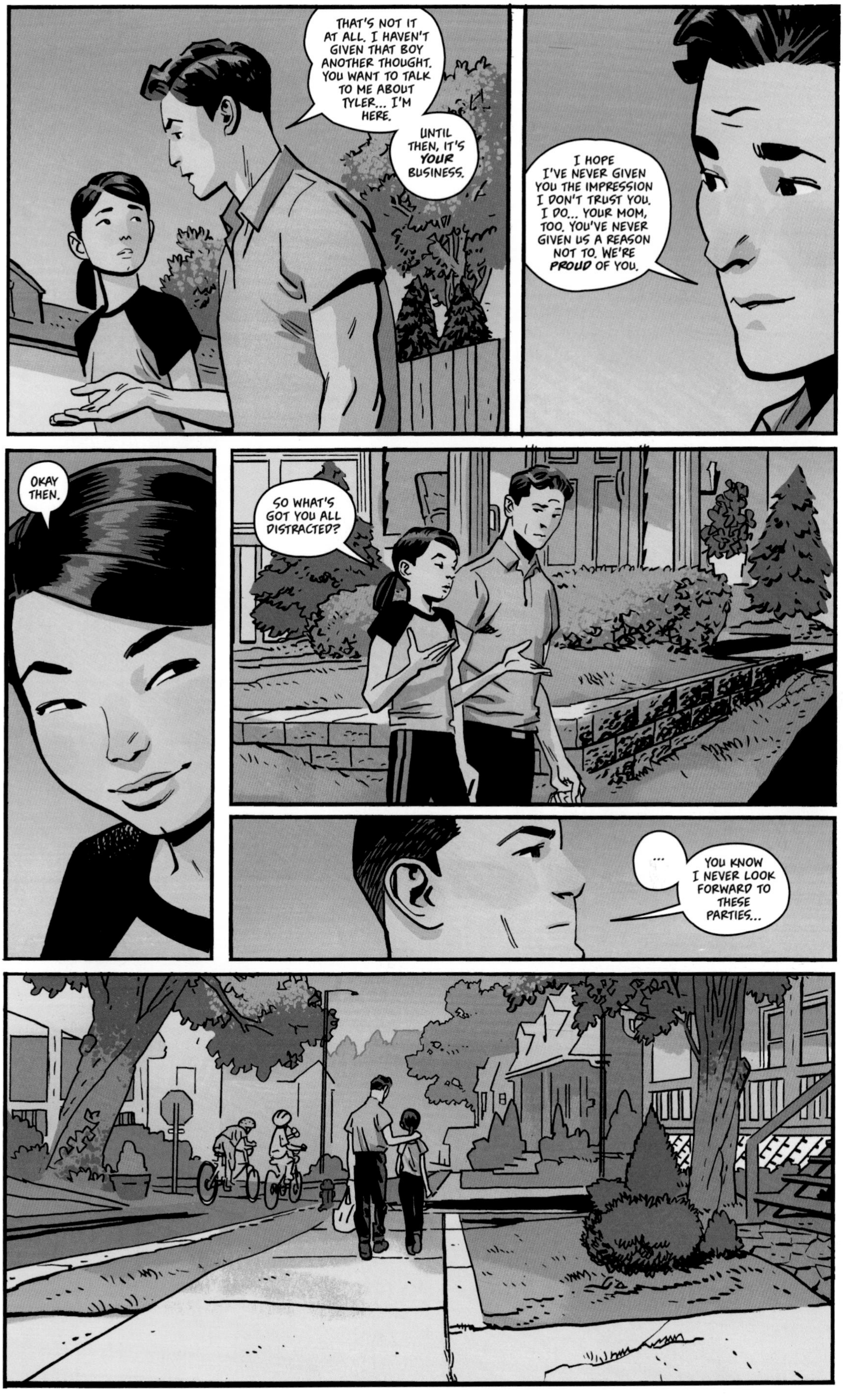
THAT'S NOT IT AT ALL. I HAVEN'T GIVEN THAT BOY ANOTHER THOUGHT. YOU WANT TO TALK TO ME ABOUT TYLER... I'M HERE.
UNTIL THEN, IT'S ***YOUR*** BUSINESS.
I HOPE I'VE NEVER GIVEN YOU THE IMPRESSION I DON'T TRUST YOU. I DO... YOUR MOM, TOO. YOU'VE NEVER GIVEN US A REASON NOT TO. WE'RE ***PROUD*** OF YOU.
OKAY THEN.
SO WHAT'S GOT YOU ALL DISTRACTED?
...
YOU KNOW I NEVER LOOK FORWARD TO THESE PARTIES...

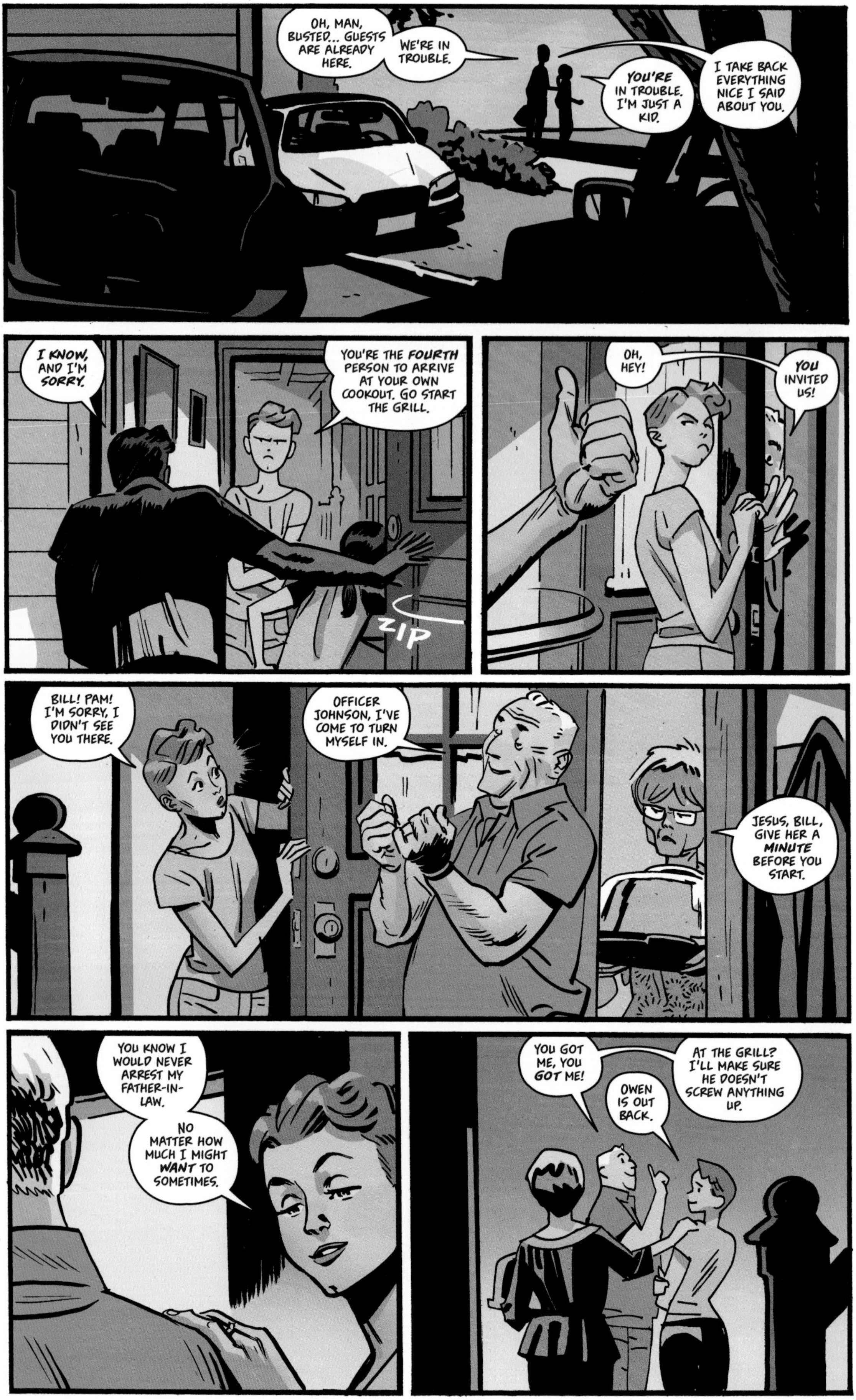
OH, MAN, BUSTED... GUESTS ARE ALREADY HERE.
WE'RE IN TROUBLE.
YOU'RE IN TROUBLE. I'M JUST A KID.
I TAKE BACK EVERYTHING NICE I SAID ABOUT YOU.
I KNOW, AND I'M SORRY.
YOU'RE THE FOURTH PERSON TO ARRIVE AT YOUR OWN COOKOUT. GO START THE GRILL.
ZIP
OH, HEY!
YOU INVITED US!
BILL! PAM! I'M SORRY, I DIDN'T SEE YOU THERE.
OFFICER JOHNSON, I'VE COME TO TURN MYSELF IN.
JESUS, BILL, GIVE HER A MINUTE BEFORE YOU START.
YOU KNOW I WOULD NEVER ARREST MY FATHER-IN-LAW.
NO MATTER HOW MUCH I MIGHT WANT TO SOMETIMES.
YOU GOT ME, YOU GOT ME!
OWEN IS OUT BACK.
AT THE GRILL? I'LL MAKE SURE HE DOESN'T SCREW ANYTHING UP.

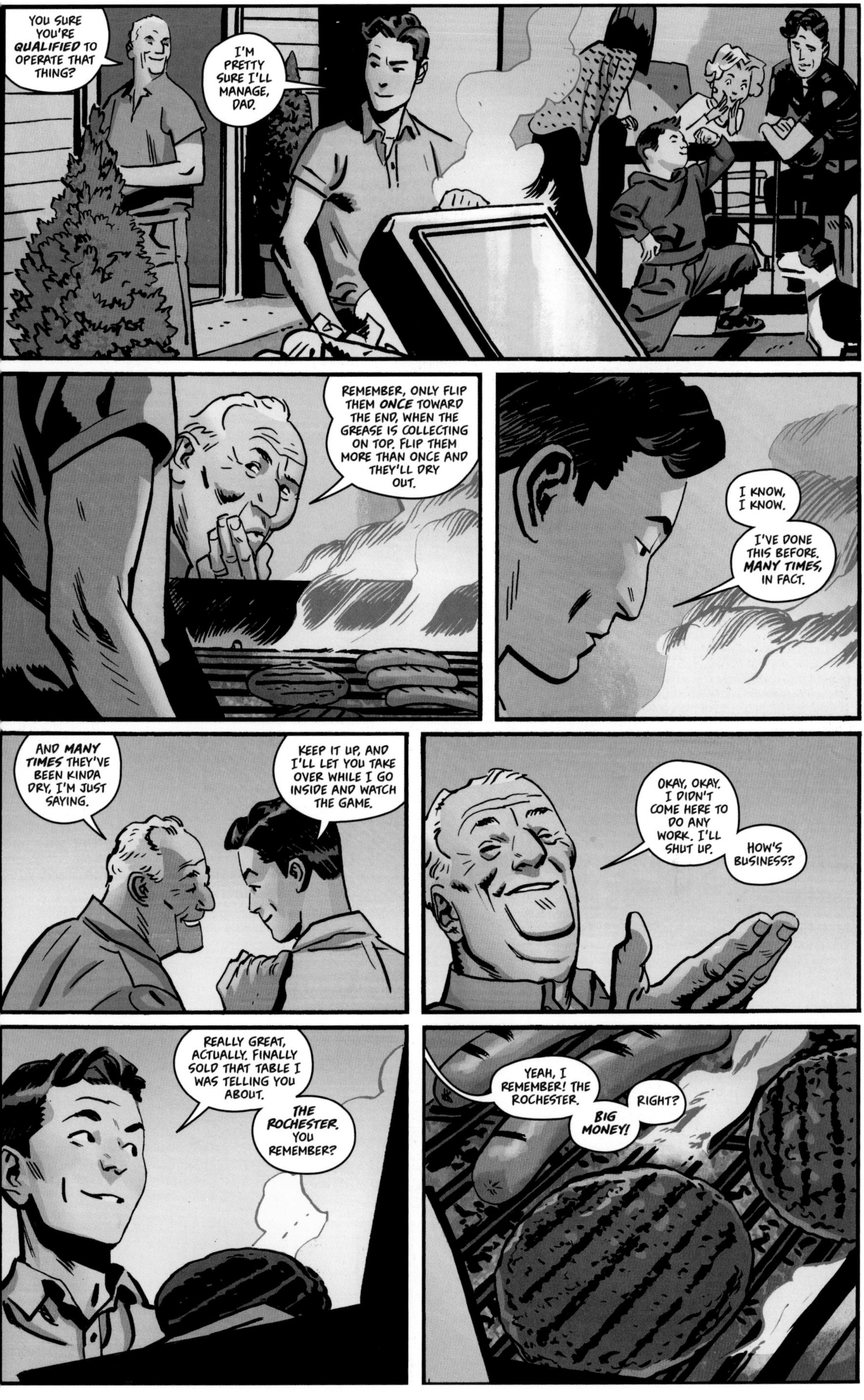
YOU SURE YOU'RE QUALIFIED TO OPERATE THAT THING?
I'M PRETTY SURE I'LL MANAGE, DAD.
REMEMBER, ONLY FLIP THEM ONCE TOWARD THE END, WHEN THE GREASE IS COLLECTING ON TOP. FLIP THEM MORE THAN ONCE AND THEY'LL DRY OUT.
I KNOW, I KNOW.
I'VE DONE THIS BEFORE. MANY TIMES, IN FACT.
AND MANY TIMES THEY'VE BEEN KINDA DRY, I'M JUST SAYING.
KEEP IT UP, AND I'LL LET YOU TAKE OVER WHILE I GO INSIDE AND WATCH THE GAME.
OKAY, OKAY. I DIDN'T COME HERE TO DO ANY WORK. I'LL SHUT UP.
HOW'S BUSINESS?
REALLY GREAT, ACTUALLY. FINALLY SOLD THAT TABLE I WAS TELLING YOU ABOUT.
THE ROCHESTER. YOU REMEMBER?
YEAH, I REMEMBER! THE ROCHESTER.
RIGHT?
BIG MONEY!

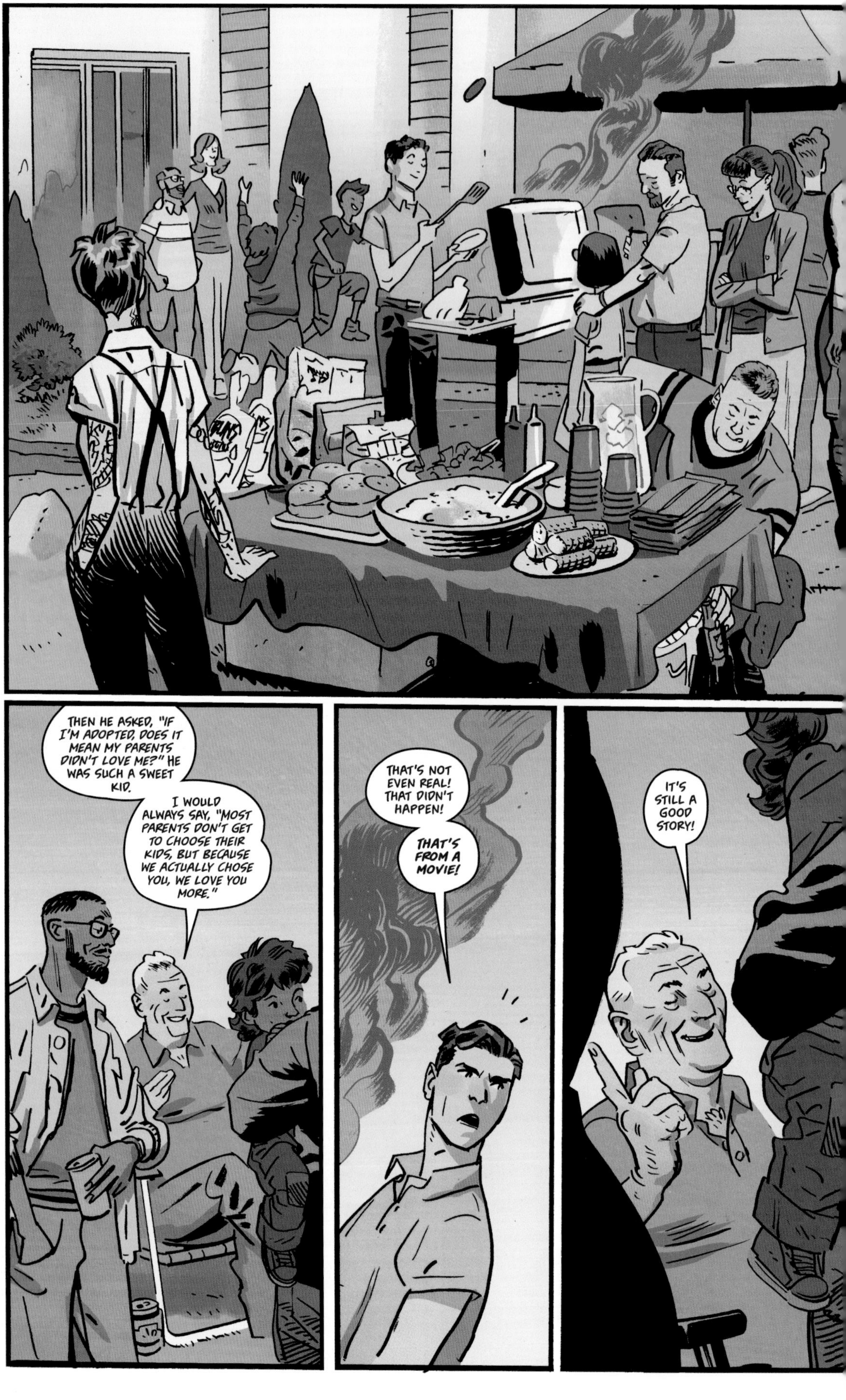
THEN HE ASKED, "IF I'M ADOPTED, DOES IT MEAN MY PARENTS DIDN'T LOVE ME?" HE WAS SUCH A SWEET KID.
I WOULD ALWAYS SAY, "MOST PARENTS DON'T GET TO CHOOSE THEIR KIDS, BUT BECAUSE WE ACTUALLY CHOSE YOU, WE LOVE YOU MORE."
THAT'S NOT EVEN REAL! THAT DIDN'T HAPPEN!
THAT'S FROM A MOVIE!
IT'S STILL A GOOD STORY!

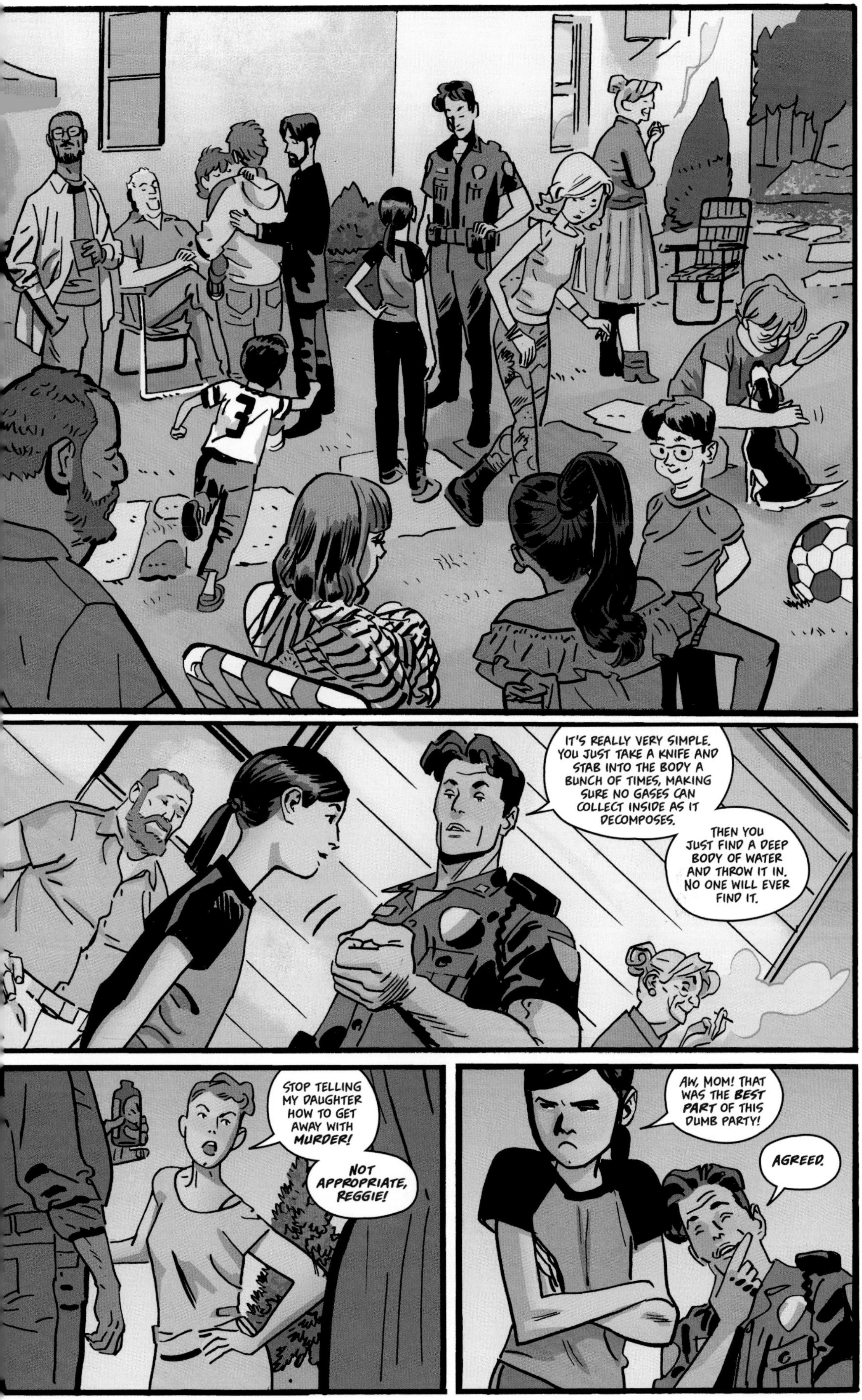
IT'S REALLY VERY SIMPLE. YOU JUST TAKE A KNIFE AND STAB INTO THE BODY A BUNCH OF TIMES, MAKING SURE NO GASES CAN COLLECT INSIDE AS IT DECOMPOSES.
THEN YOU JUST FIND A DEEP BODY OF WATER AND THROW IT IN. NO ONE WILL EVER FIND IT.
STOP TELLING MY DAUGHTER HOW TO GET AWAY WITH MURDER!
NOT APPROPRIATE, REGGIE!
AW, MOM! THAT WAS THE BEST PART OF THIS DUMB PARTY!
AGREED.

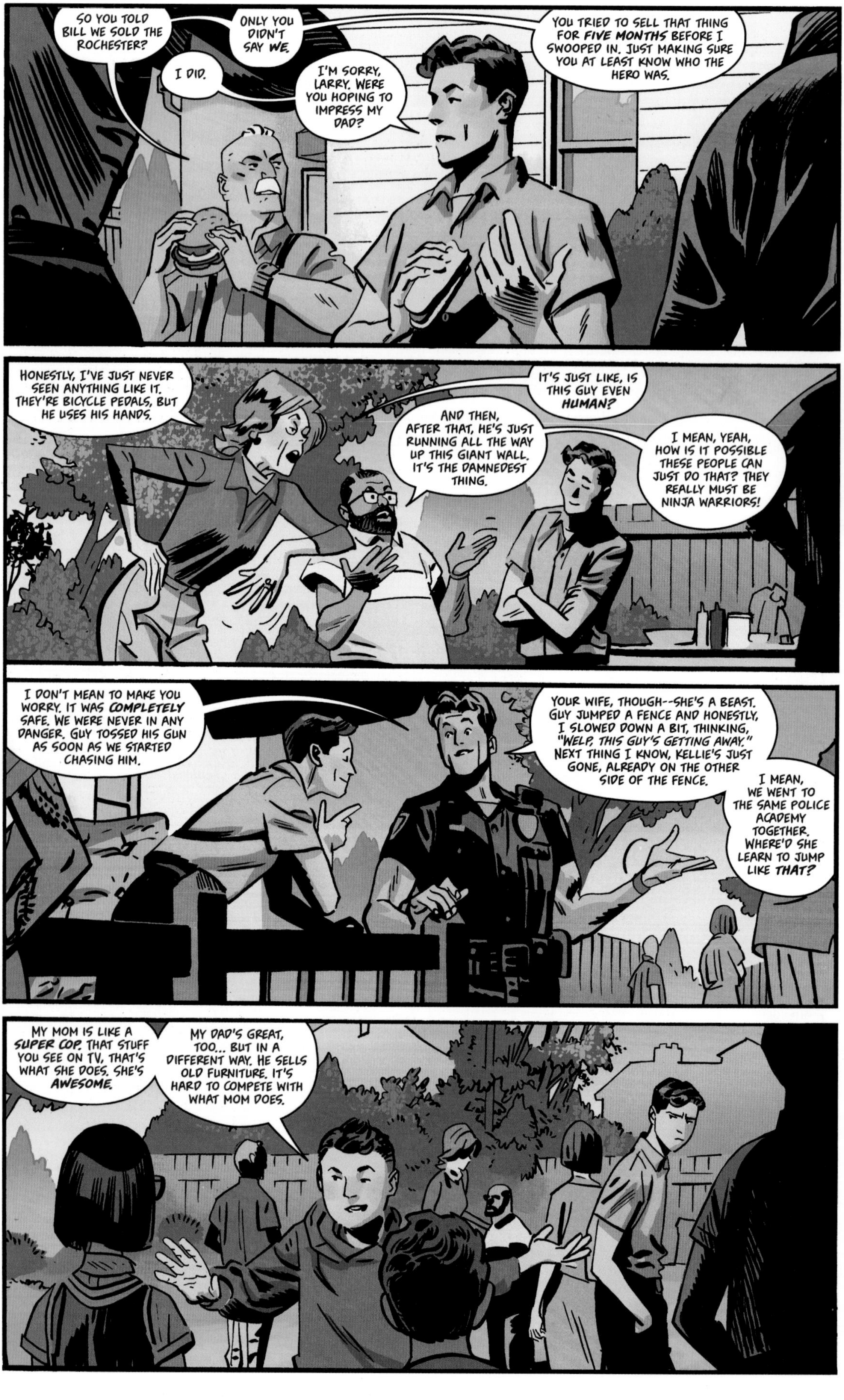
SO YOU TOLD BILL WE SOLD THE ROCHESTER?
I DID.
ONLY YOU DIDN'T SAY WE.
I'M SORRY, LARRY. WERE YOU HOPING TO IMPRESS MY DAD?
YOU TRIED TO SELL THAT THING FOR FIVE MONTHS BEFORE I SWOOPED IN. JUST MAKING SURE YOU AT LEAST KNOW WHO THE HERO WAS.
HONESTLY, I'VE JUST NEVER SEEN ANYTHING LIKE IT. THEY'RE BICYCLE PEDALS, BUT HE USES HIS HANDS.
IT'S JUST LIKE, IS THIS GUY EVEN HUMAN?
AND THEN, AFTER THAT, HE'S JUST RUNNING ALL THE WAY UP THIS GIANT WALL. IT'S THE DAMNEDEST THING.
I MEAN, YEAH, HOW IS IT POSSIBLE THESE PEOPLE CAN JUST DO THAT? THEY REALLY MUST BE NINJA WARRIORS!
I DON'T MEAN TO MAKE YOU WORRY. IT WAS COMPLETELY SAFE. WE WERE NEVER IN ANY DANGER. GUY TOSSED HIS GUN AS SOON AS WE STARTED CHASING HIM.
YOUR WIFE, THOUGH--SHE'S A BEAST. GUY JUMPED A FENCE AND HONESTLY, I SLOWED DOWN A BIT, THINKING, "WELP, THIS GUY'S GETTING AWAY." NEXT THING I KNOW, KELLIE'S JUST GONE, ALREADY ON THE OTHER SIDE OF THE FENCE.
I MEAN, WE WENT TO THE SAME POLICE ACADEMY TOGETHER. WHERE'D SHE LEARN TO JUMP LIKE THAT?
MY MOM IS LIKE A SUPER COP. THAT STUFF YOU SEE ON TV, THAT'S WHAT SHE DOES. SHE'S AWESOME.
MY DAD'S GREAT, TOO... BUT IN A DIFFERENT WAY. HE SELLS OLD FURNITURE. IT'S HARD TO COMPETE WITH WHAT MOM DOES.

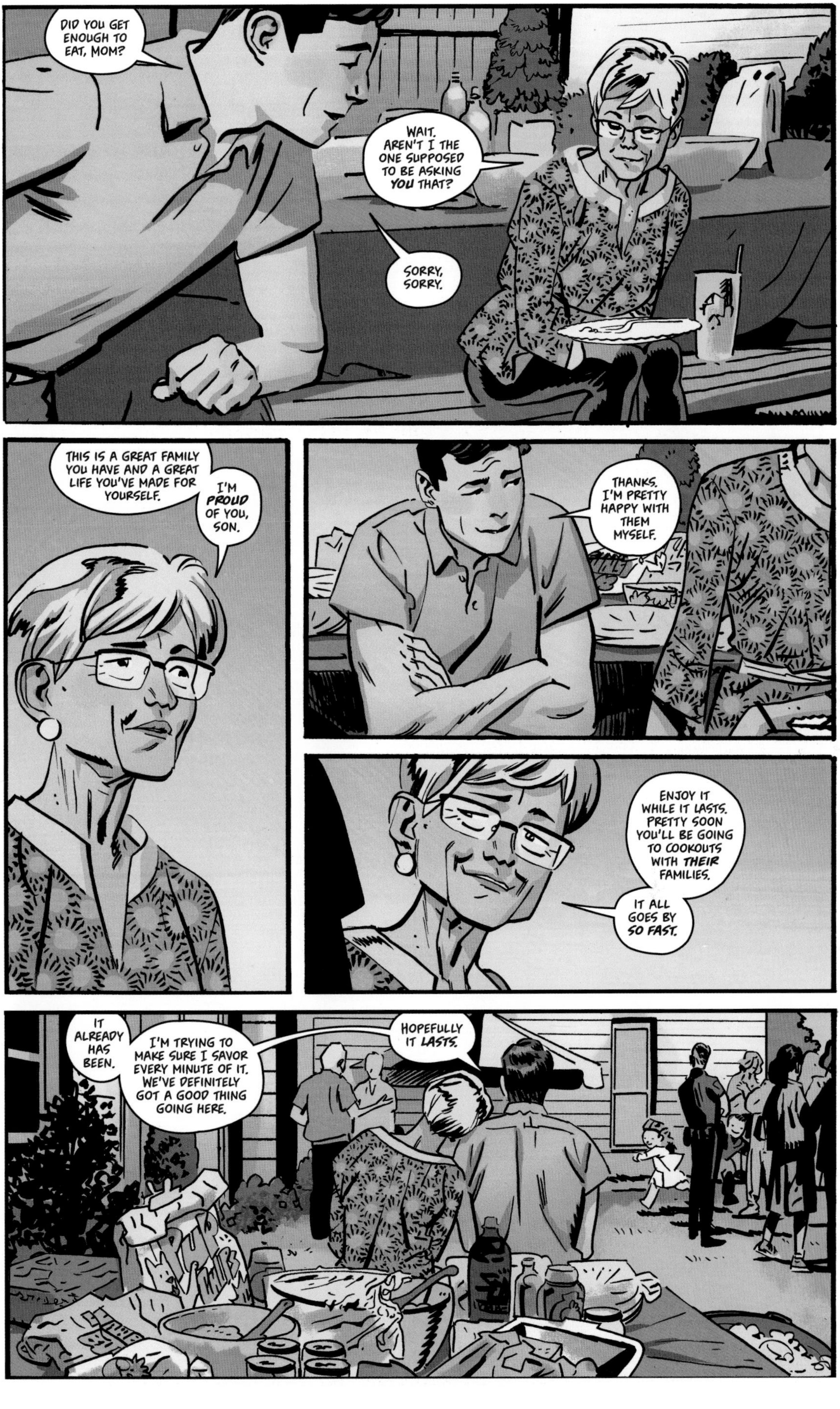
DID YOU GET ENOUGH TO EAT, MOM?
WAIT. AREN'T I THE ONE SUPPOSED TO BE ASKING YOU THAT?
SORRY, SORRY.
THIS IS A GREAT FAMILY YOU HAVE AND A GREAT LIFE YOU'VE MADE FOR YOURSELF.
I'M PROUD OF YOU, SON.
THANKS. I'M PRETTY HAPPY WITH THEM MYSELF.
ENJOY IT WHILE IT LASTS. PRETTY SOON YOU'LL BE GOING TO COOKOUTS WITH THEIR FAMILIES.
IT ALL GOES BY SO FAST.
IT ALREADY HAS BEEN.
I'M TRYING TO MAKE SURE I SAVOR EVERY MINUTE OF IT. WE'VE DEFINITELY GOT A GOOD THING GOING HERE.
HOPEFULLY IT LASTS.

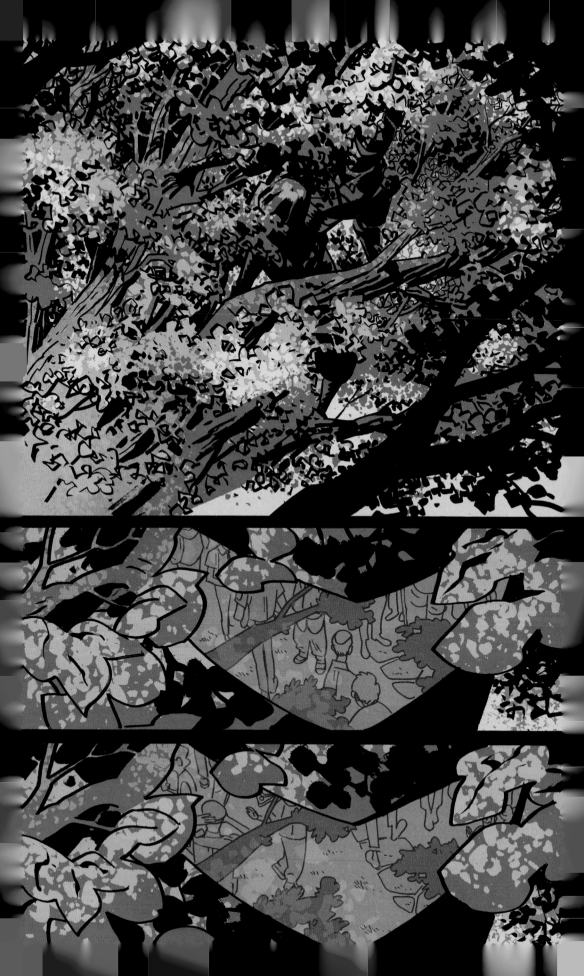

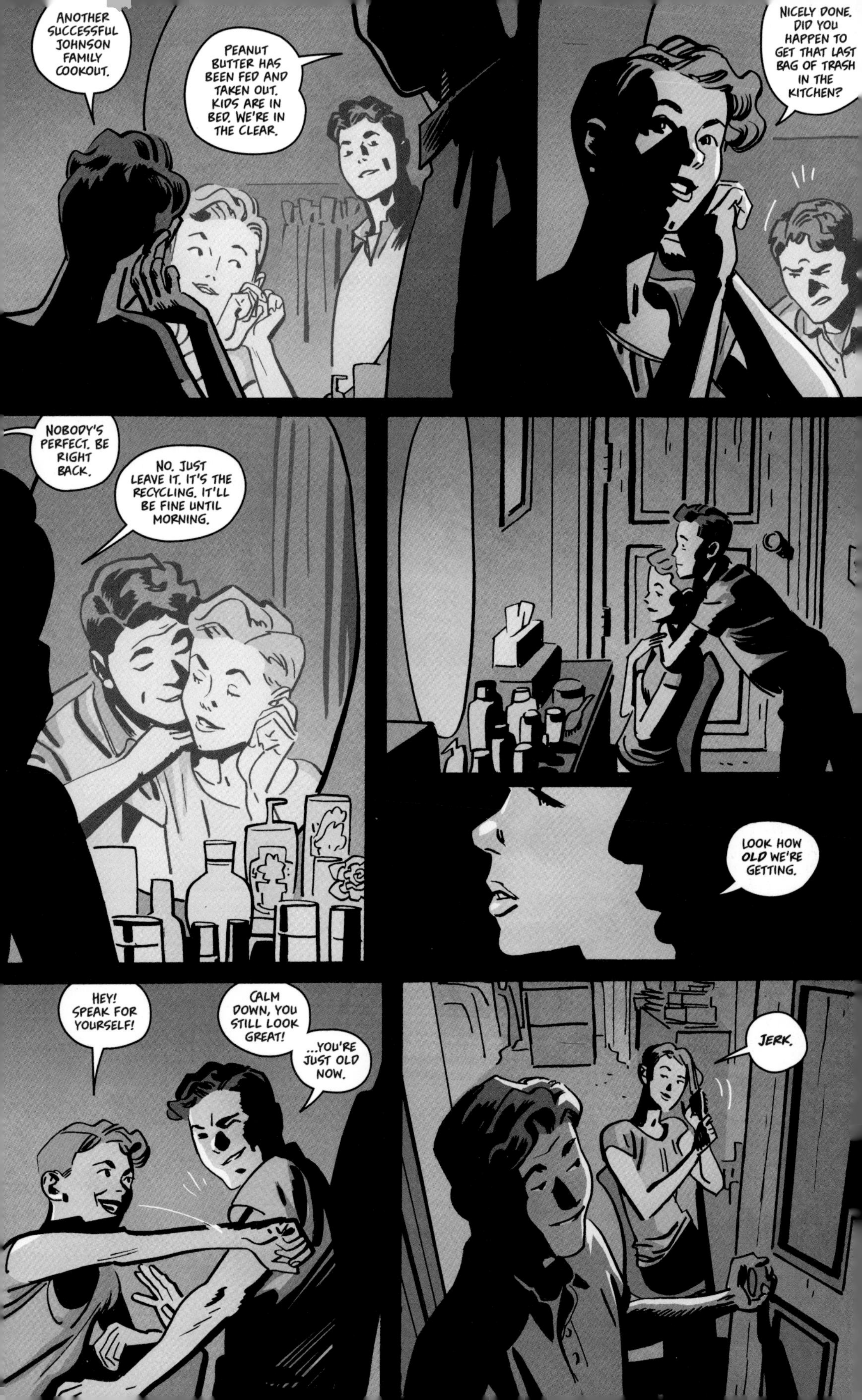
ANOTHER SUCCESSFUL JOHNSON FAMILY COOKOUT.
PEANUT BUTTER HAS BEEN FED AND TAKEN OUT. KIDS ARE IN BED. WE'RE IN THE CLEAR.
NICELY DONE. DID YOU HAPPEN TO GET THAT LAST BAG OF TRASH IN THE KITCHEN?
NOBODY'S PERFECT. BE RIGHT BACK.
NO. JUST LEAVE IT. IT'S THE RECYCLING. IT'LL BE FINE UNTIL MORNING.
LOOK HOW OLD WE'RE GETTING.
HEY! SPEAK FOR YOURSELF!
CALM DOWN, YOU STILL LOOK GREAT!
...YOU'RE JUST OLD NOW.
JERK.

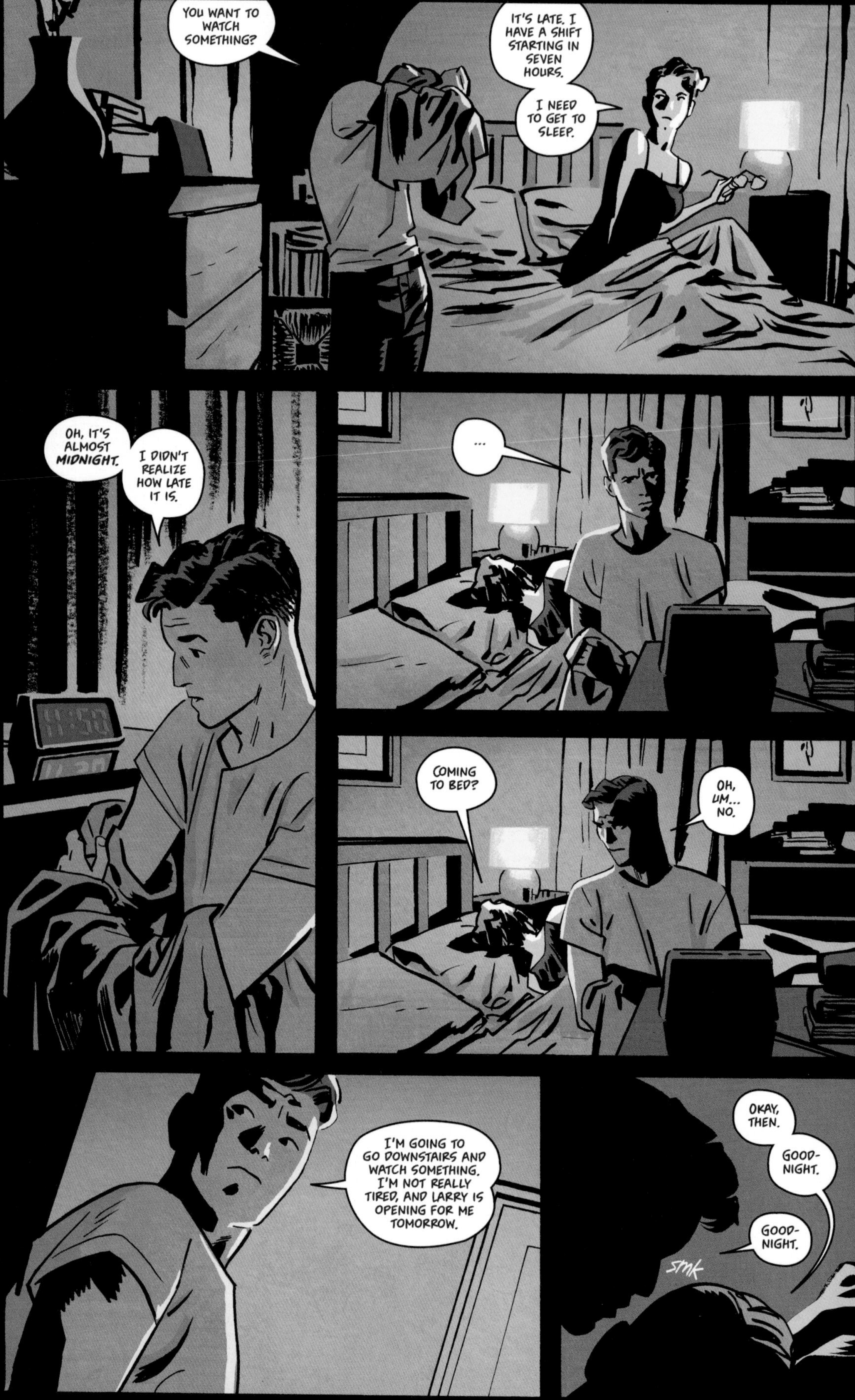

YOU WANT TO WATCH SOMETHING?
IT'S LATE. I HAVE A SHIFT STARTING IN SEVEN HOURS.
I NEED TO GET TO SLEEP.
OH, IT'S ALMOST MIDNIGHT.
I DIDN'T REALIZE HOW LATE IT IS.
...
COMING TO BED?
OH, UM... NO.
I'M GOING TO GO DOWNSTAIRS AND WATCH SOMETHING. I'M NOT REALLY TIRED, AND LARRY IS OPENING FOR ME TOMORROW.
OKAY, THEN.
GOOD-NIGHT.
GOOD-NIGHT.
smk

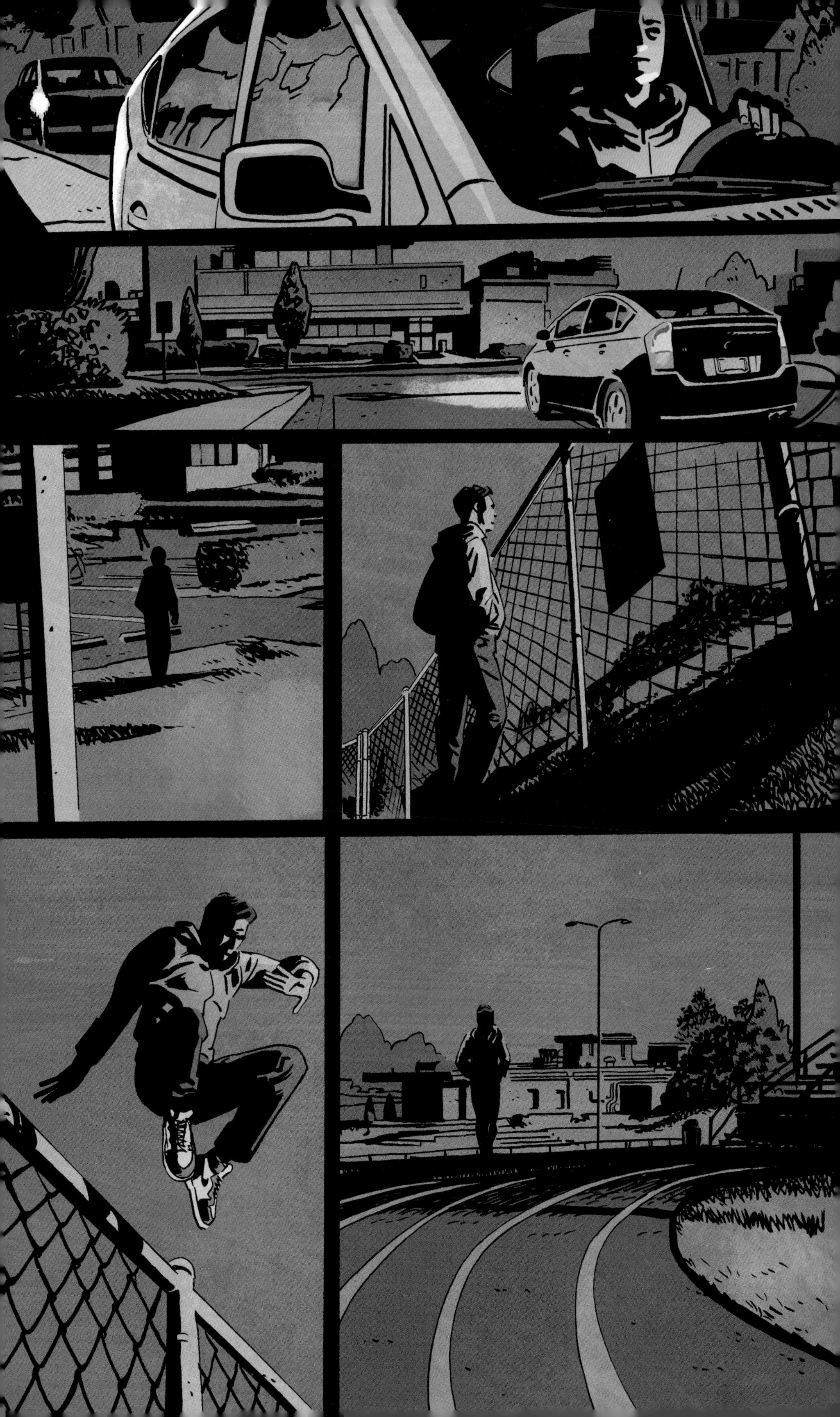

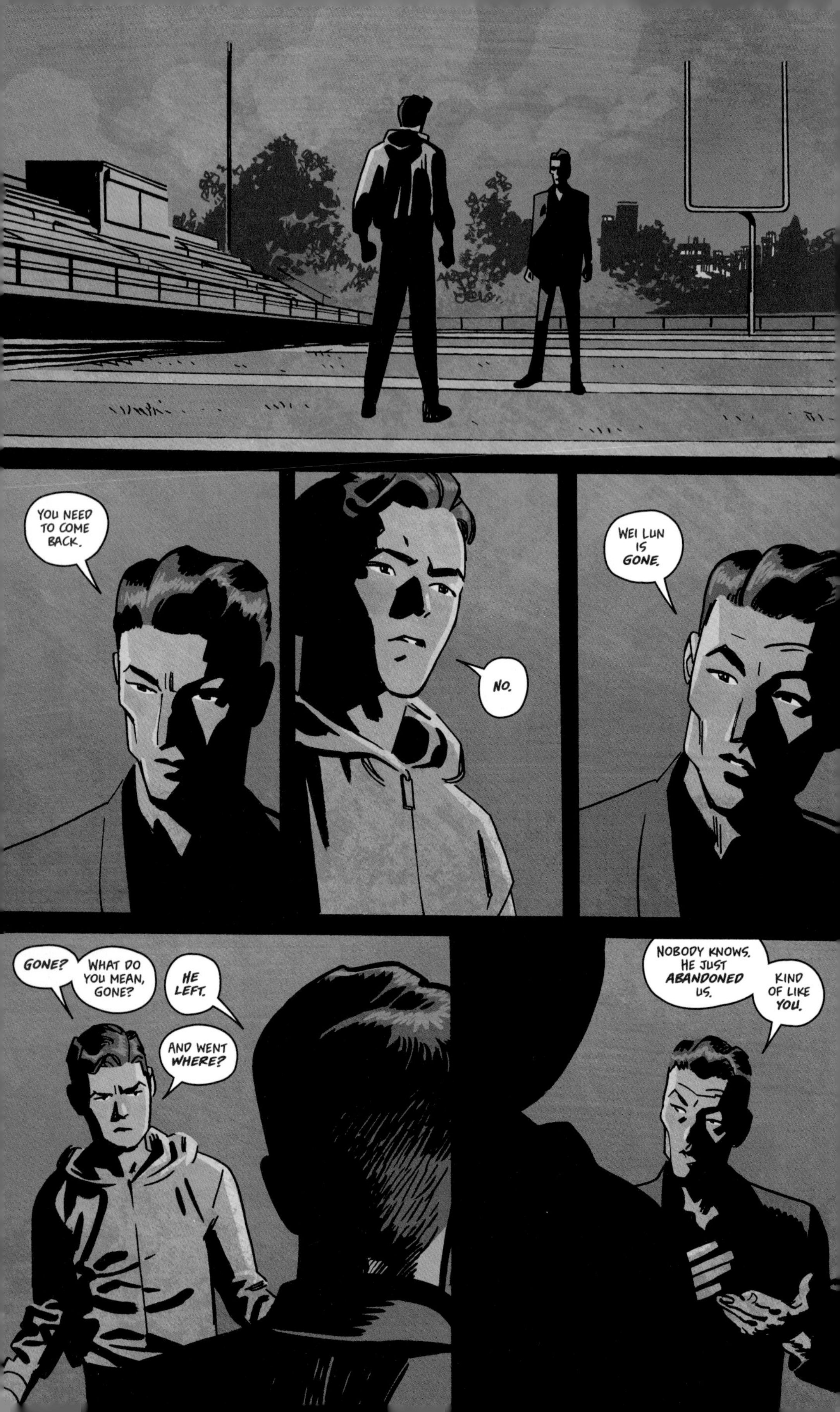

YOU NEED TO COME BACK.
NO.
WEI LUN IS GONE.
GONE?
WHAT DO YOU MEAN, GONE?
HE LEFT.
AND WENT WHERE?
NOBODY KNOWS. HE JUST ABANDONED US.
KIND OF LIKE YOU.

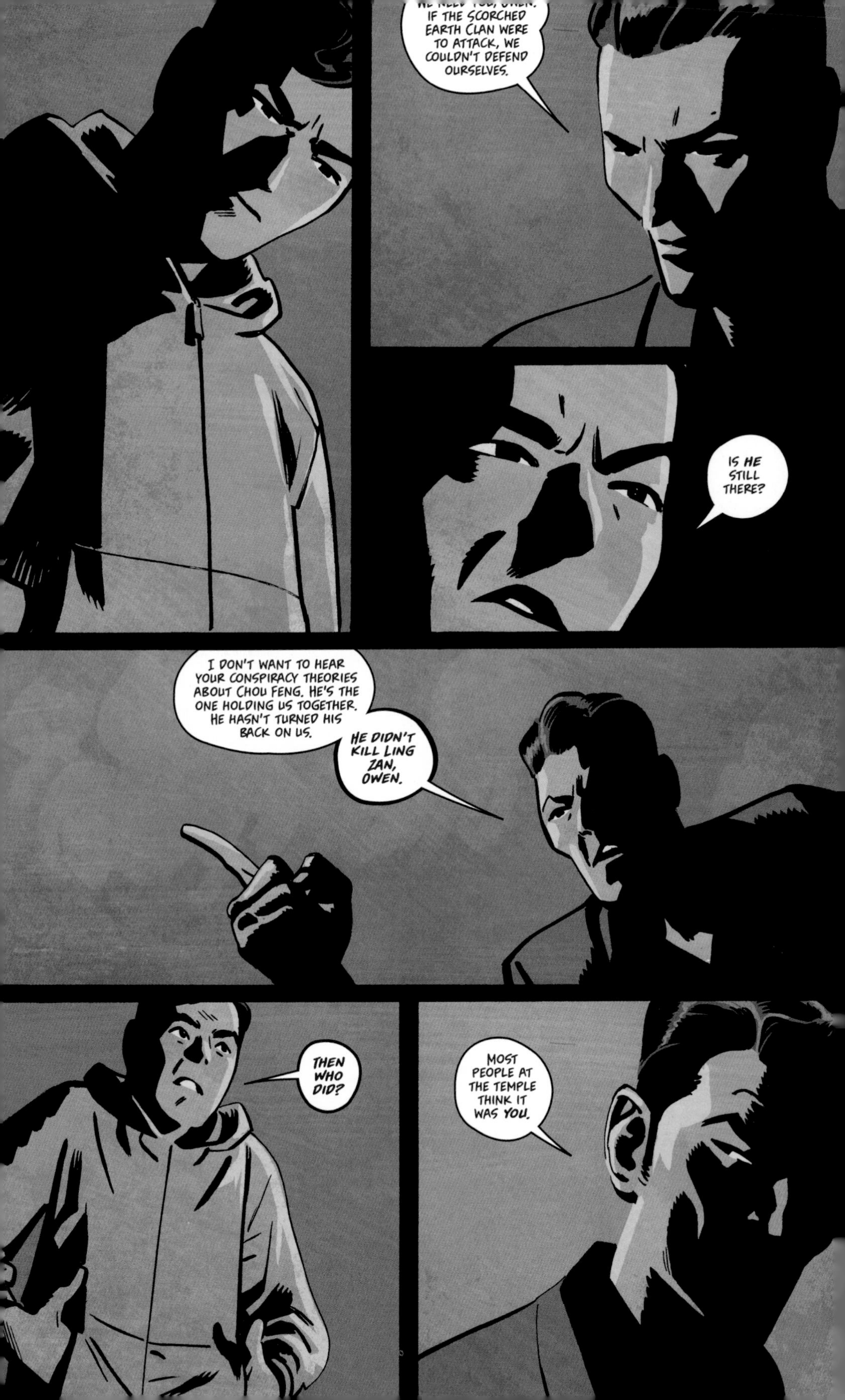
IF THE SCORCHED EARTH CLAN WERE TO ATTACK, WE COULDN'T DEFEND OURSELVES.
IS HE STILL THERE?
I DON'T WANT TO HEAR YOUR CONSPIRACY THEORIES ABOUT CHOU FENG. HE'S THE ONE HOLDING US TOGETHER. HE HASN'T TURNED HIS BACK ON US.
HE DIDN'T KILL LING ZAN, OWEN.
THEN WHO DID?
MOST PEOPLE AT THE TEMPLE THINK IT WAS YOU.

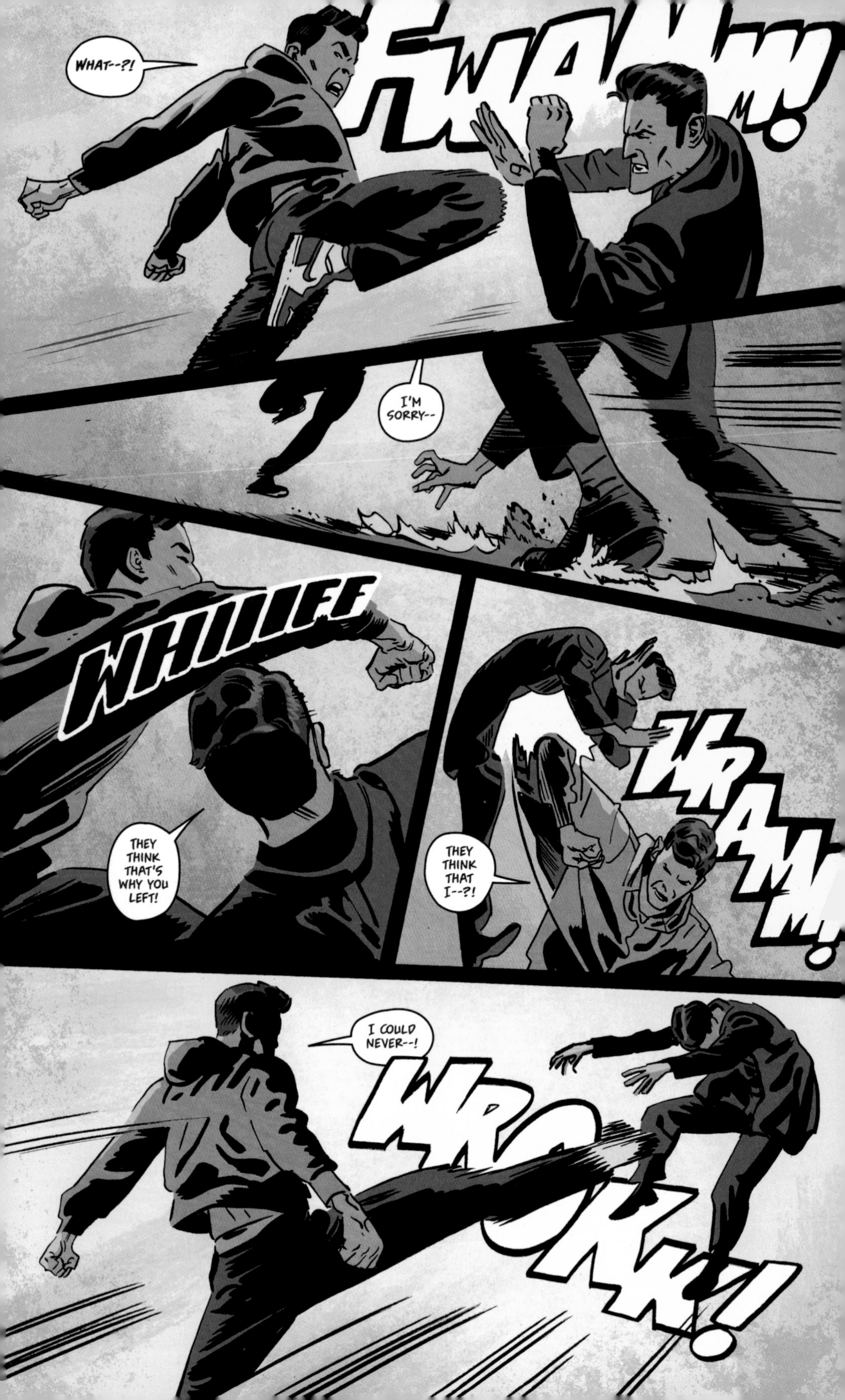
WHAT--?!
FWAMM!
I'M SORRY--
WHIIIIFF
THEY THINK THAT'S WHY YOU LEFT!
THEY THINK THAT I--?!
WRAMM!
I COULD NEVER--!
WROKK!!

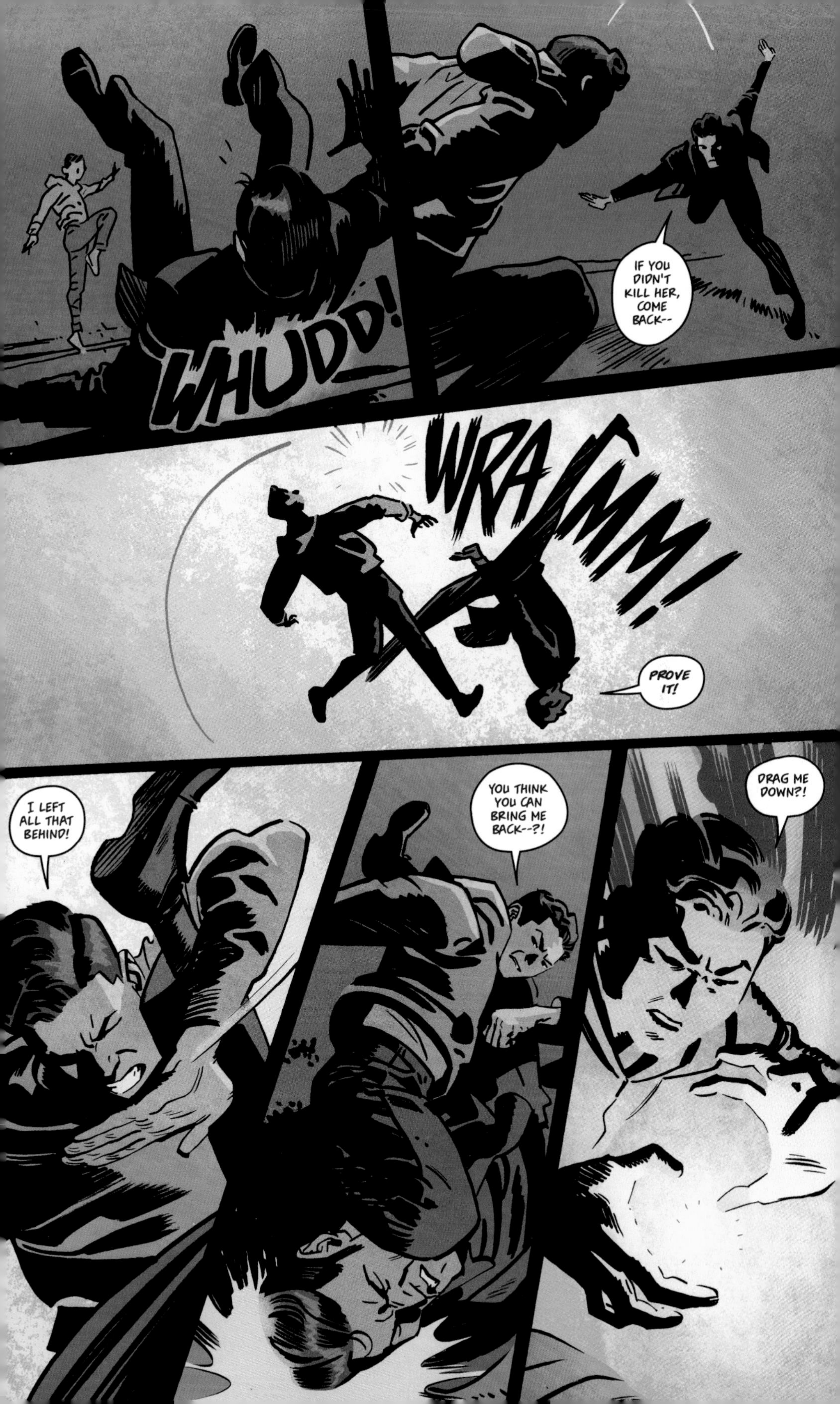
WHUDD!
IF YOU DIDN'T KILL HER, COME BACK--
WRAMMM!
PROVE IT!
I LEFT ALL THAT BEHIND!
YOU THINK YOU CAN BRING ME BACK--?!
DRAG ME DOWN?!

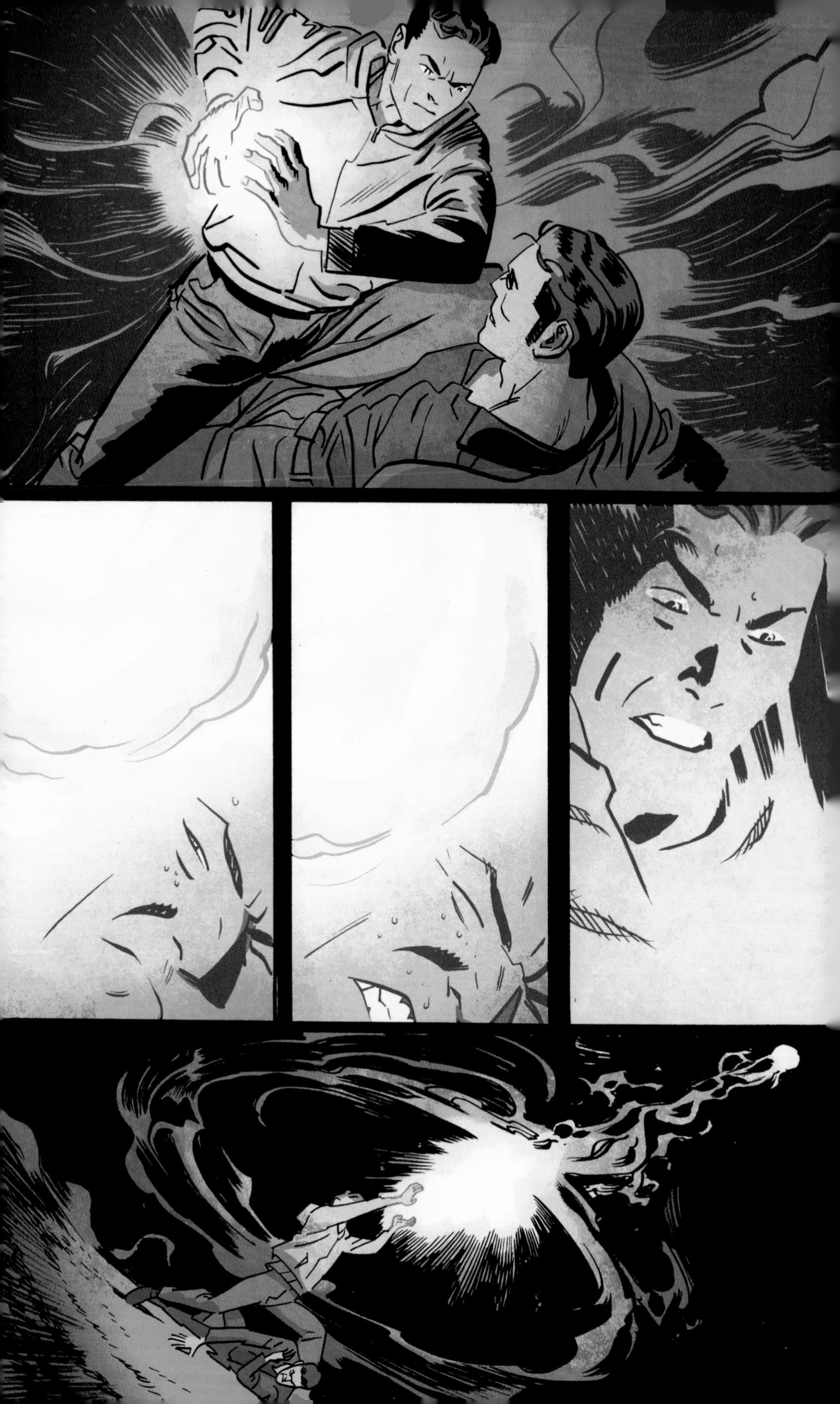

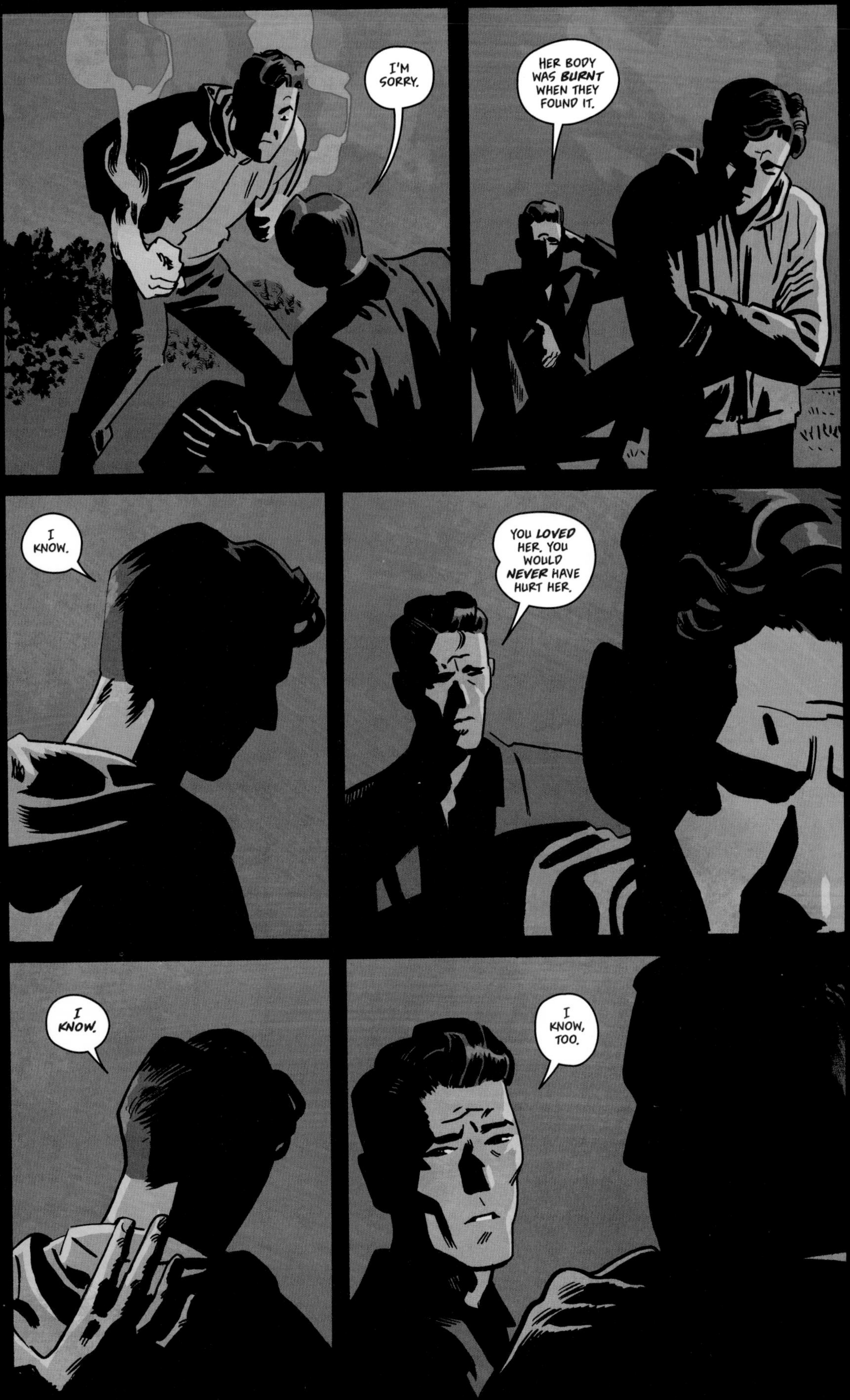
I'M SORRY.
HER BODY WAS BURNT WHEN THEY FOUND IT.
I KNOW.
YOU LOVED HER. YOU WOULD NEVER HAVE HURT HER.
I KNOW.
I KNOW, TOO.

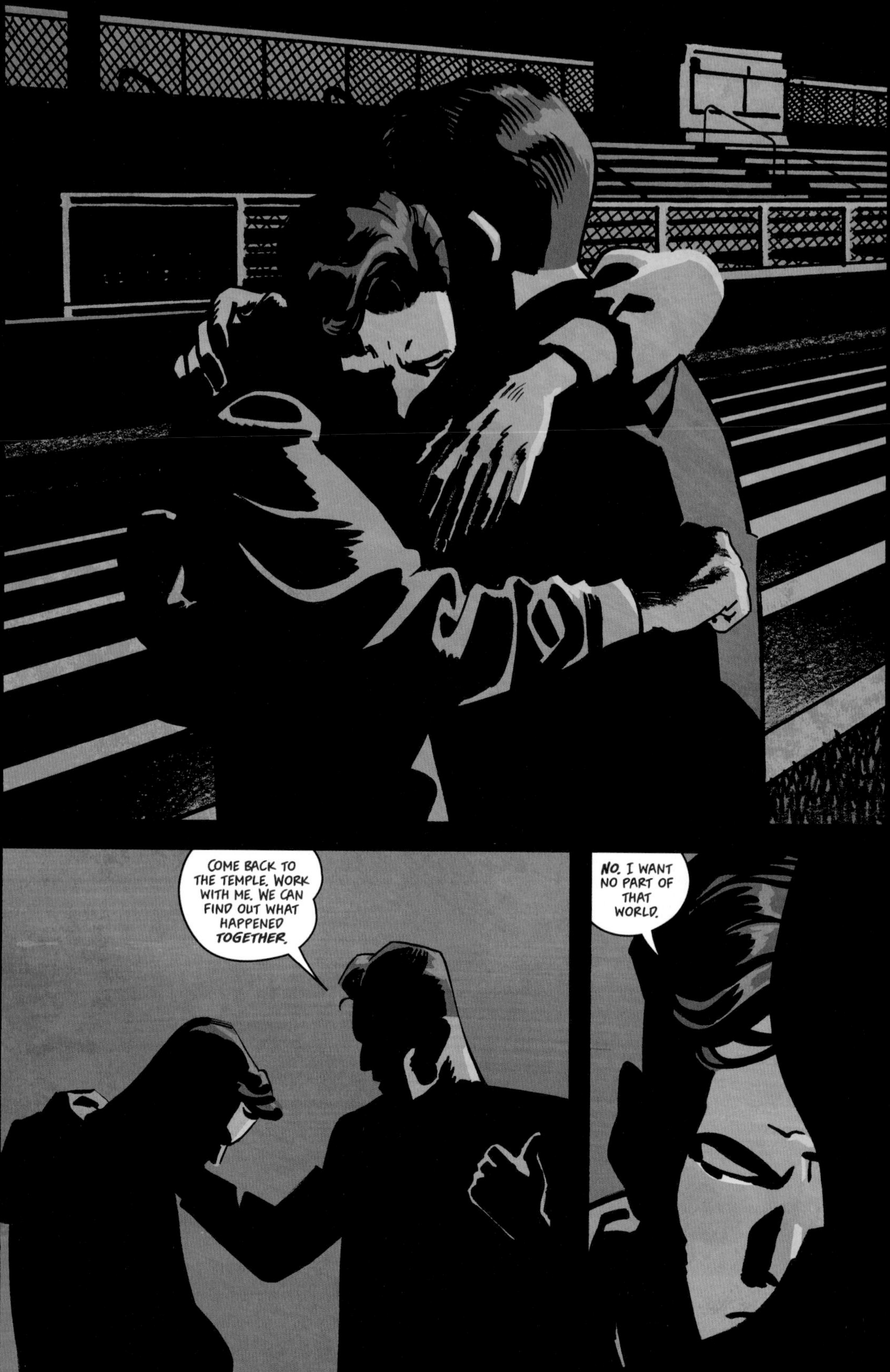
COME BACK TO THE TEMPLE. WORK WITH ME. WE CAN FIND OUT WHAT HAPPENED *TOGETHER*.
NO. I WANT NO PART OF THAT WORLD.

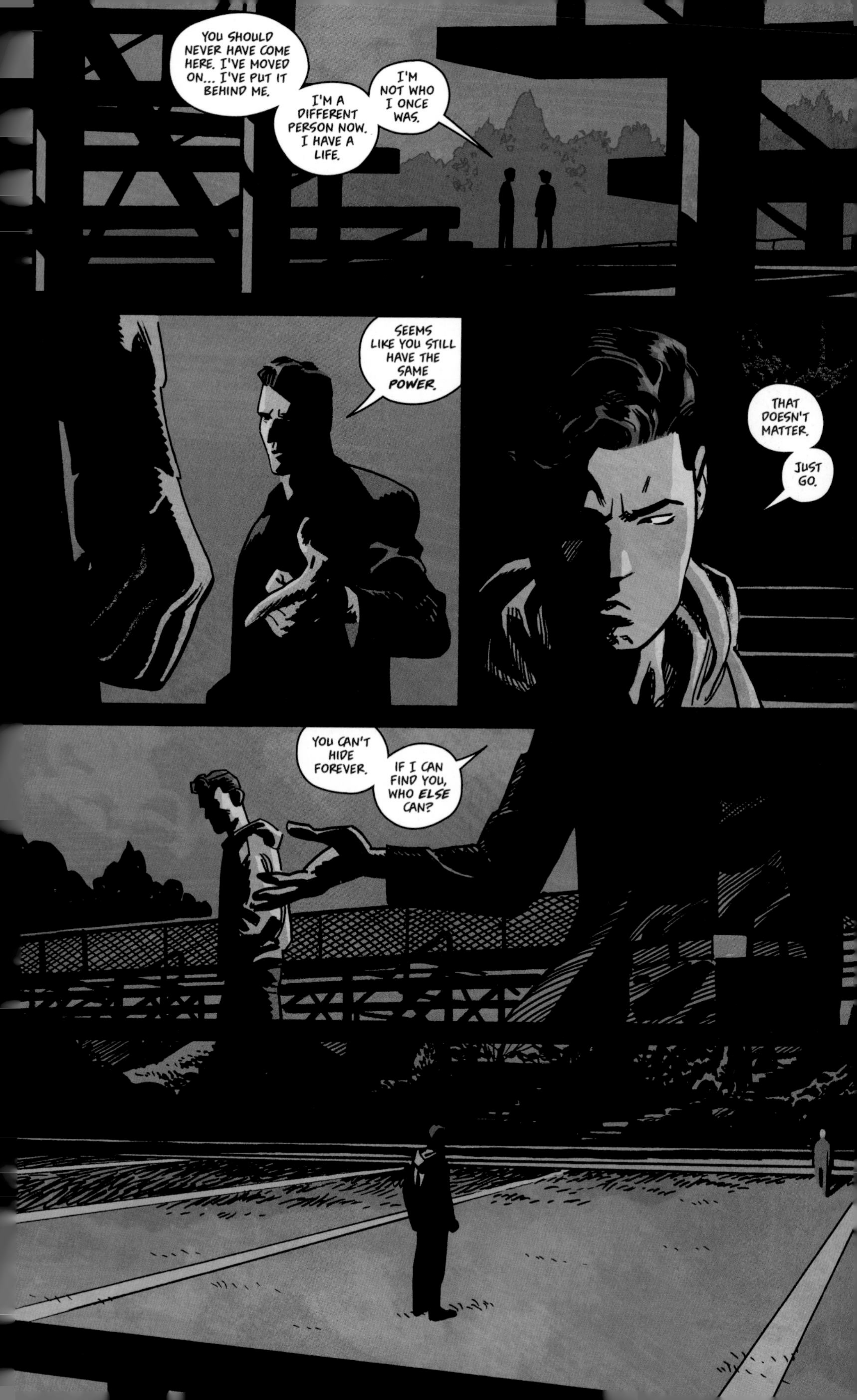
YOU SHOULD NEVER HAVE COME HERE. I'VE MOVED ON... I'VE PUT IT BEHIND ME.
I'M A DIFFERENT PERSON NOW. I HAVE A LIFE.
I'M NOT WHO I ONCE WAS.
SEEMS LIKE YOU STILL HAVE THE SAME POWER.
THAT DOESN'T MATTER.
JUST GO.
YOU CAN'T HIDE FOREVER.
IF I CAN FIND YOU, WHO ELSE CAN?

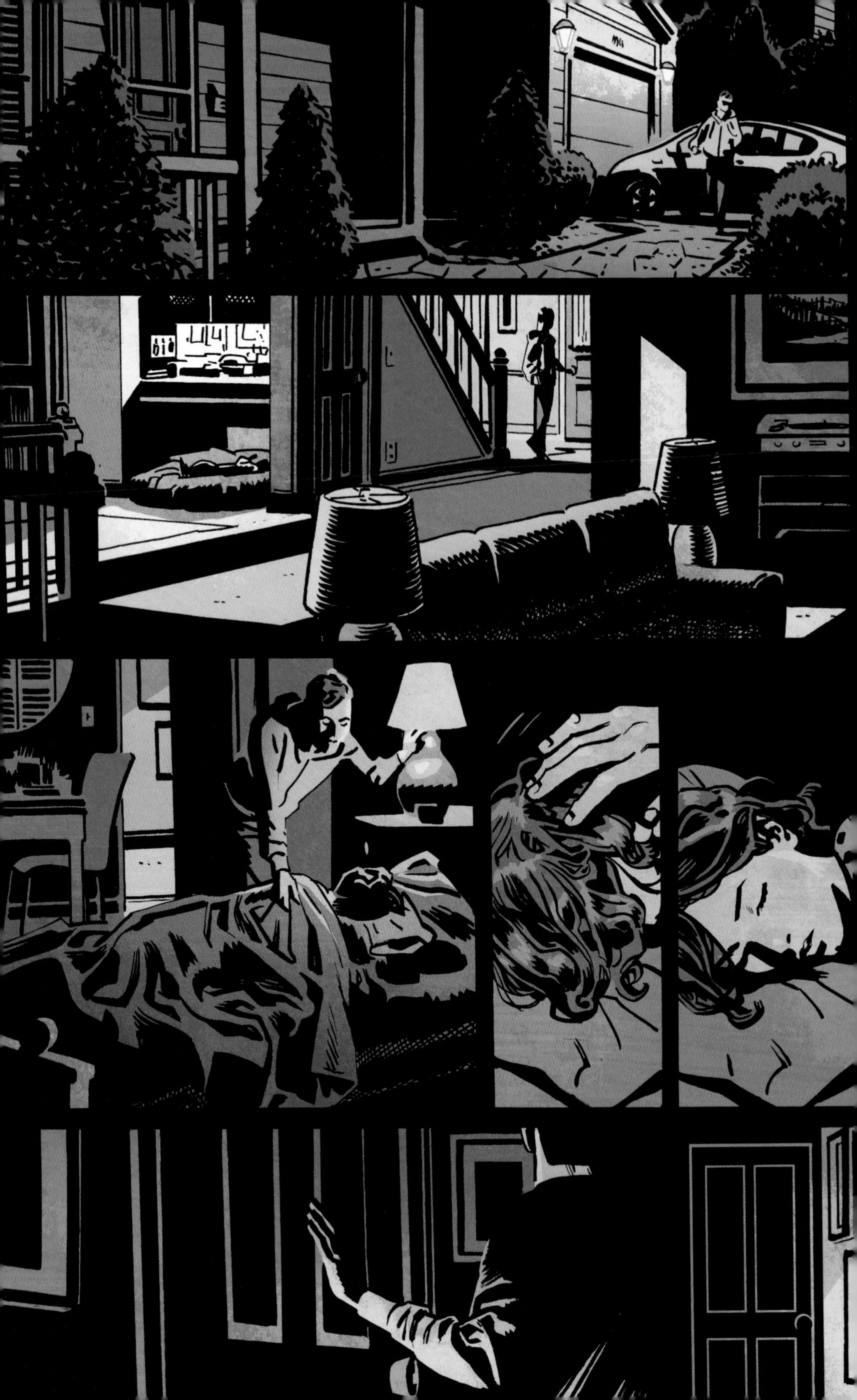

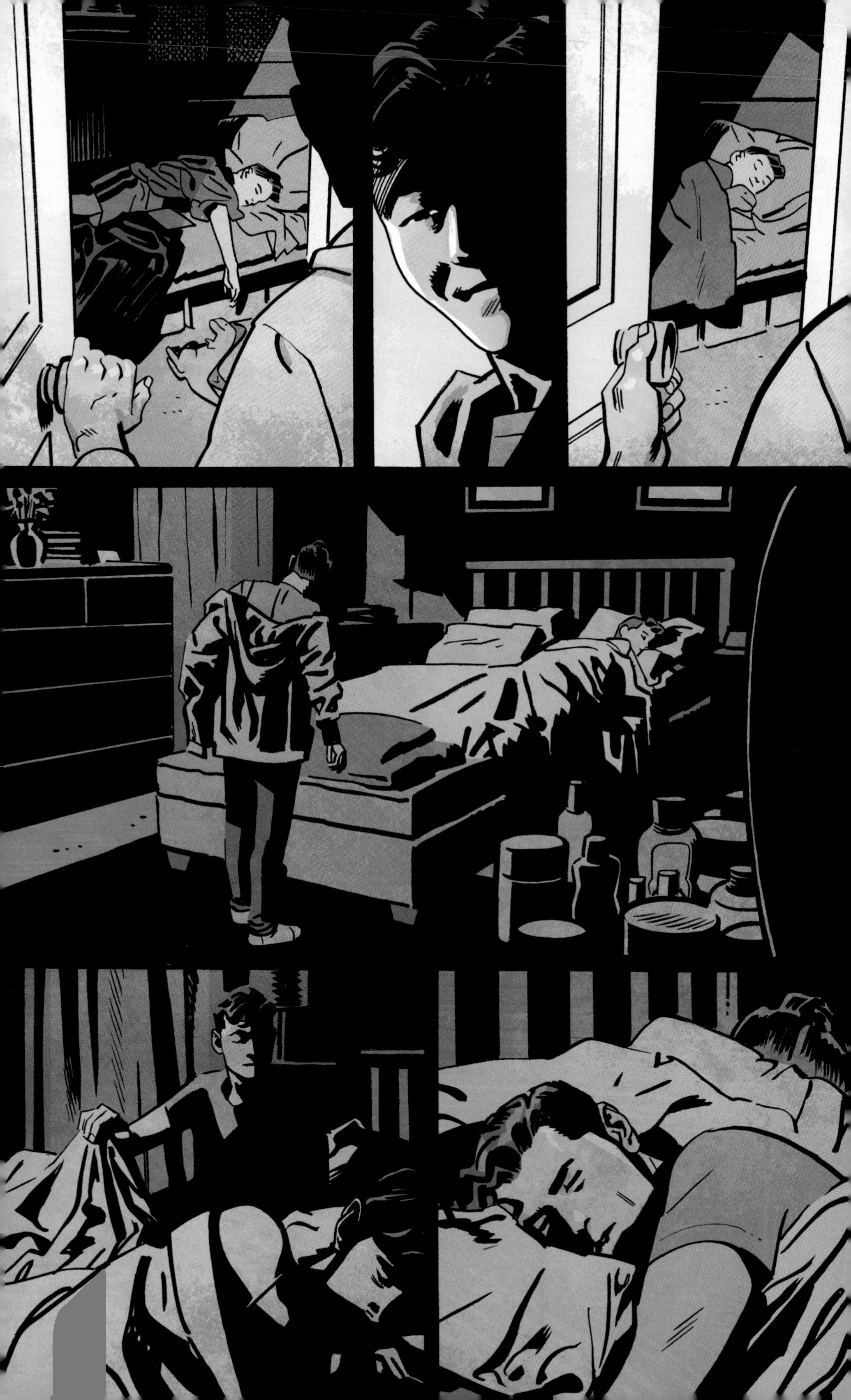

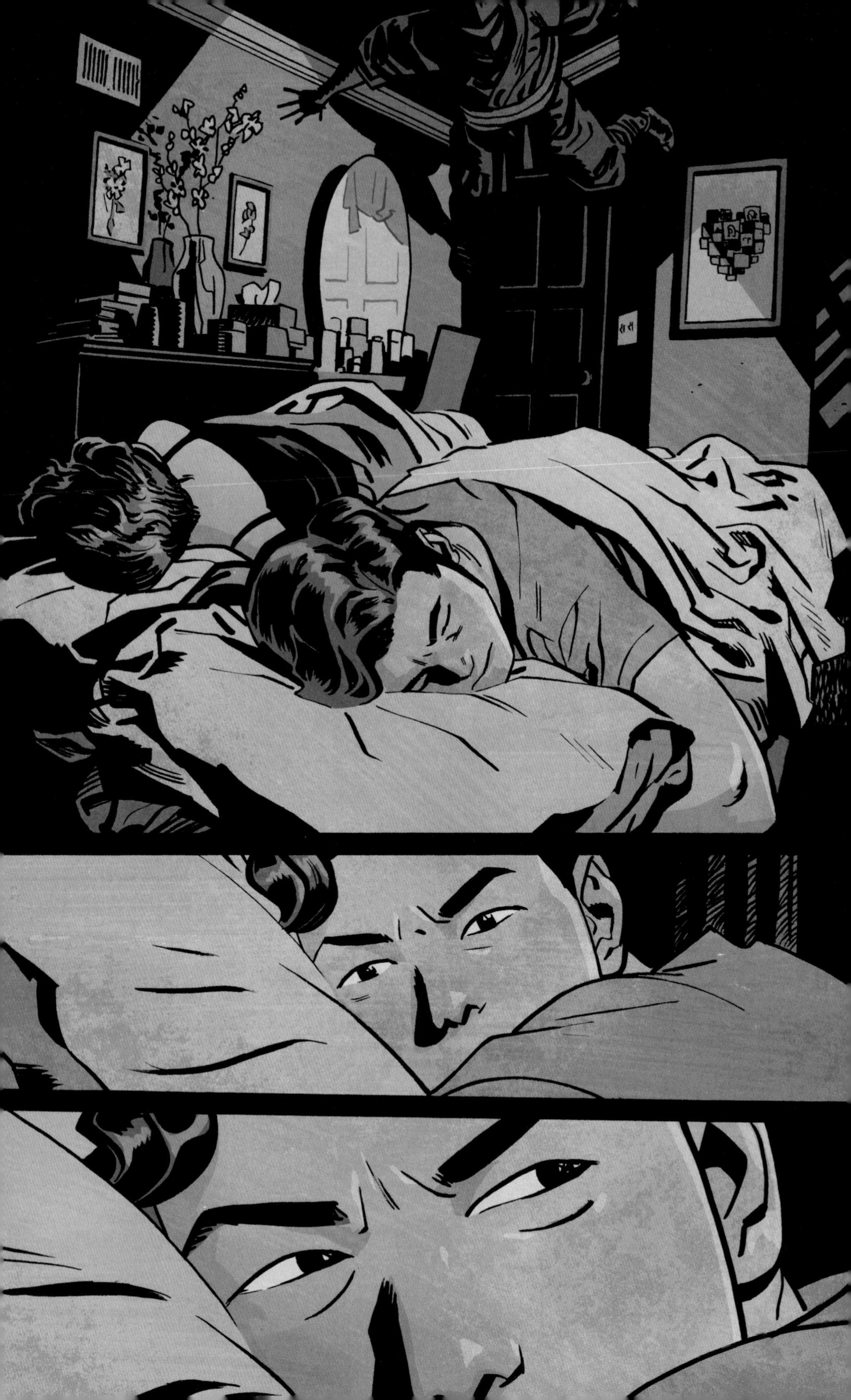

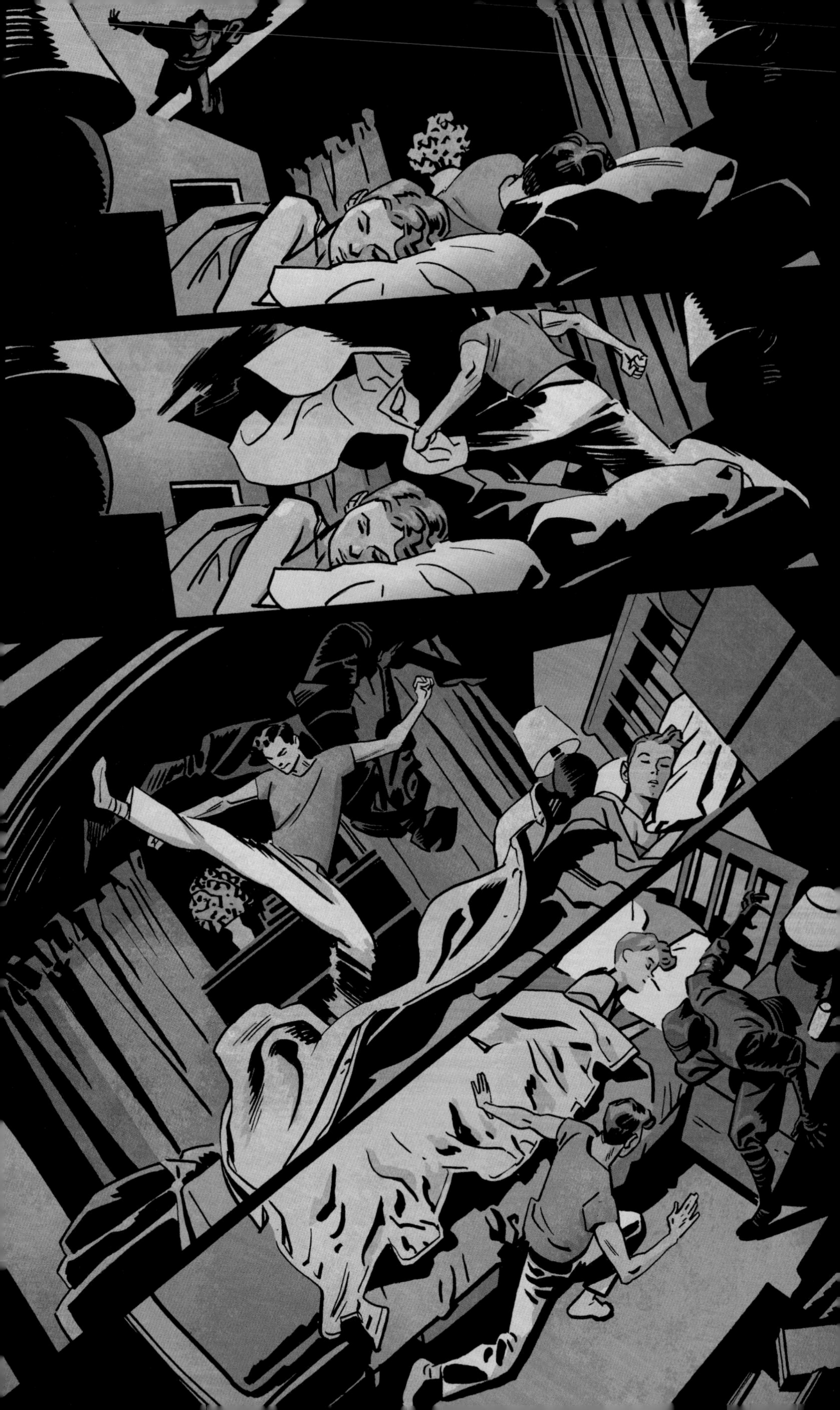

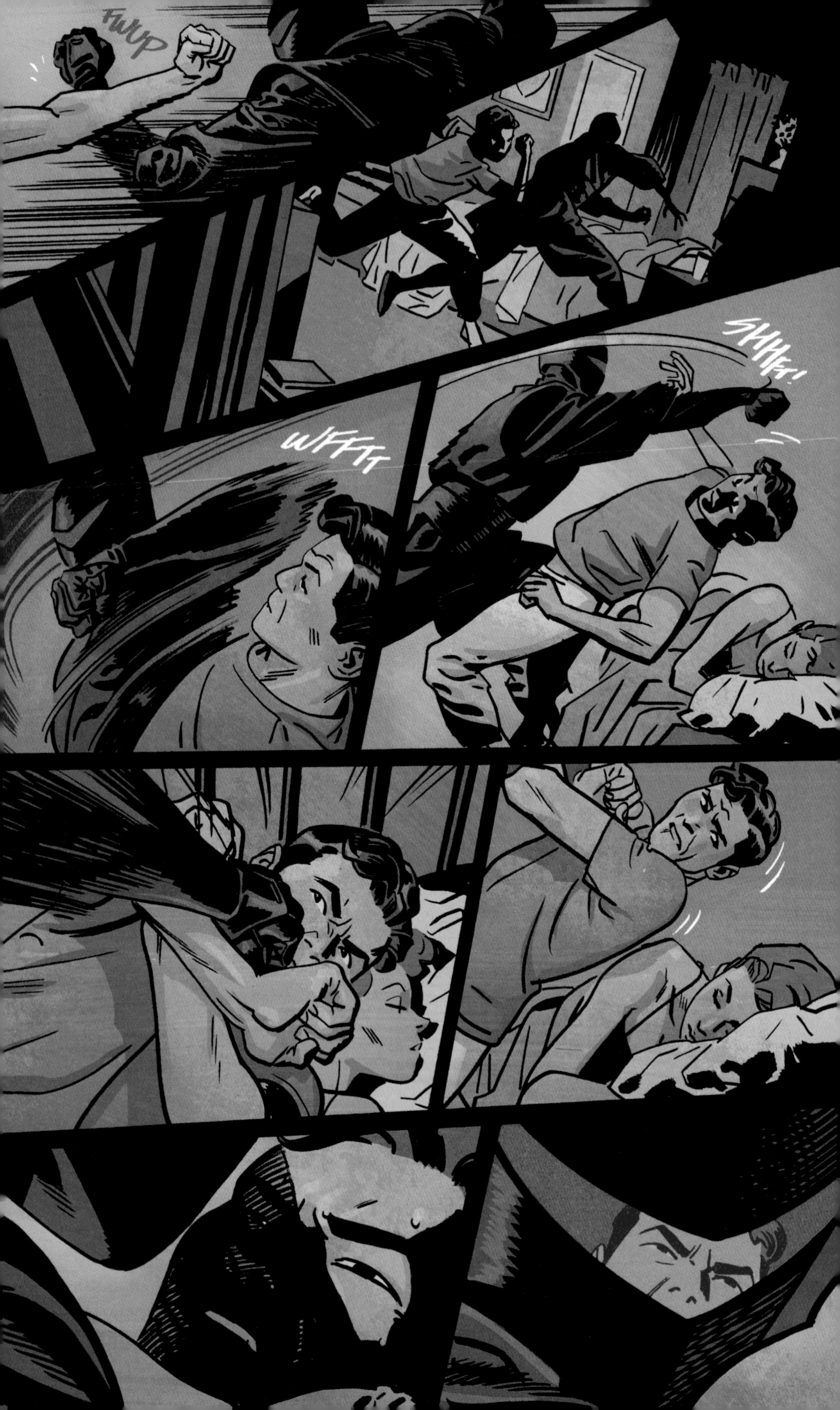
FWUP
WFFTT
SHHFT!

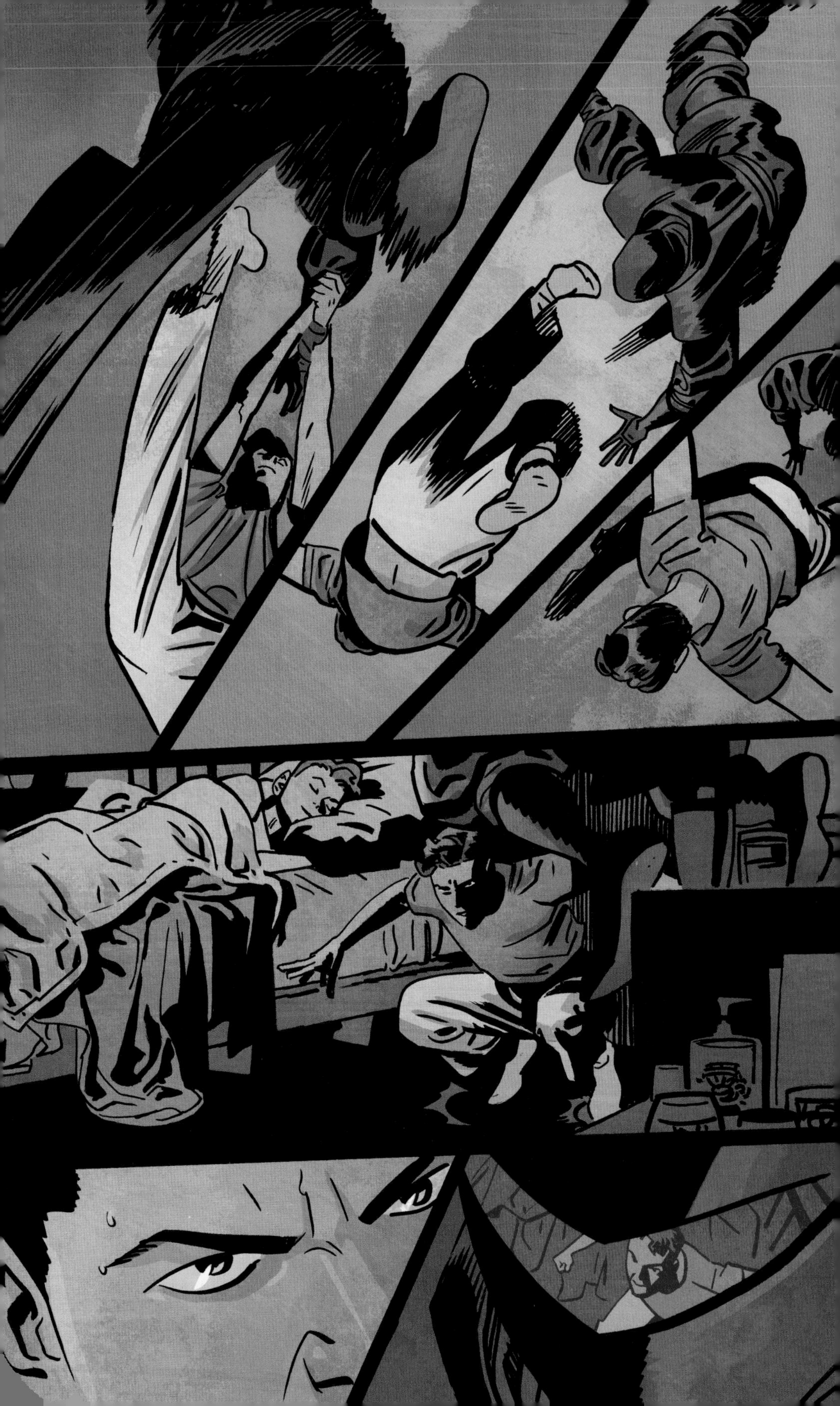

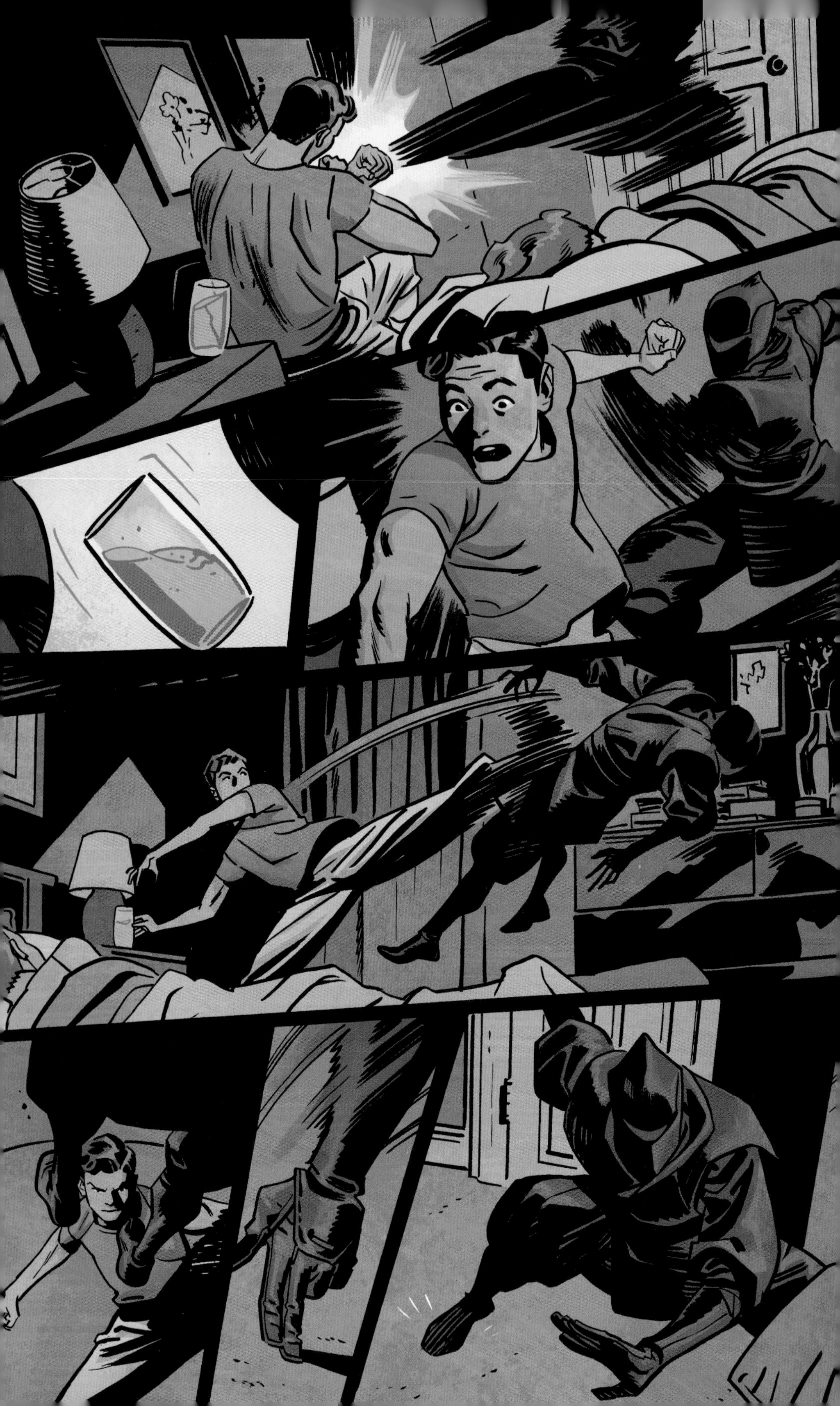

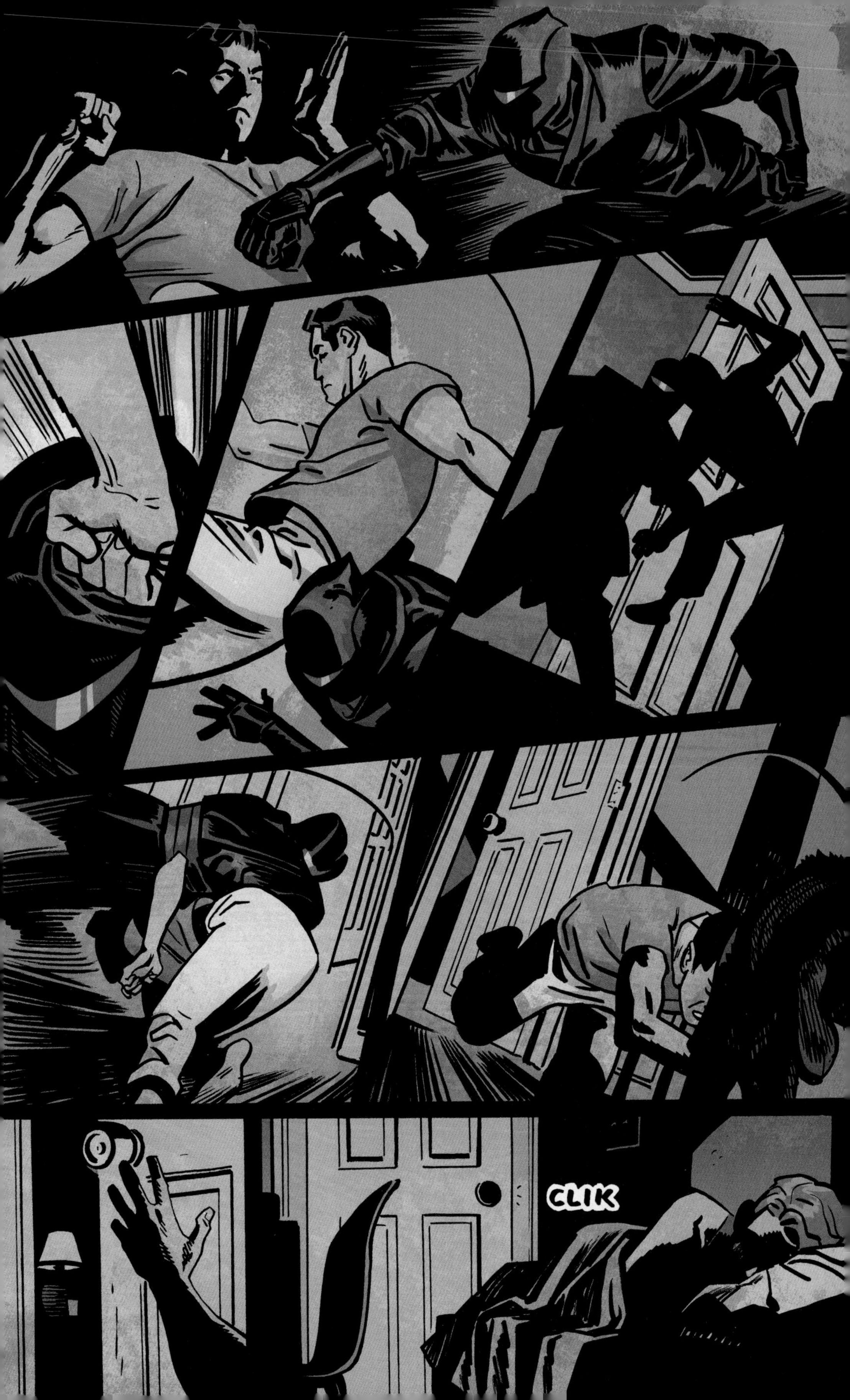
CLIK

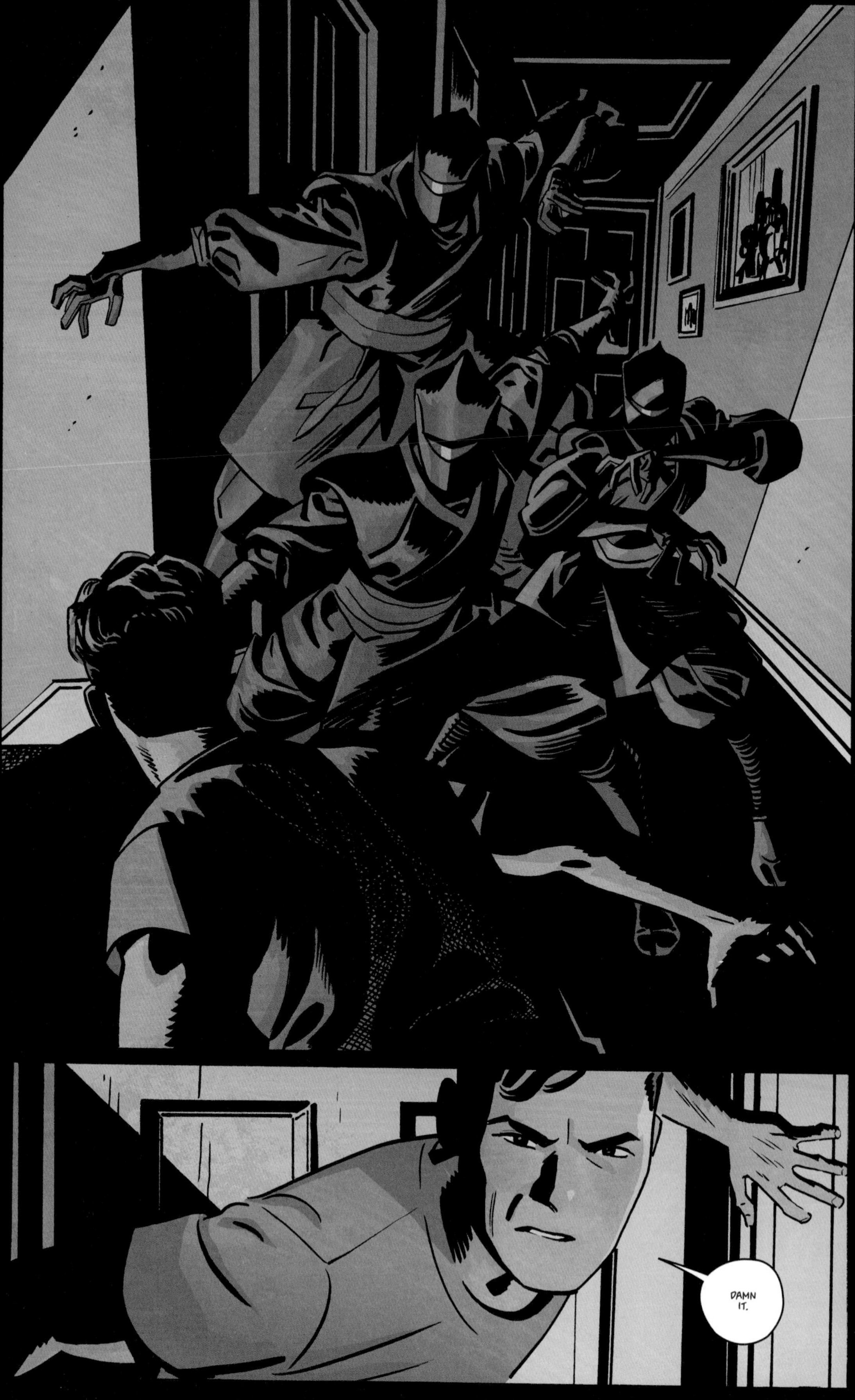
DAMN IT.

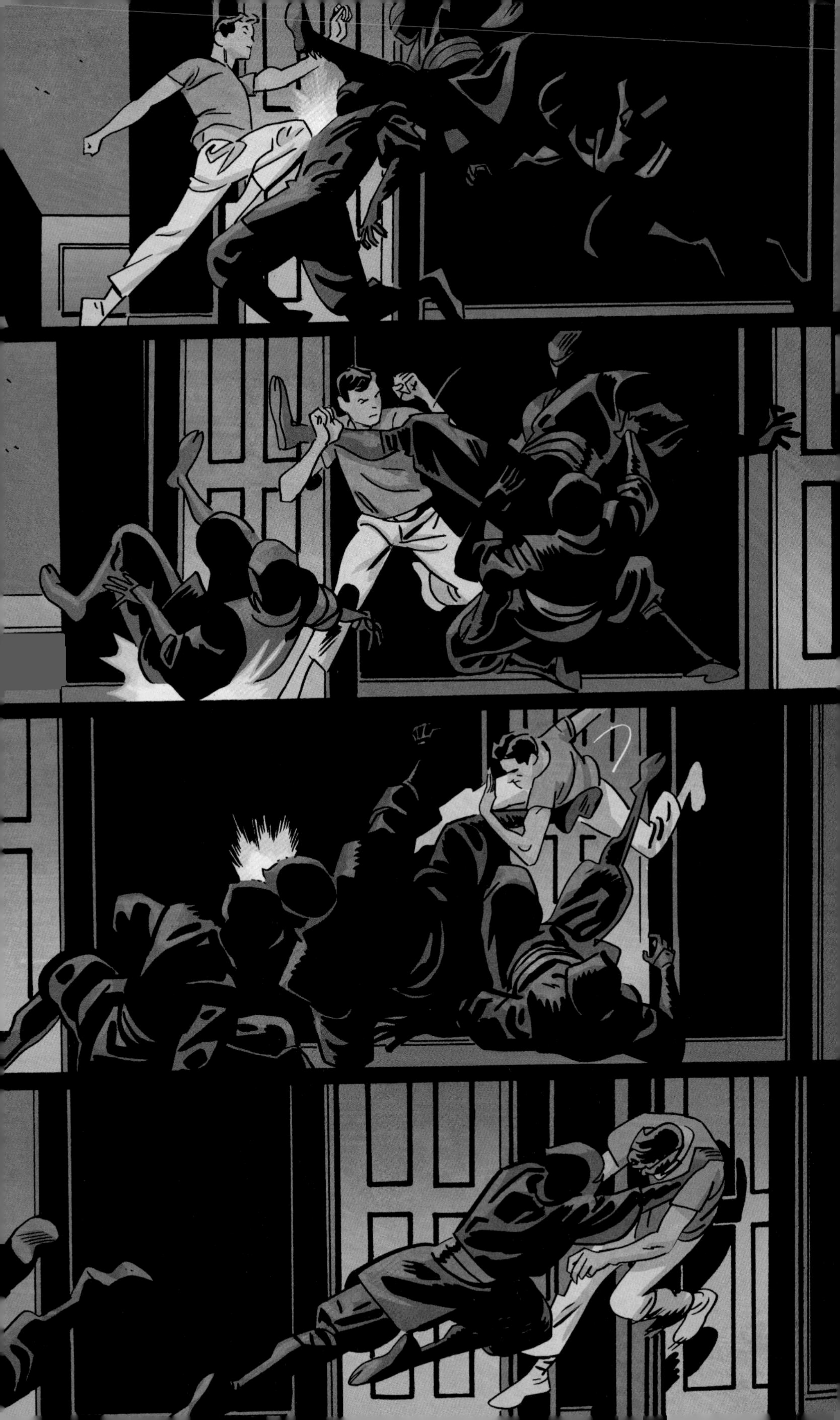

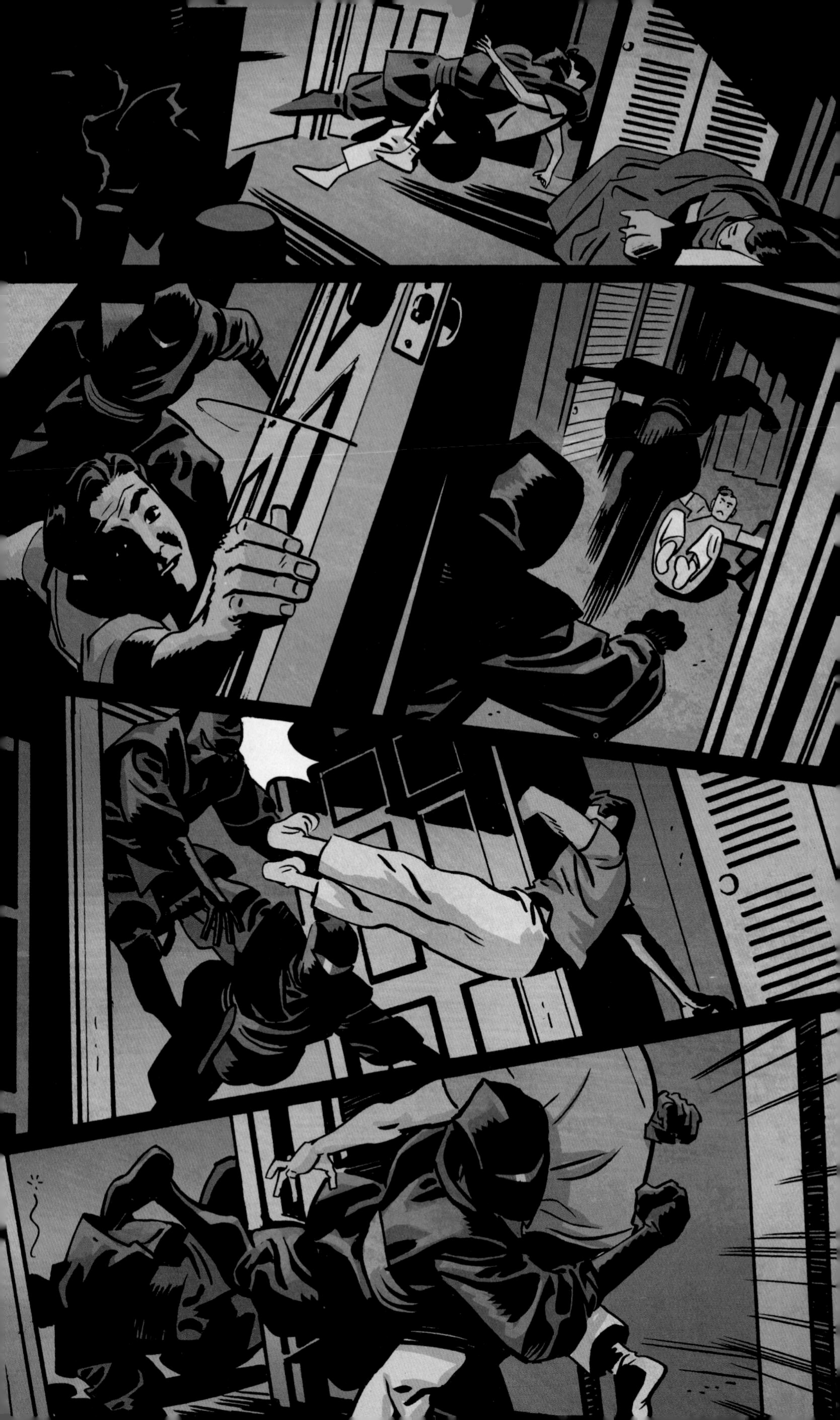

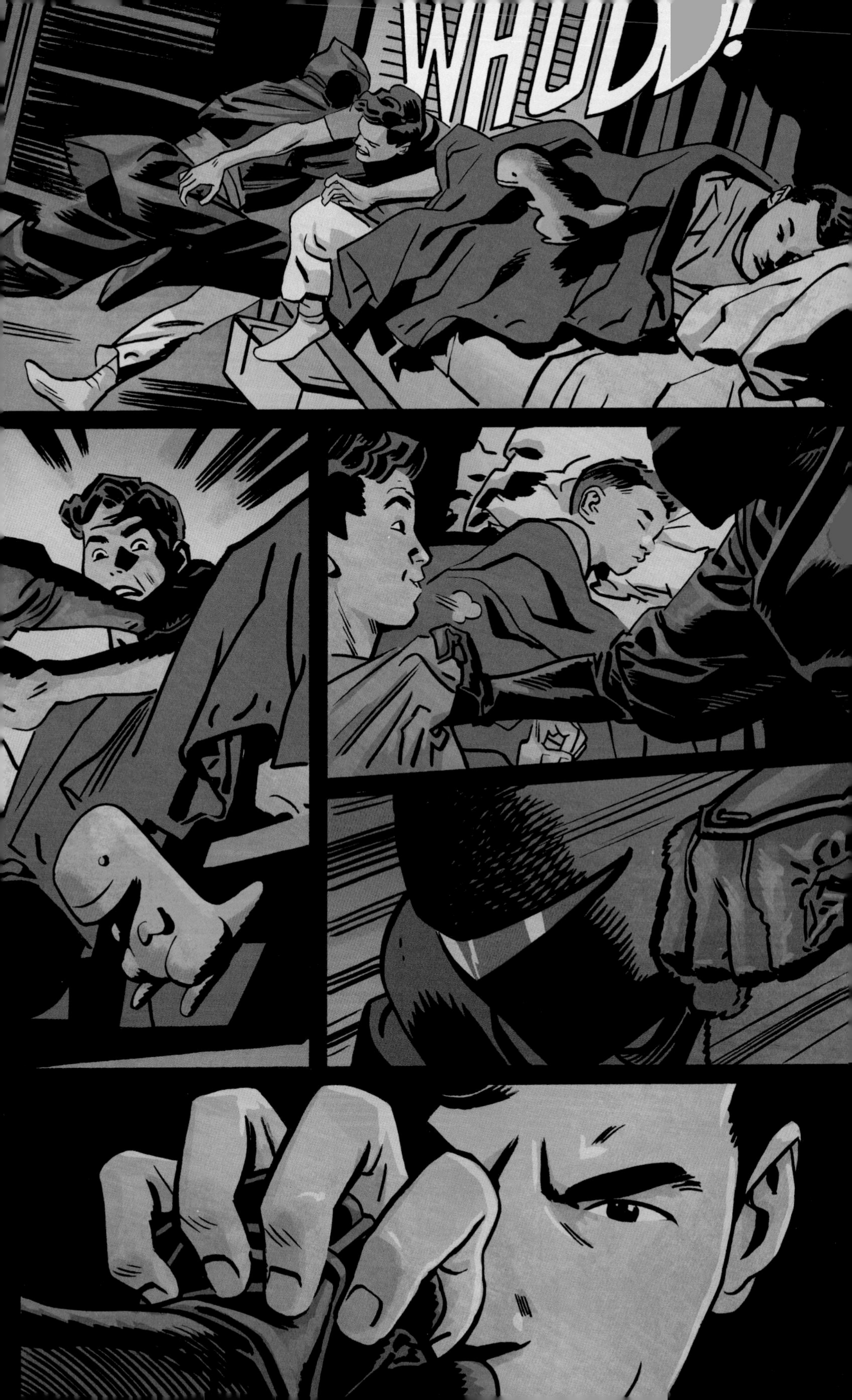
WHUD!

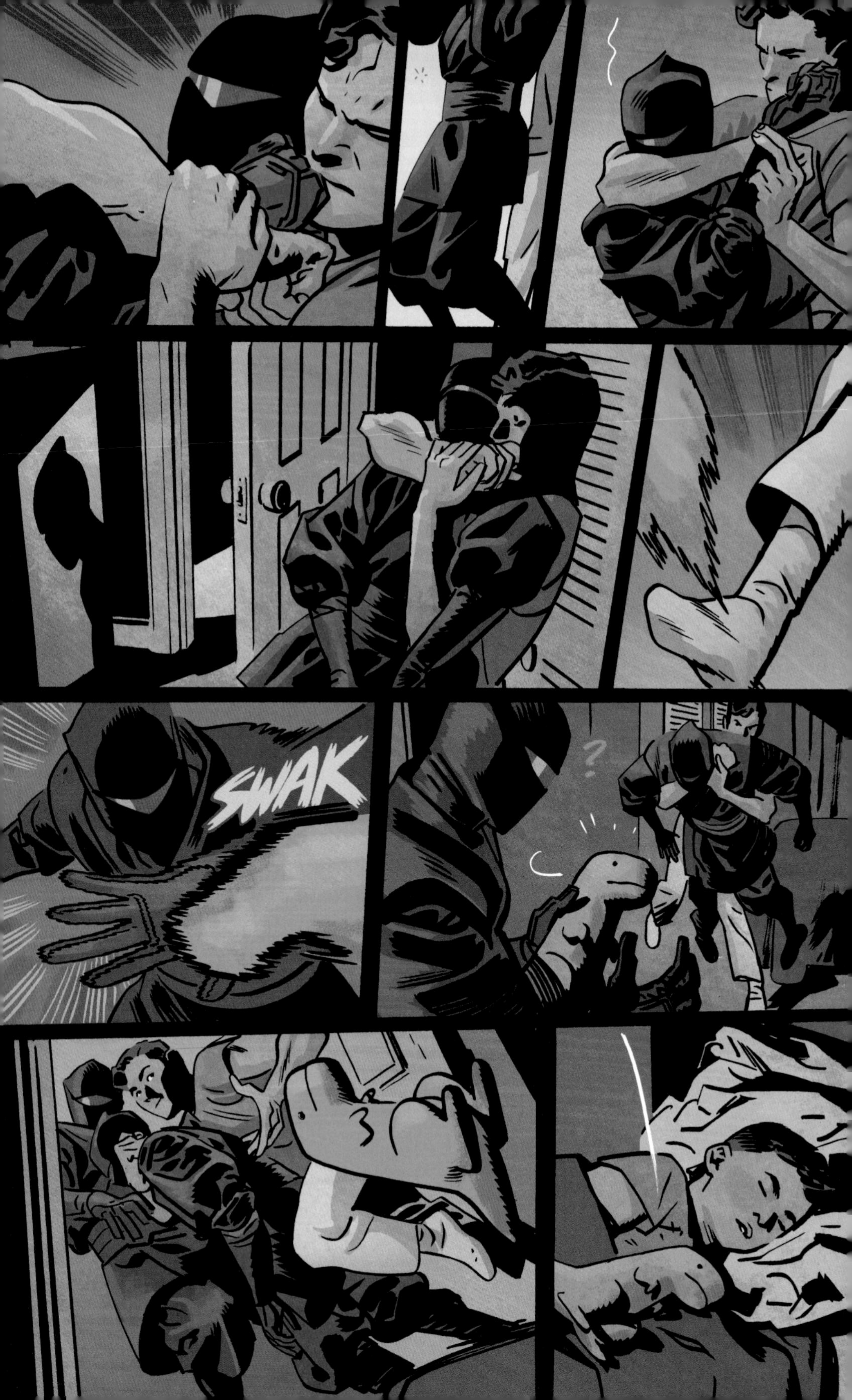
SWAK
?

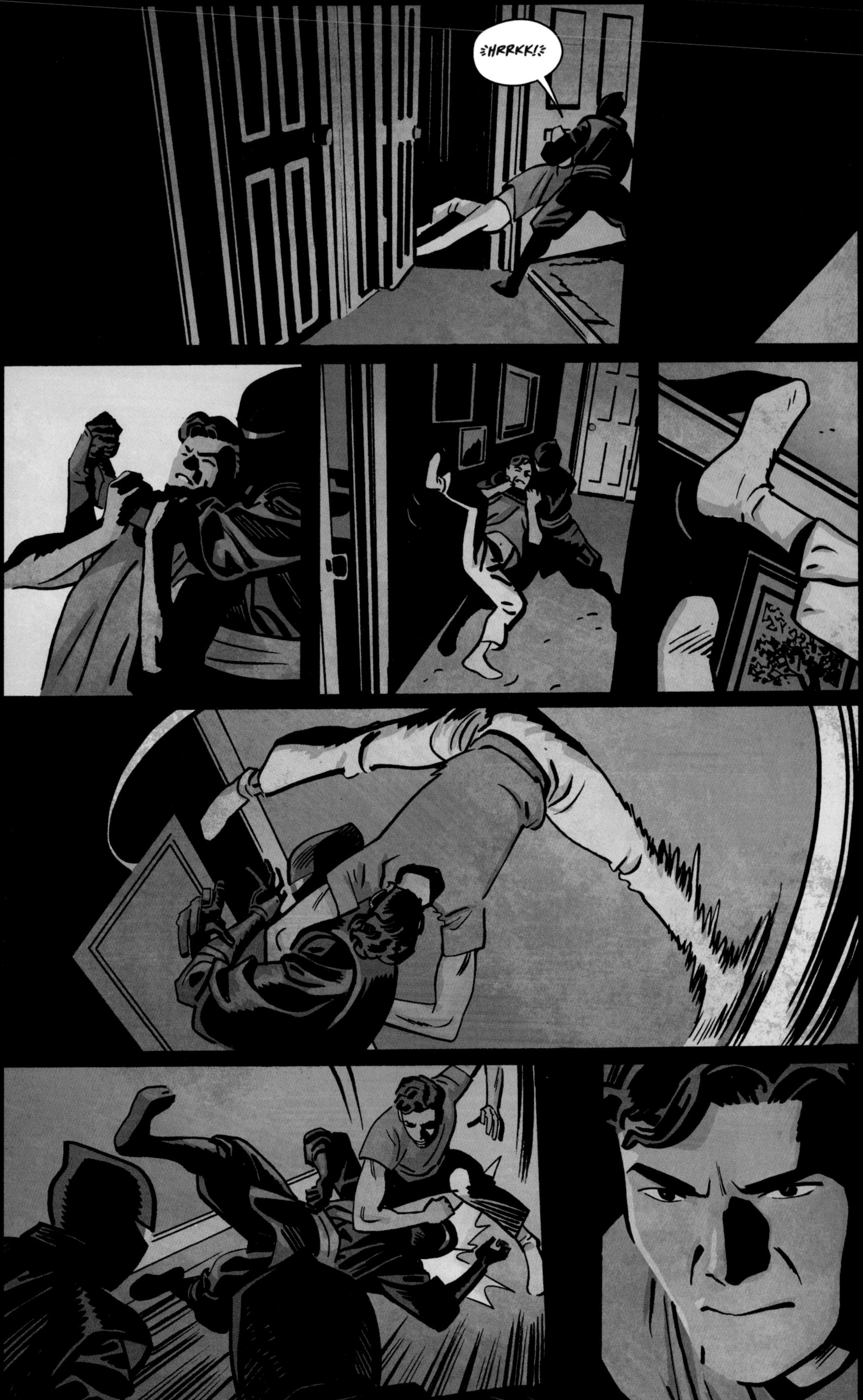
HRRKK!

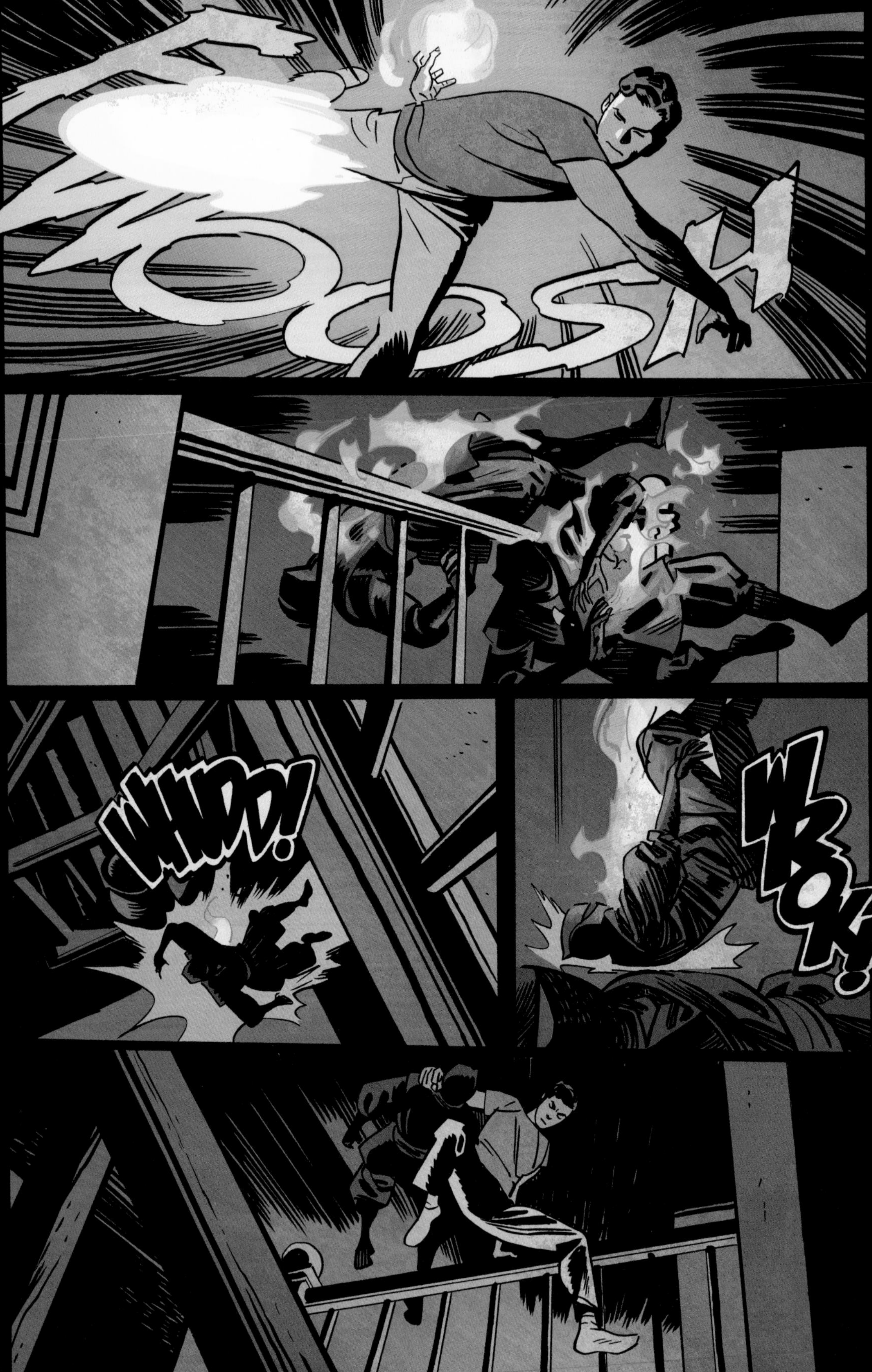
WHUD!
WBOK!

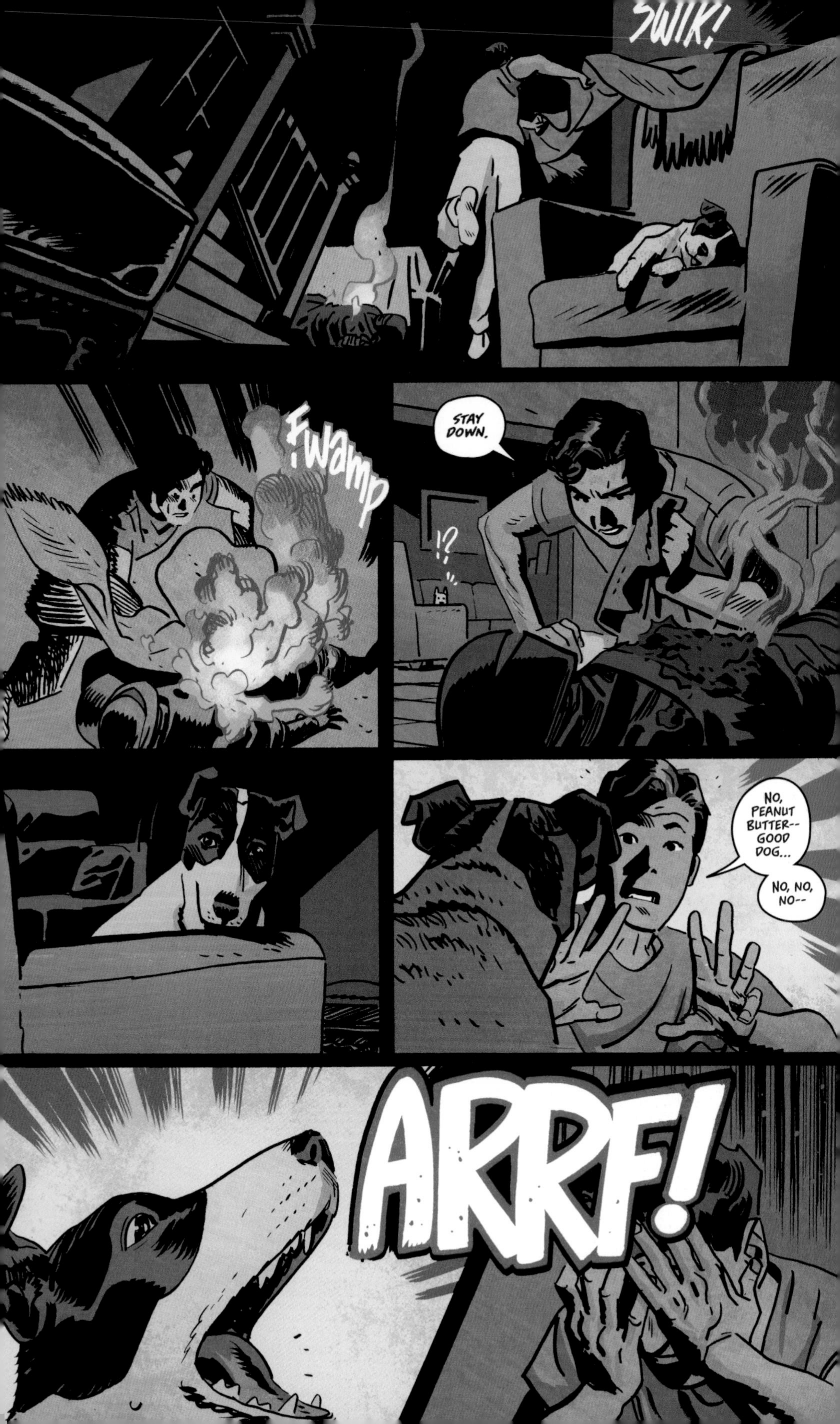
SWIK!
FWAMP
STAY DOWN.
!?
NO, PEANUT BUTTER-- GOOD DOG...
NO, NO, NO--
ARRF!

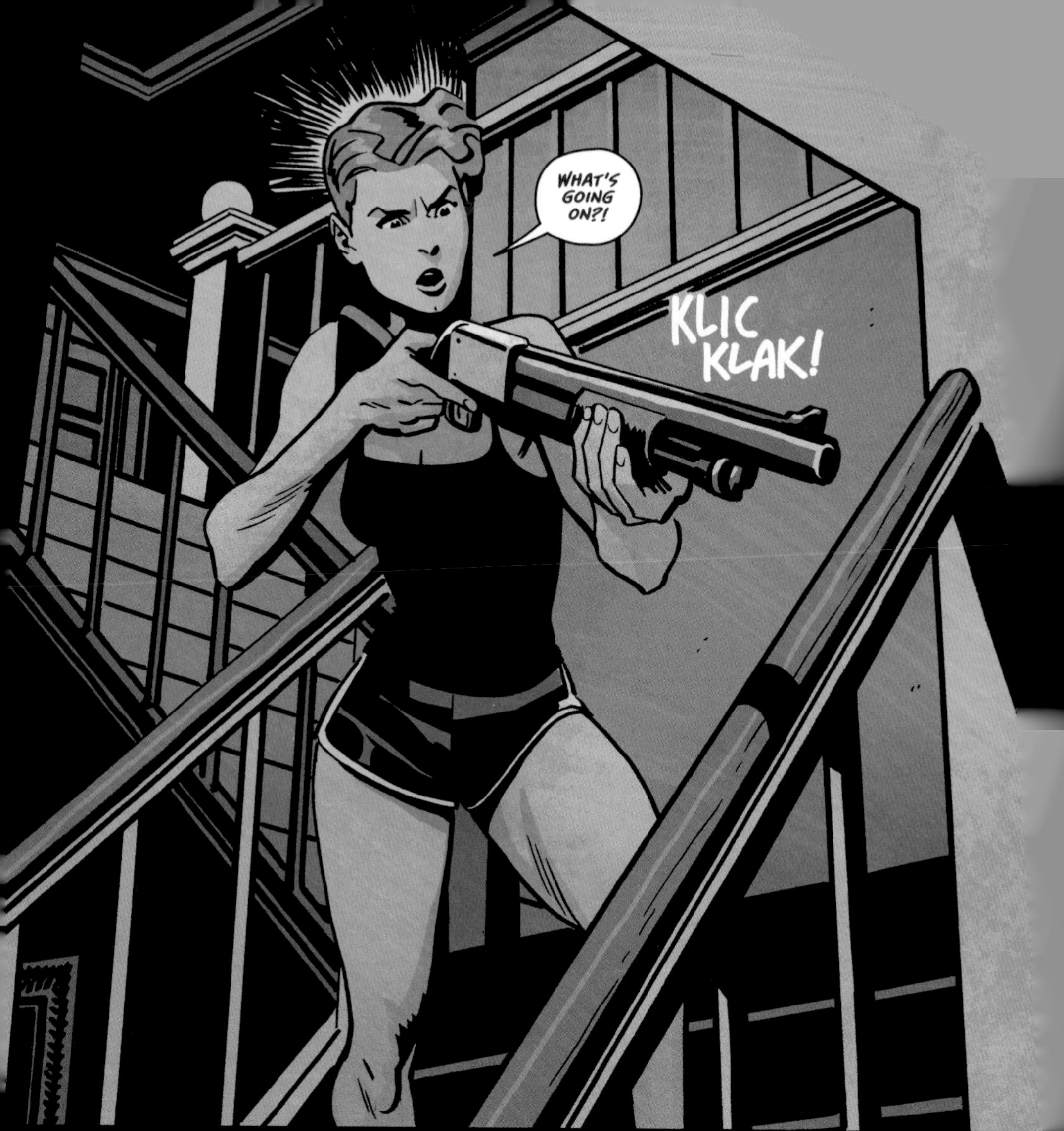
WHAT'S GOING ON?!
KLIC KLAK!

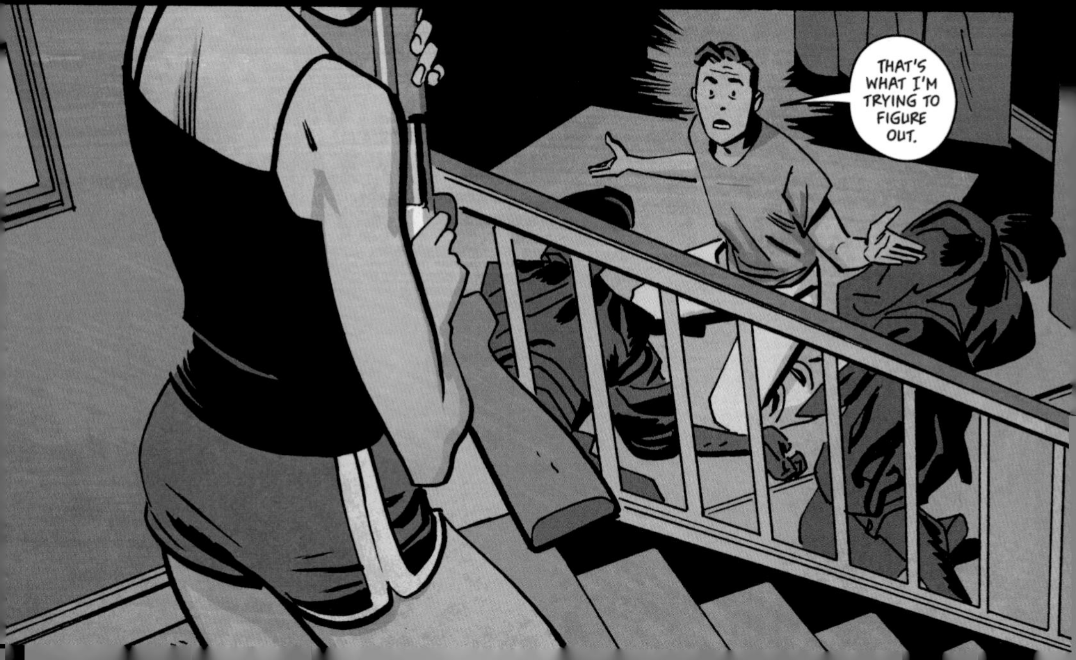
THAT'S WHAT I'M TRYING TO FIGURE OUT.

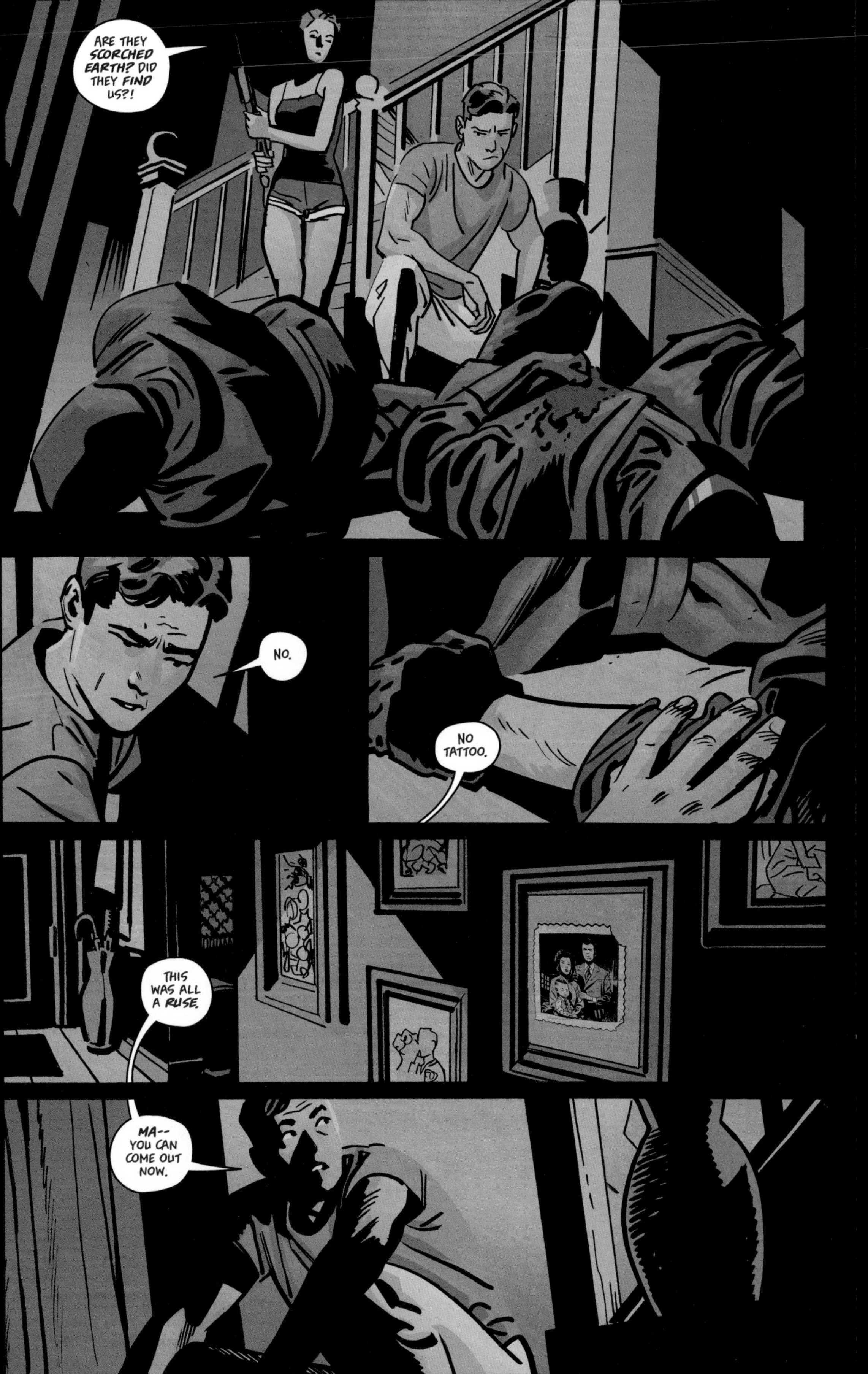
ARE THEY SCORCHED EARTH? DID THEY FIND US?!
NO.
NO TATTOO.
THIS WAS ALL A RUSE.
MA-- YOU CAN COME OUT NOW.

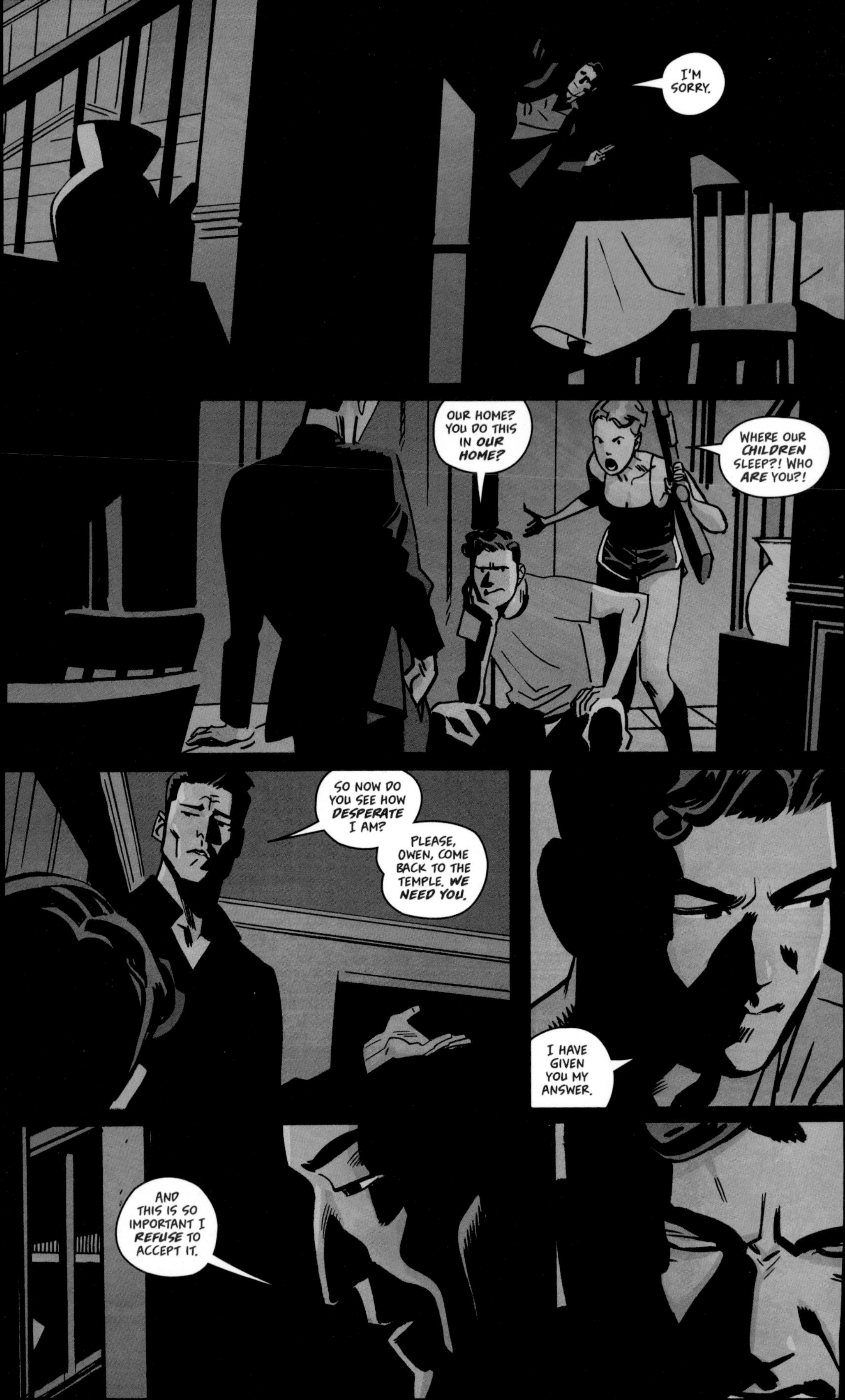

I'M SORRY.
OUR HOME? YOU DO THIS IN OUR HOME?
WHERE OUR CHILDREN SLEEP?! WHO ARE YOU?!
SO NOW DO YOU SEE HOW DESPERATE I AM?
PLEASE, OWEN, COME BACK TO THE TEMPLE. WE NEED YOU.
I HAVE GIVEN YOU MY ANSWER.
AND THIS IS SO IMPORTANT I REFUSE TO ACCEPT IT.

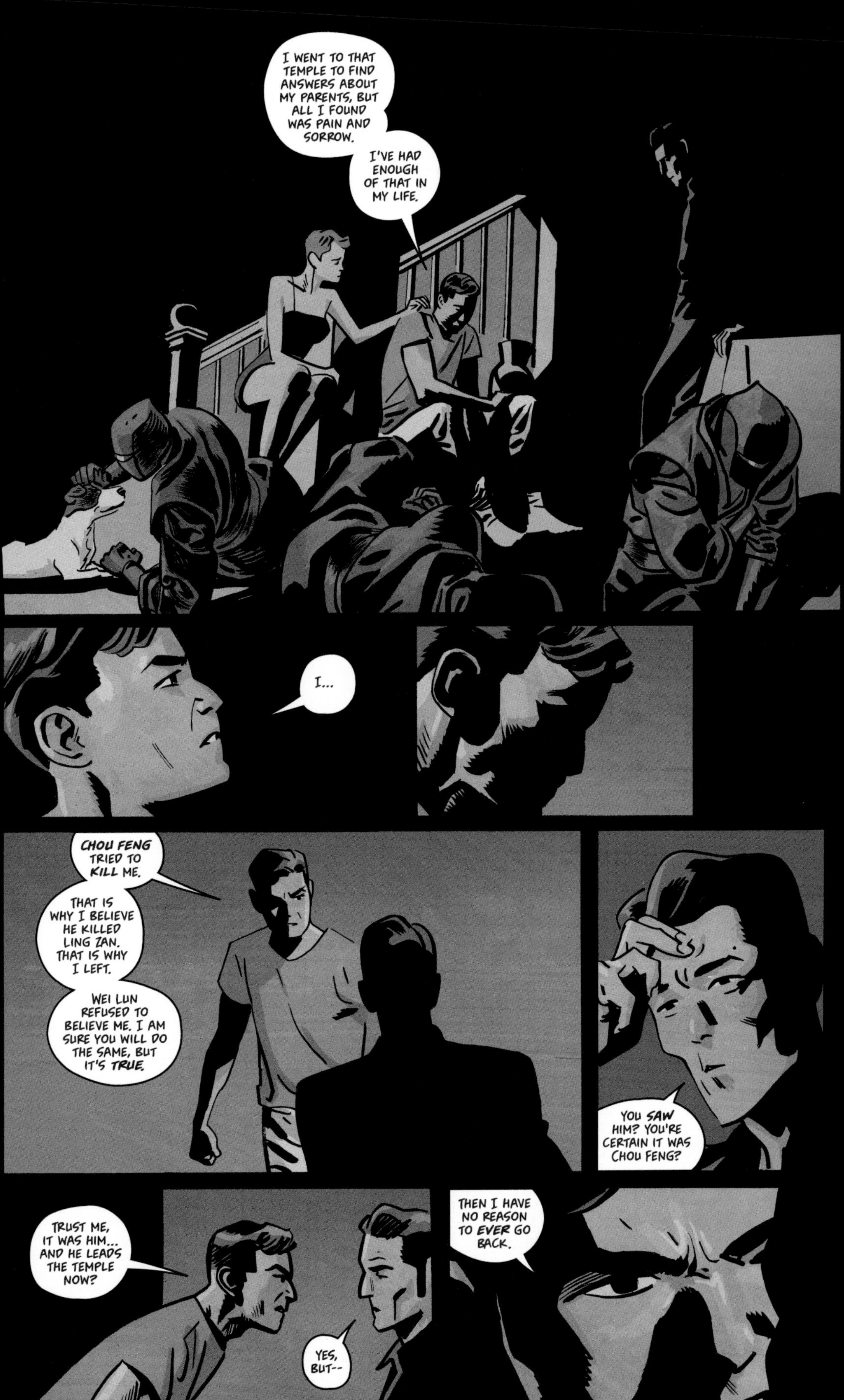
I WENT TO THAT TEMPLE TO FIND ANSWERS ABOUT MY PARENTS, BUT ALL I FOUND WAS PAIN AND SORROW.
I'VE HAD ENOUGH OF THAT IN MY LIFE.
I...
CHOU FENG TRIED TO KILL ME.
THAT IS WHY I BELIEVE HE KILLED LING ZAN. THAT IS WHY I LEFT.
WEI LUN REFUSED TO BELIEVE ME. I AM SURE YOU WILL DO THE SAME, BUT IT'S TRUE.
YOU SAW HIM? YOU'RE CERTAIN IT WAS CHOU FENG?
TRUST ME, IT WAS HIM... AND HE LEADS THE TEMPLE NOW?
YES, BUT--
THEN I HAVE NO REASON TO EVER GO BACK.

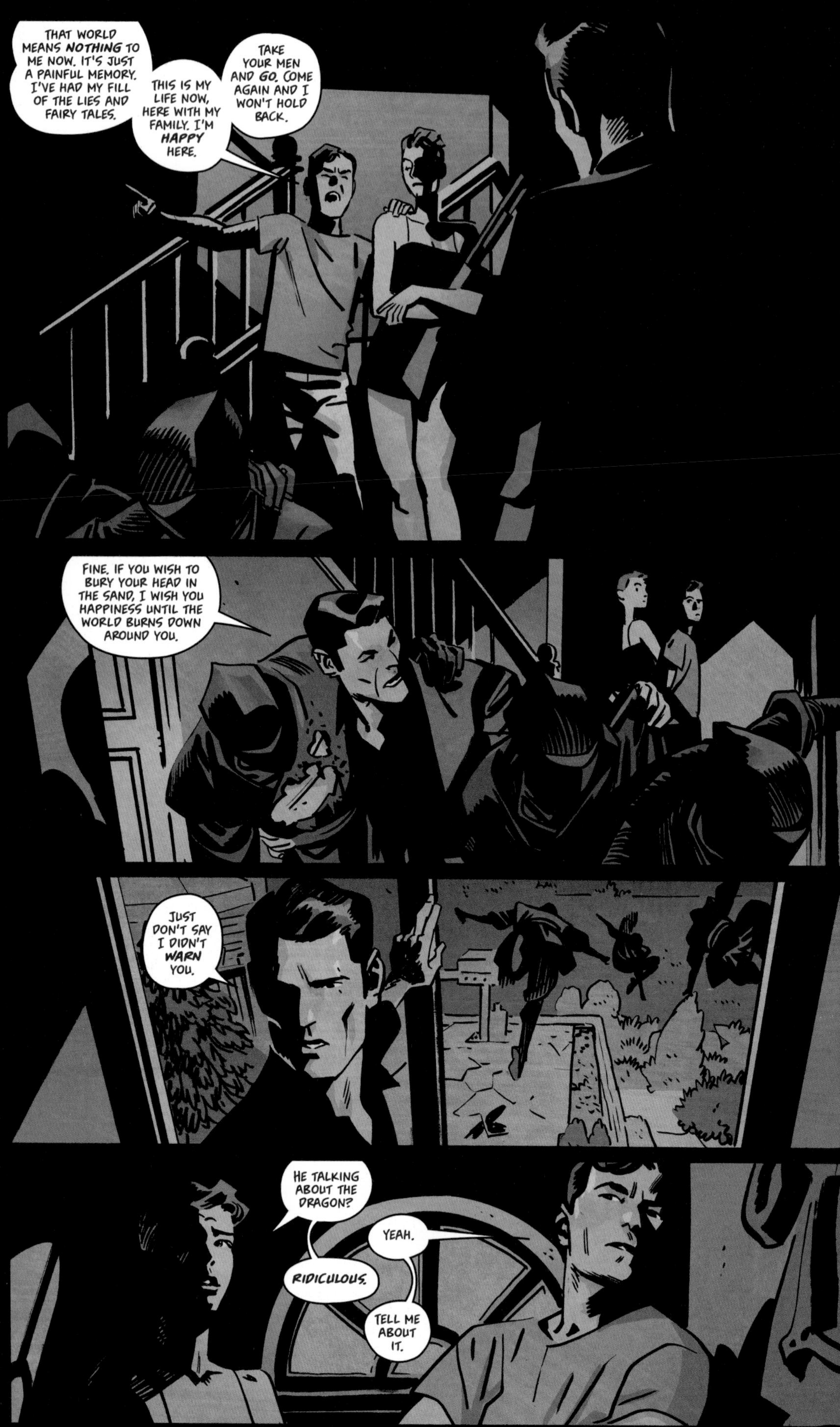
THAT WORLD MEANS NOTHING TO ME NOW. IT'S JUST A PAINFUL MEMORY. I'VE HAD MY FILL OF THE LIES AND FAIRY TALES.
THIS IS MY LIFE NOW, HERE WITH MY FAMILY. I'M HAPPY HERE.
TAKE YOUR MEN AND GO. COME AGAIN AND I WON'T HOLD BACK.
FINE. IF YOU WISH TO BURY YOUR HEAD IN THE SAND, I WISH YOU HAPPINESS UNTIL THE WORLD BURNS DOWN AROUND YOU.
JUST DON'T SAY I DIDN'T WARN YOU.
HE TALKING ABOUT THE DRAGON?
YEAH.
RIDICULOUS.
TELL ME ABOUT IT.

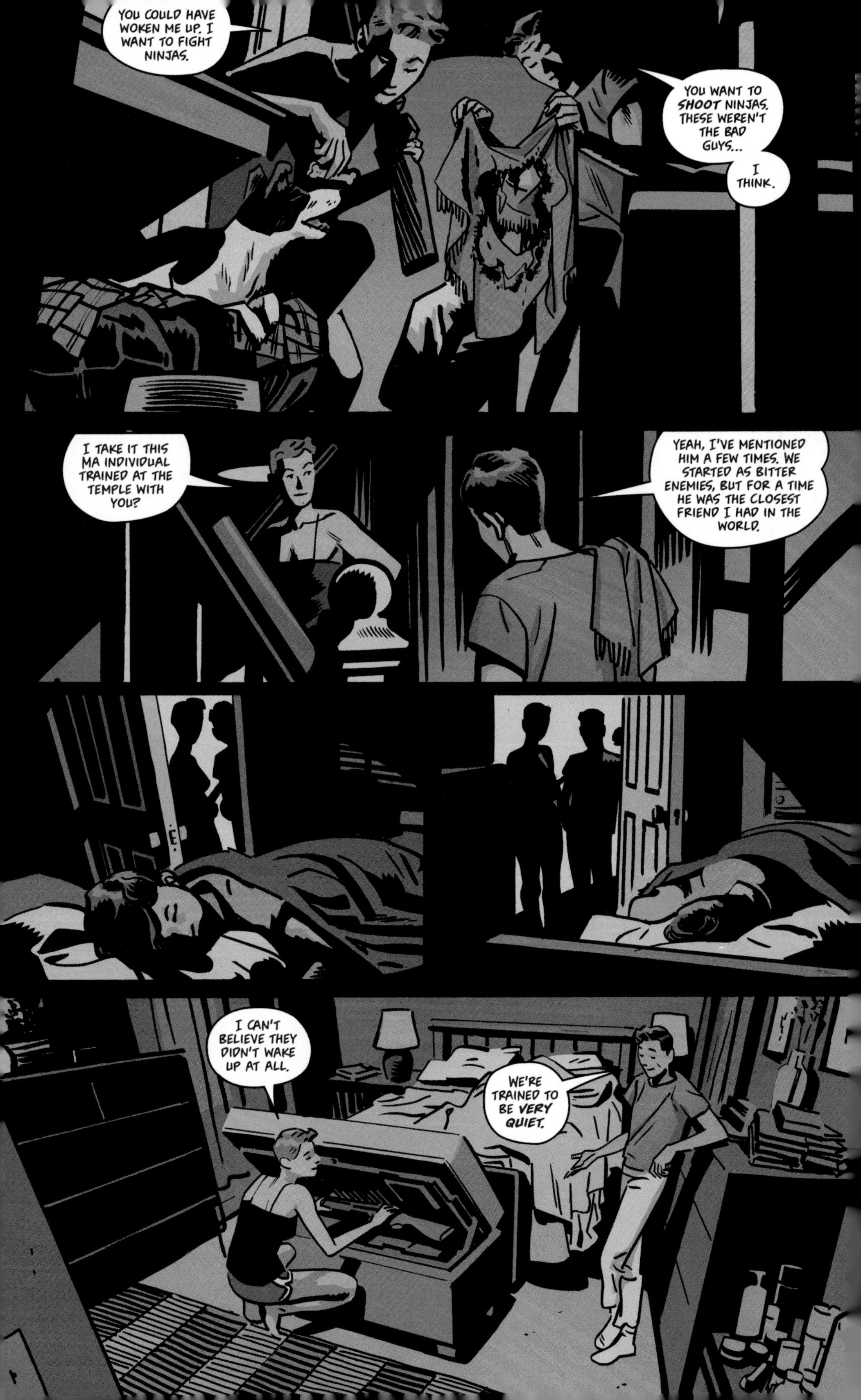
YOU COULD HAVE WOKEN ME UP. I WANT TO FIGHT NINJAS.
YOU WANT TO SHOOT NINJAS. THESE WEREN'T THE BAD GUYS...
I THINK.
I TAKE IT THIS MA INDIVIDUAL TRAINED AT THE TEMPLE WITH YOU?
YEAH, I'VE MENTIONED HIM A FEW TIMES. WE STARTED AS BITTER ENEMIES, BUT FOR A TIME HE WAS THE CLOSEST FRIEND I HAD IN THE WORLD.
I CAN'T BELIEVE THEY DIDN'T WAKE UP AT ALL.
WE'RE TRAINED TO BE VERY QUIET.

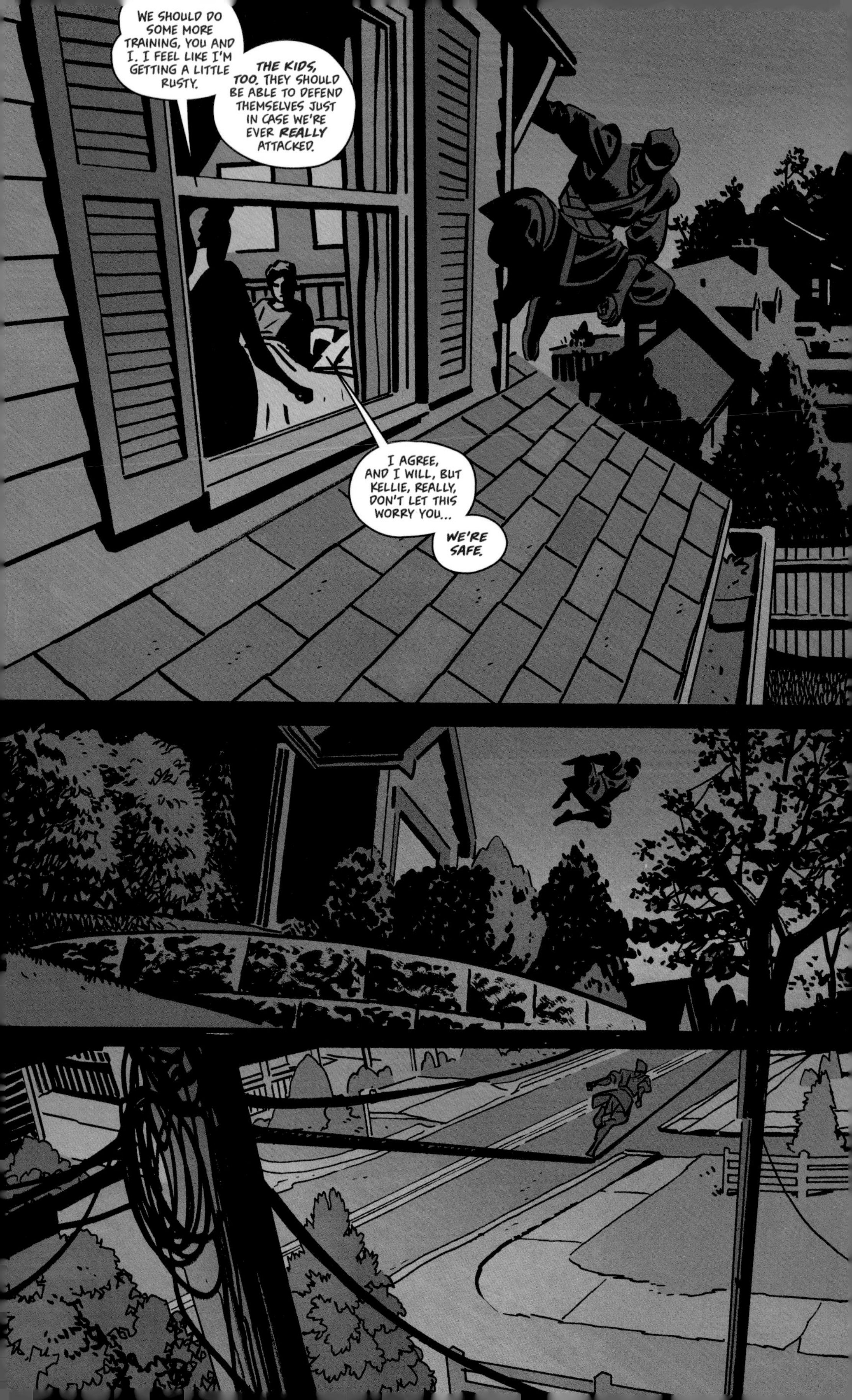
WE SHOULD DO SOME MORE TRAINING, YOU AND I. I FEEL LIKE I'M GETTING A LITTLE RUSTY.
THE KIDS, TOO. THEY SHOULD BE ABLE TO DEFEND THEMSELVES JUST IN CASE WE'RE EVER REALLY ATTACKED.
I AGREE, AND I WILL, BUT KELLIE, REALLY, DON'T LET THIS WORRY YOU...
WE'RE SAFE.

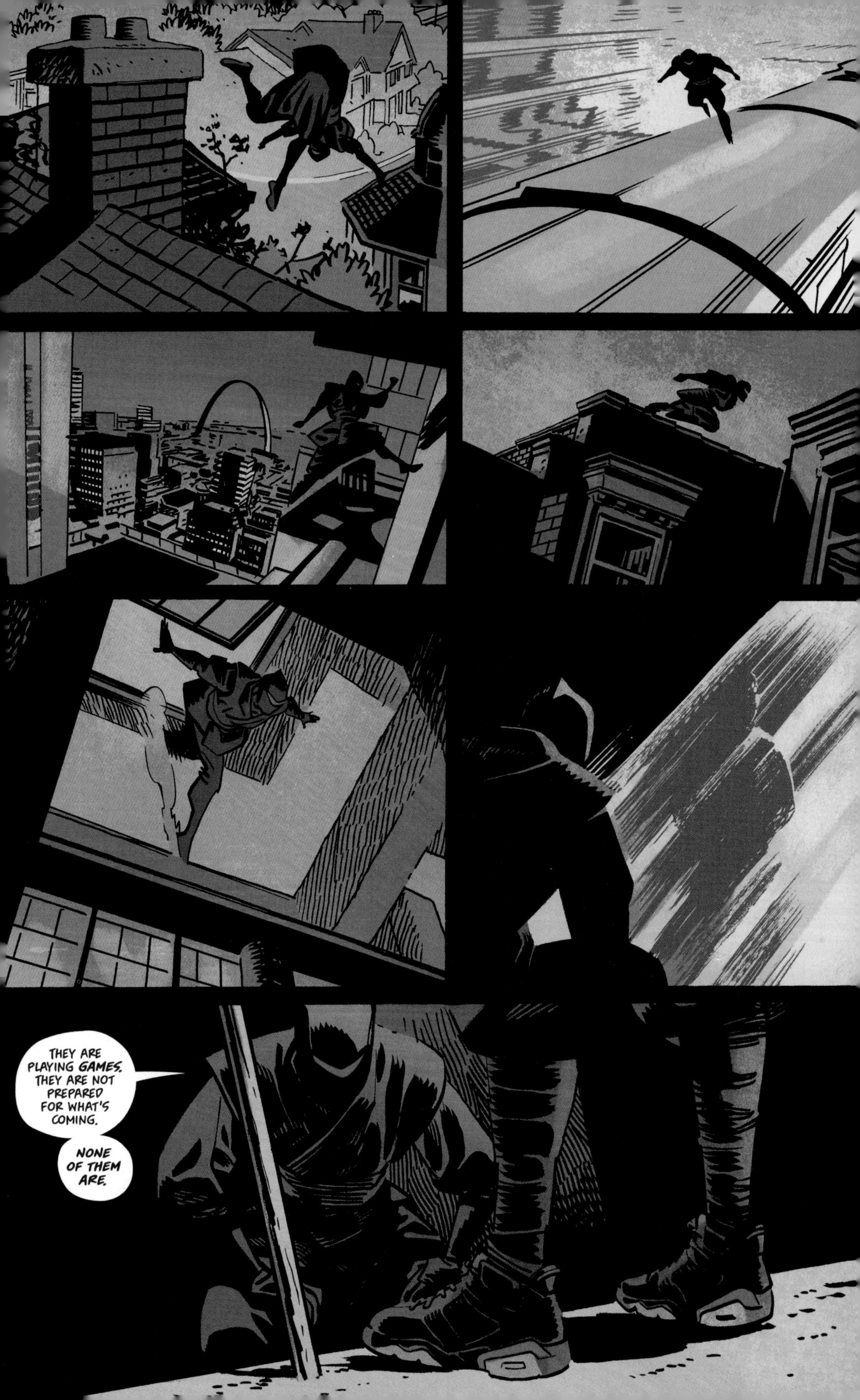
THEY ARE PLAYING GAMES. THEY ARE NOT PREPARED FOR WHAT'S COMING.
NONE OF THEM ARE.

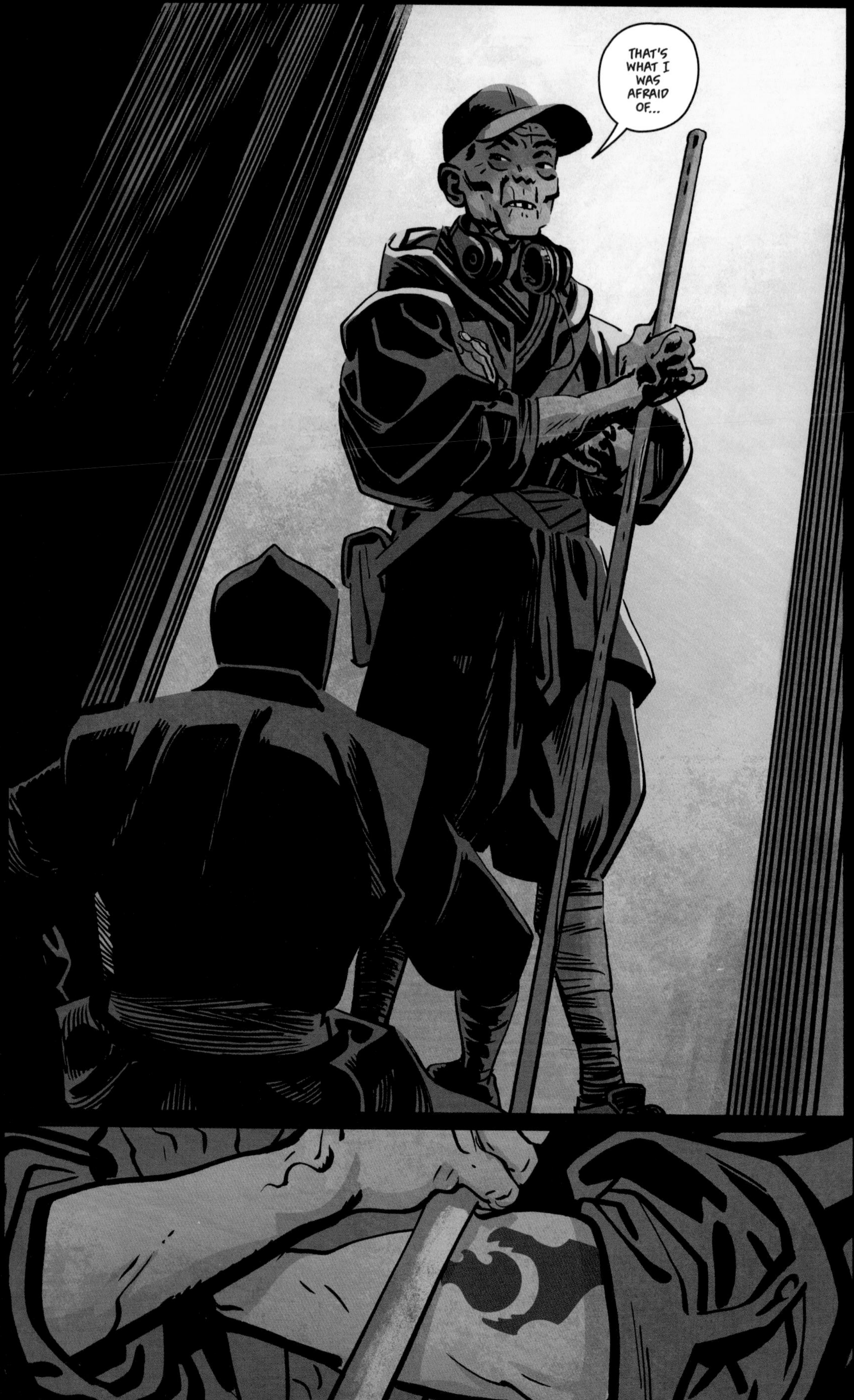
THAT'S WHAT I WAS AFRAID OF...

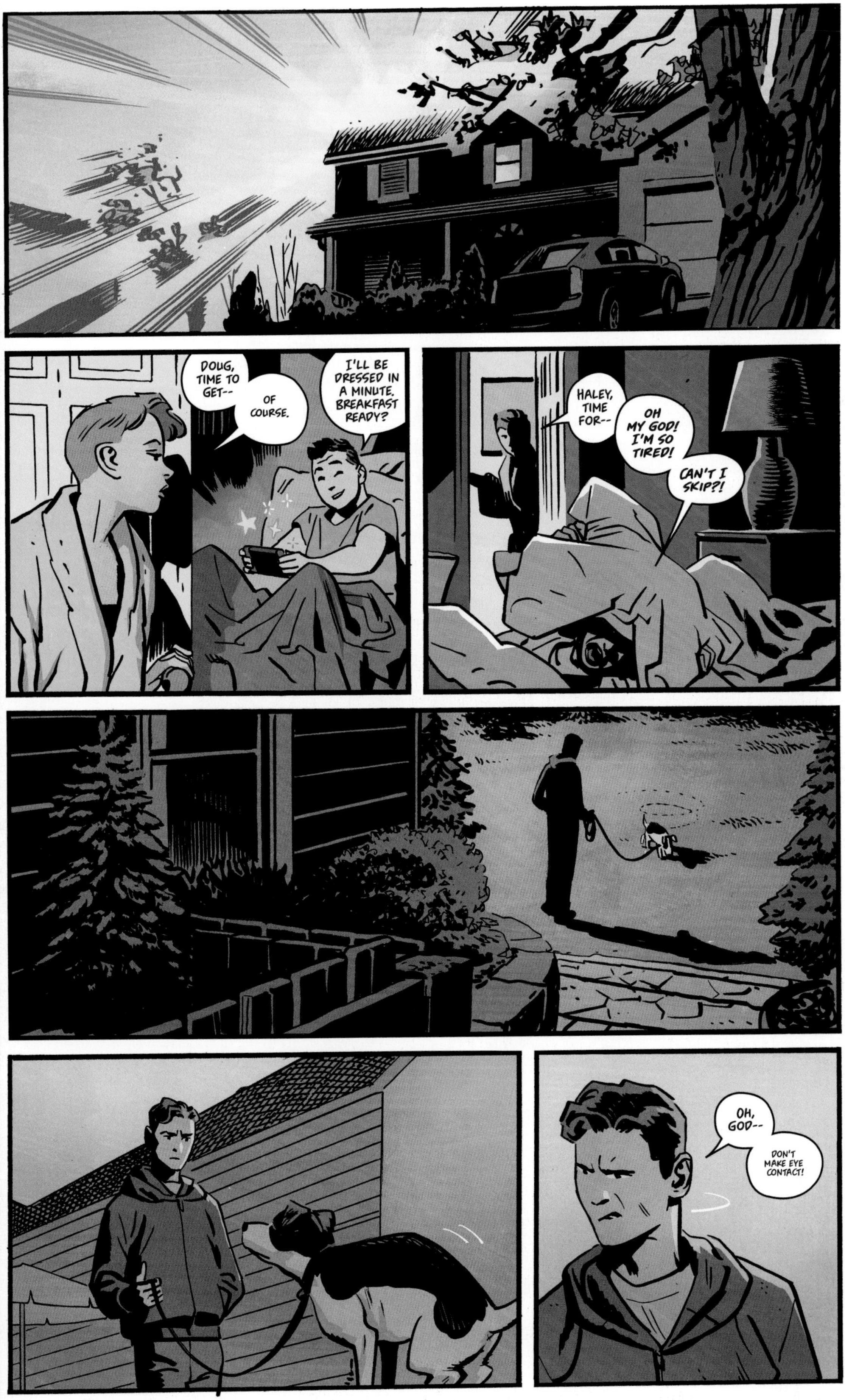
DOUG, TIME TO GET--
OF COURSE.
I'LL BE DRESSED IN A MINUTE. BREAKFAST READY?
HALEY, TIME FOR--
OH MY GOD! I'M SO TIRED!
CAN'T I SKIP?!
OH, GOD--
DON'T MAKE EYE CONTACT!

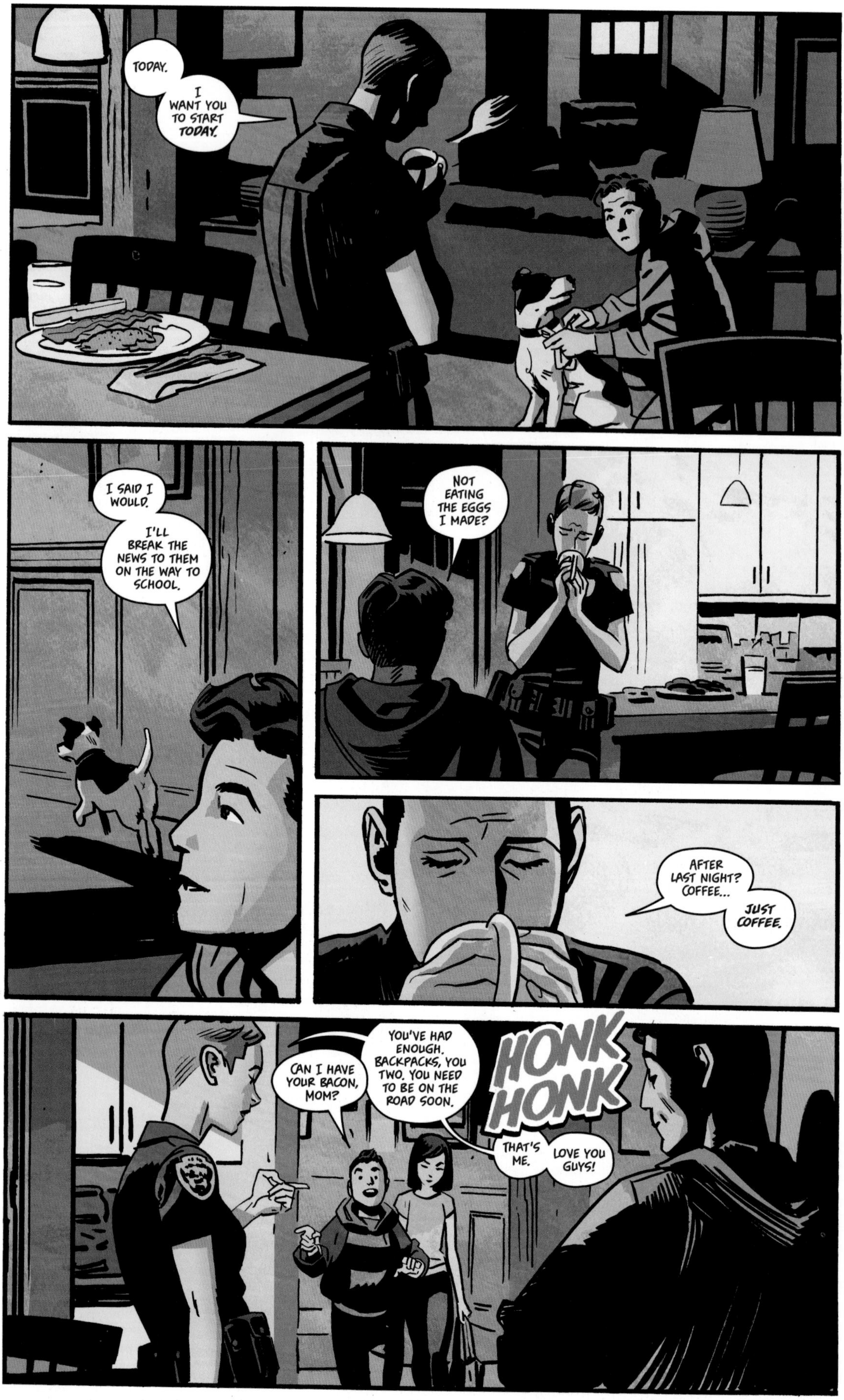
TODAY.
I WANT YOU TO START *TODAY.*
I SAID I WOULD.
I'LL BREAK THE NEWS TO THEM ON THE WAY TO SCHOOL.
NOT EATING THE EGGS I MADE?
AFTER LAST NIGHT? COFFEE...
JUST *COFFEE.*
CAN I HAVE YOUR BACON, MOM?
YOU'VE HAD ENOUGH. BACKPACKS, YOU TWO. YOU NEED TO BE ON THE ROAD SOON.
HONK HONK
THAT'S ME.
LOVE YOU GUYS!

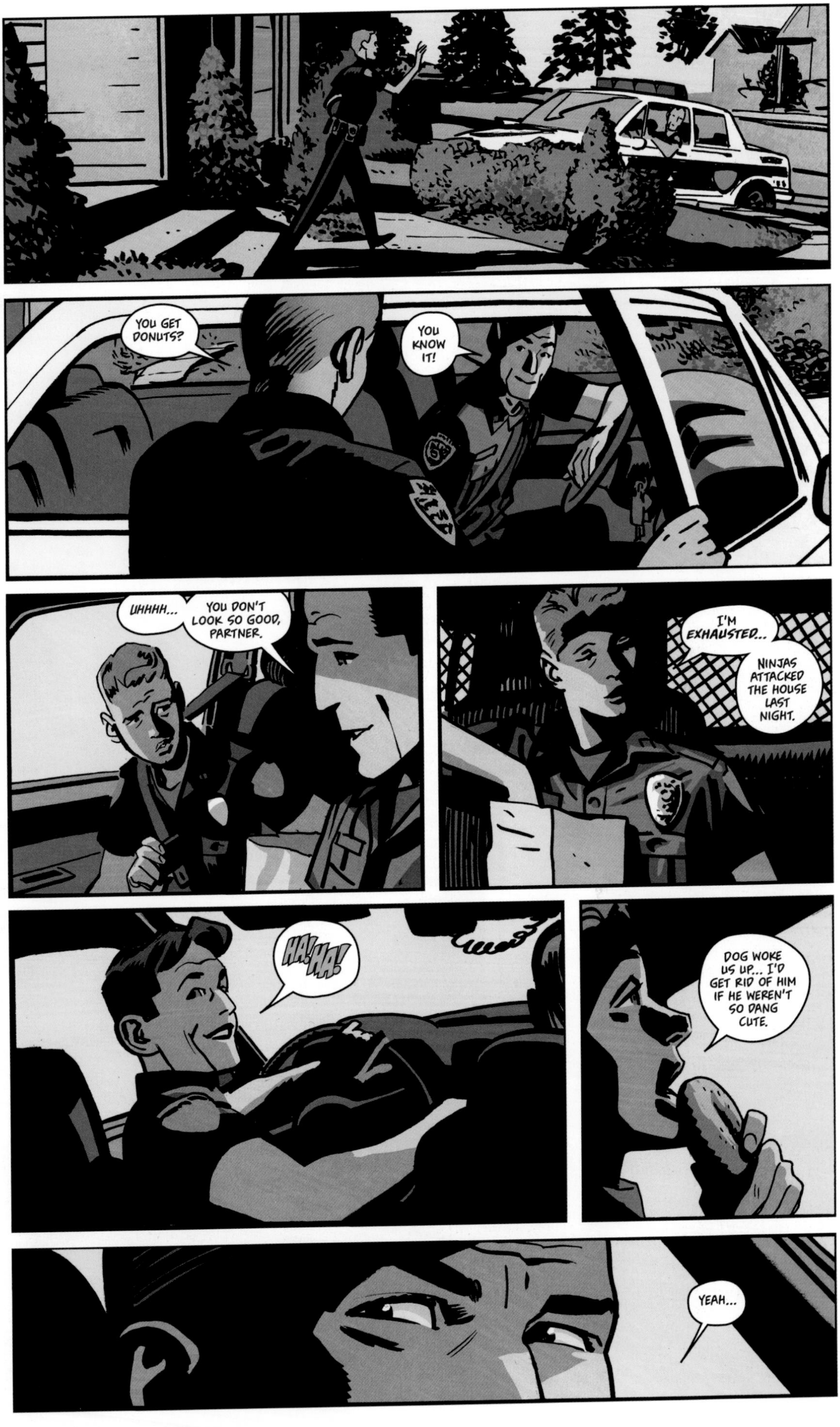
YOU GET DONUTS?
YOU KNOW IT!
UHHHH...
YOU DON'T LOOK SO GOOD, PARTNER.
I'M EXHAUSTED...
NINJAS ATTACKED THE HOUSE LAST NIGHT.
HA! HA!
DOG WOKE US UP... I'D GET RID OF HIM IF HE WEREN'T SO DANG CUTE.
YEAH...

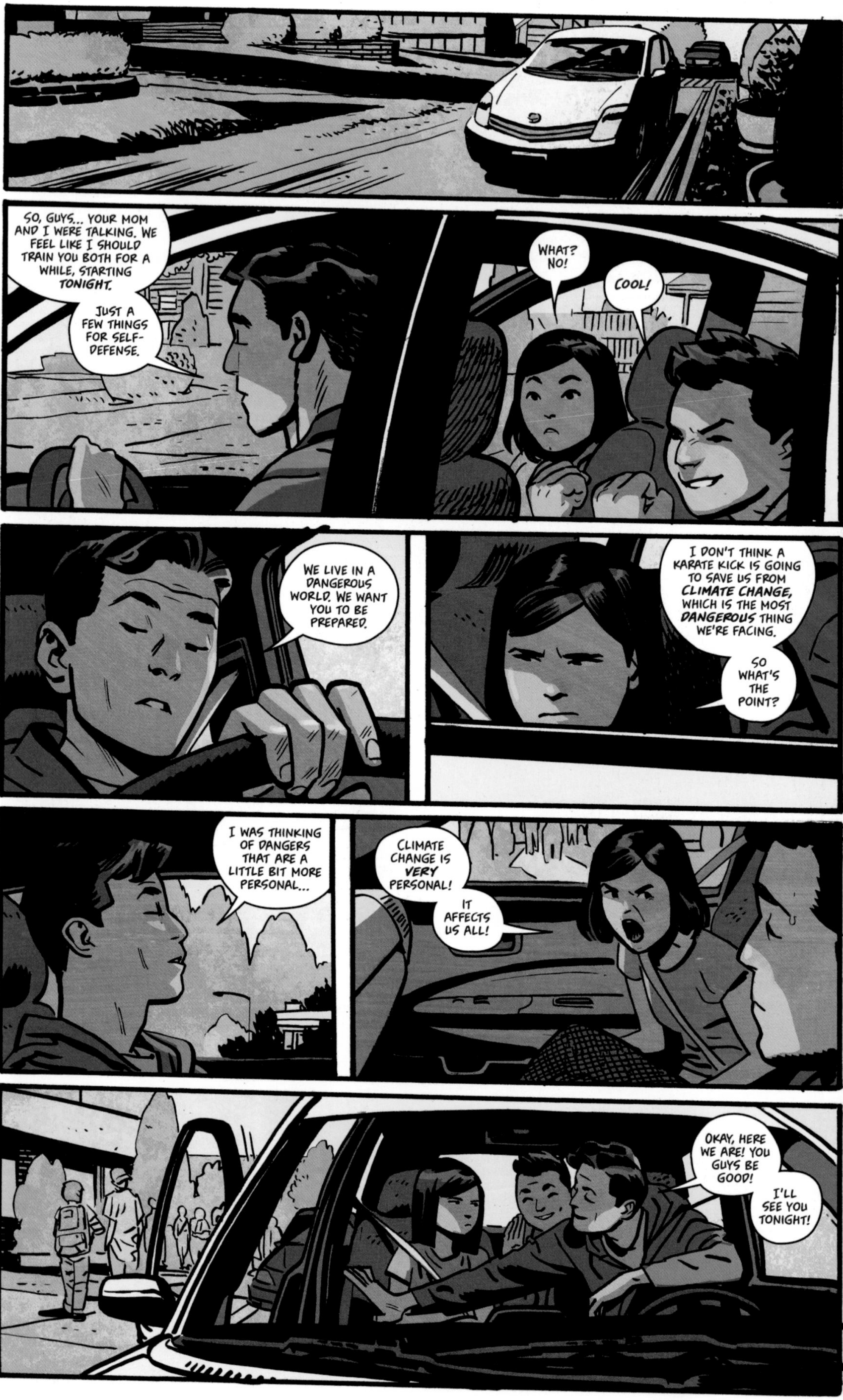
SO, GUYS... YOUR MOM AND I WERE TALKING. WE FEEL LIKE I SHOULD TRAIN YOU BOTH FOR A WHILE, STARTING TONIGHT.
JUST A FEW THINGS FOR SELF-DEFENSE.
WHAT? NO!
COOL!
WE LIVE IN A DANGEROUS WORLD. WE WANT YOU TO BE PREPARED.
I DON'T THINK A KARATE KICK IS GOING TO SAVE US FROM CLIMATE CHANGE, WHICH IS THE MOST DANGEROUS THING WE'RE FACING.
SO WHAT'S THE POINT?
I WAS THINKING OF DANGERS THAT ARE A LITTLE BIT MORE PERSONAL...
CLIMATE CHANGE IS VERY PERSONAL!
IT AFFECTS US ALL!
OKAY, HERE WE ARE! YOU GUYS BE GOOD!
I'LL SEE YOU TONIGHT!

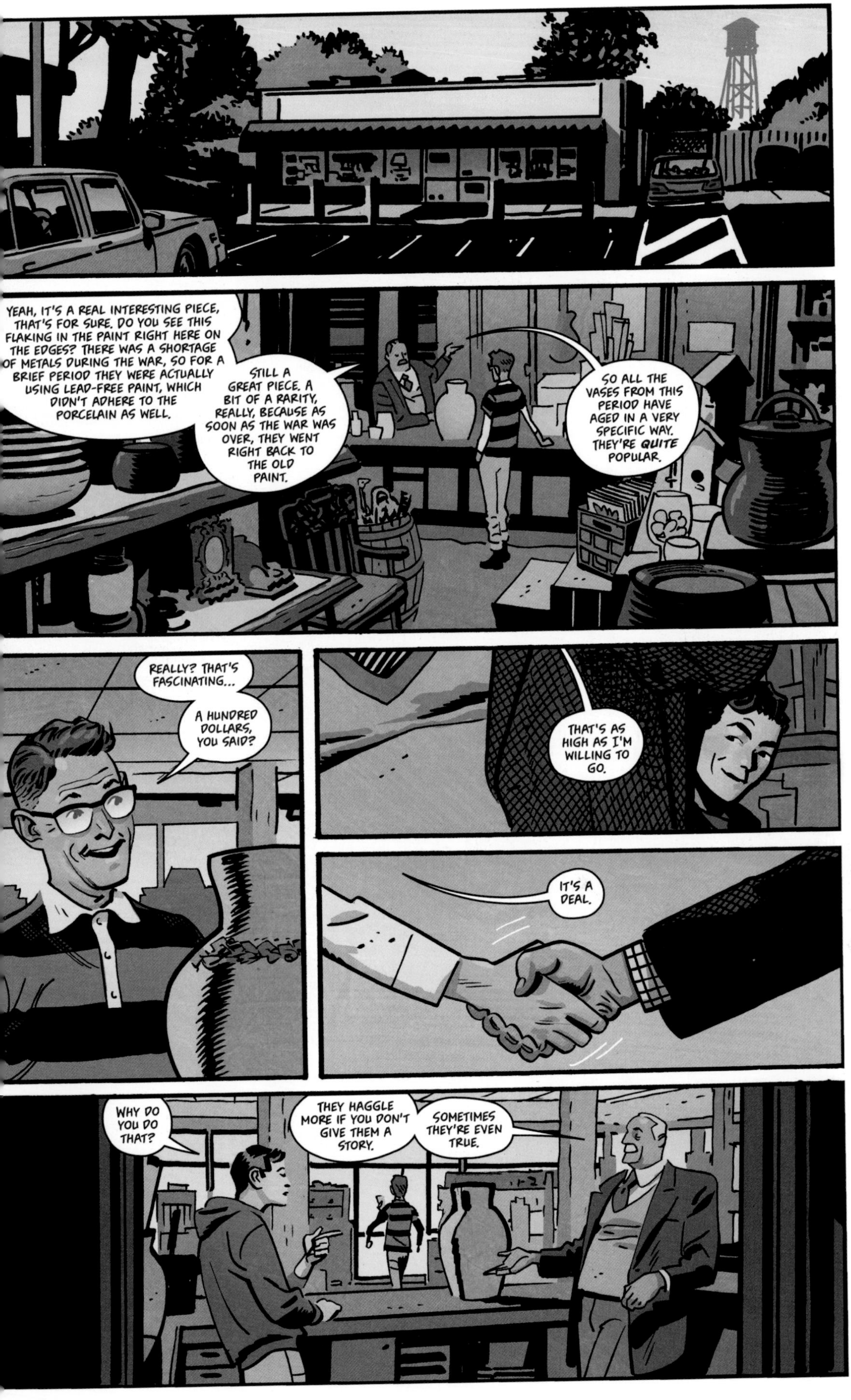
YEAH, IT'S A REAL INTERESTING PIECE, THAT'S FOR SURE. DO YOU SEE THIS FLAKING IN THE PAINT RIGHT HERE ON THE EDGES? THERE WAS A SHORTAGE OF METALS DURING THE WAR, SO FOR A BRIEF PERIOD THEY WERE ACTUALLY USING LEAD-FREE PAINT, WHICH DIDN'T ADHERE TO THE PORCELAIN AS WELL.
STILL A GREAT PIECE. A BIT OF A RARITY, REALLY, BECAUSE AS SOON AS THE WAR WAS OVER, THEY WENT RIGHT BACK TO THE OLD PAINT.
SO ALL THE VASES FROM THIS PERIOD HAVE AGED IN A VERY SPECIFIC WAY. THEY'RE QUITE POPULAR.
REALLY? THAT'S FASCINATING...
A HUNDRED DOLLARS, YOU SAID?
THAT'S AS HIGH AS I'M WILLING TO GO.
IT'S A DEAL.
WHY DO YOU DO THAT?
THEY HAGGLE MORE IF YOU DON'T GIVE THEM A STORY.
SOMETIMES THEY'RE EVEN TRUE.

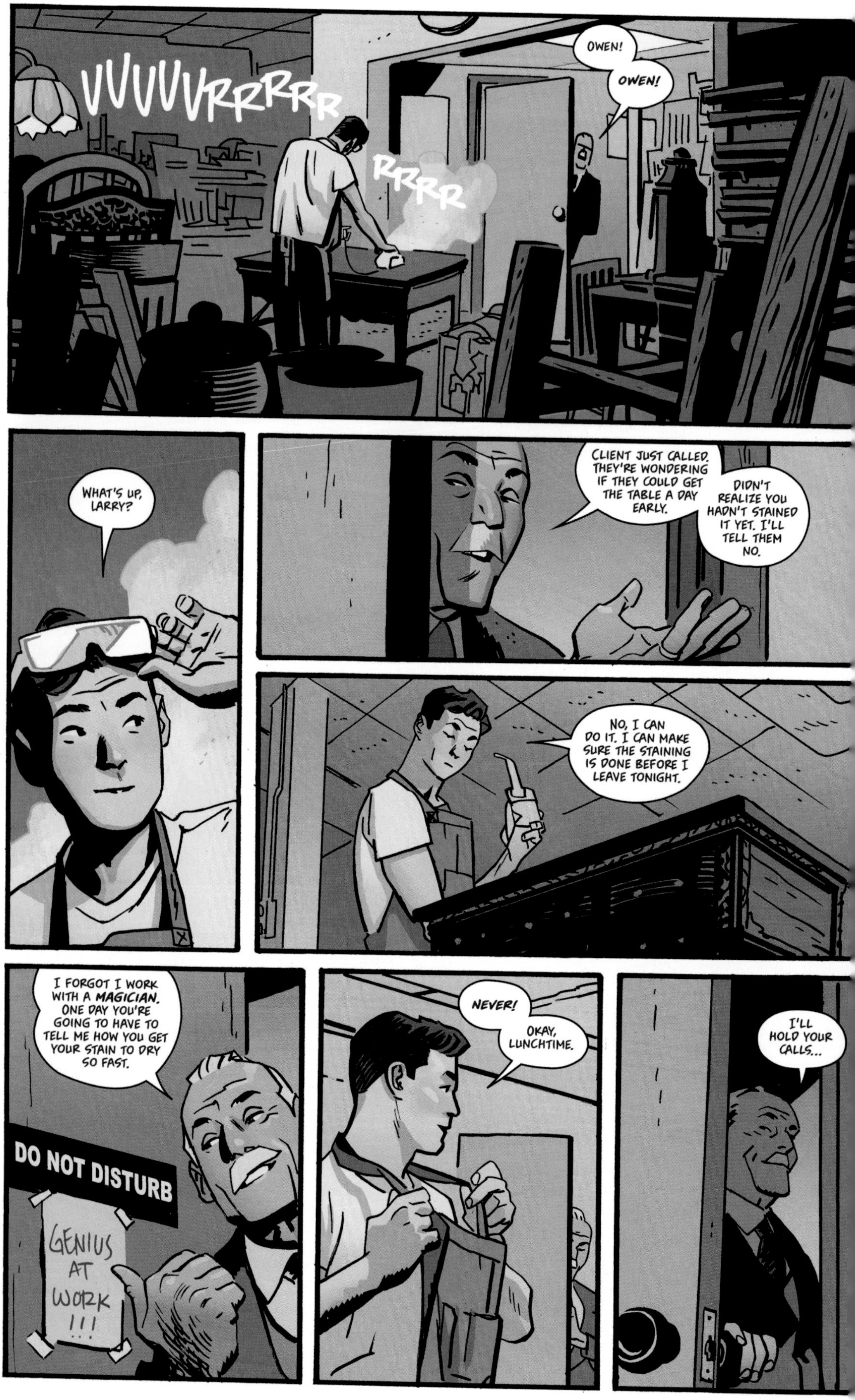
VVUUVRRRRR
RRRR
OWEN!
OWEN!
WHAT'S UP, LARRY?
CLIENT JUST CALLED. THEY'RE WONDERING IF THEY COULD GET THE TABLE A DAY EARLY.
DIDN'T REALIZE YOU HADN'T STAINED IT YET. I'LL TELL THEM NO.
NO, I CAN DO IT. I CAN MAKE SURE THE STAINING IS DONE BEFORE I LEAVE TONIGHT.
I FORGOT I WORK WITH A MAGICIAN. ONE DAY YOU'RE GOING TO HAVE TO TELL ME HOW YOU GET YOUR STAIN TO DRY SO FAST.
DO NOT DISTURB
GENIUS AT WORK !!!
NEVER!
OKAY, LUNCHTIME.
I'LL HOLD YOUR CALLS...

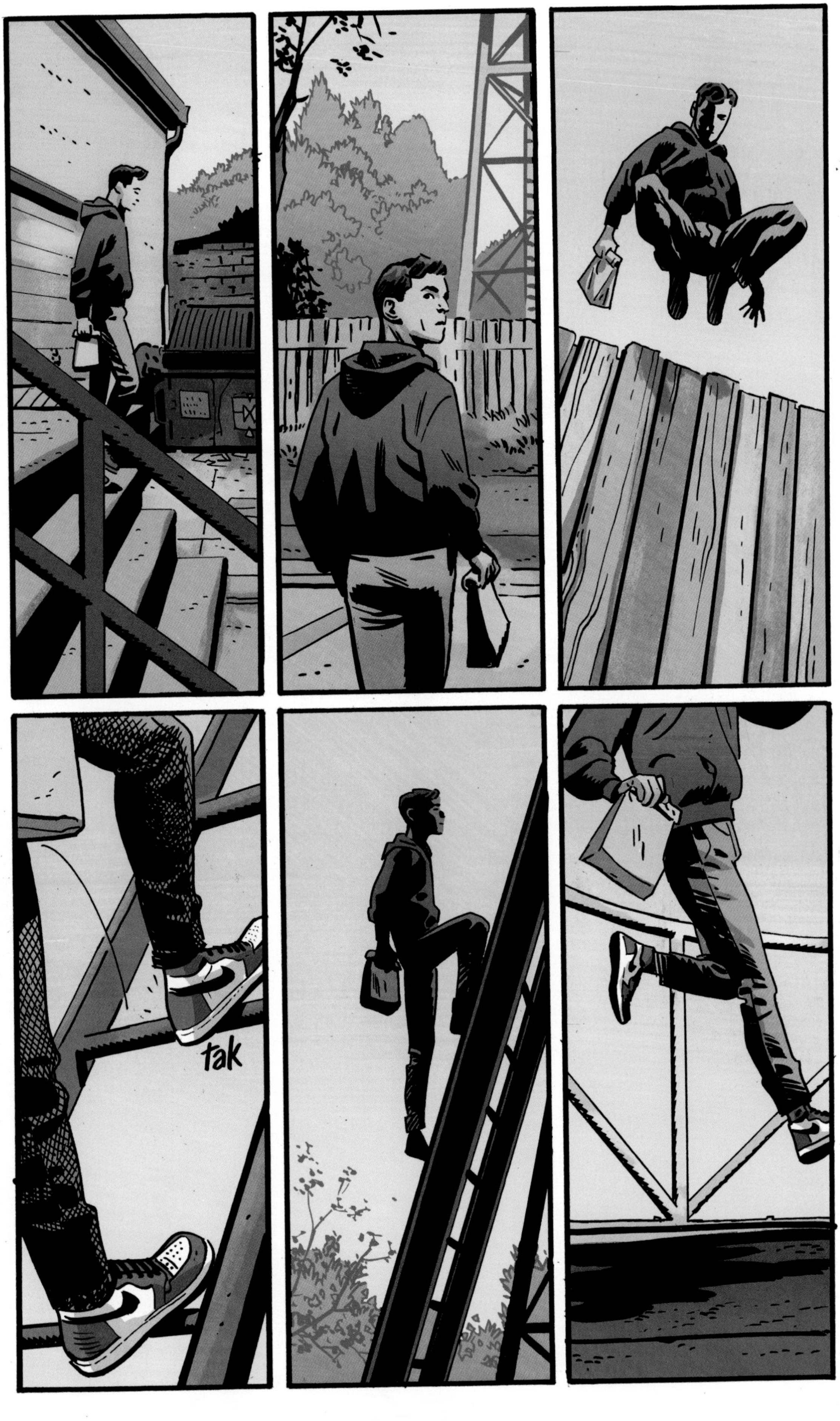
tak

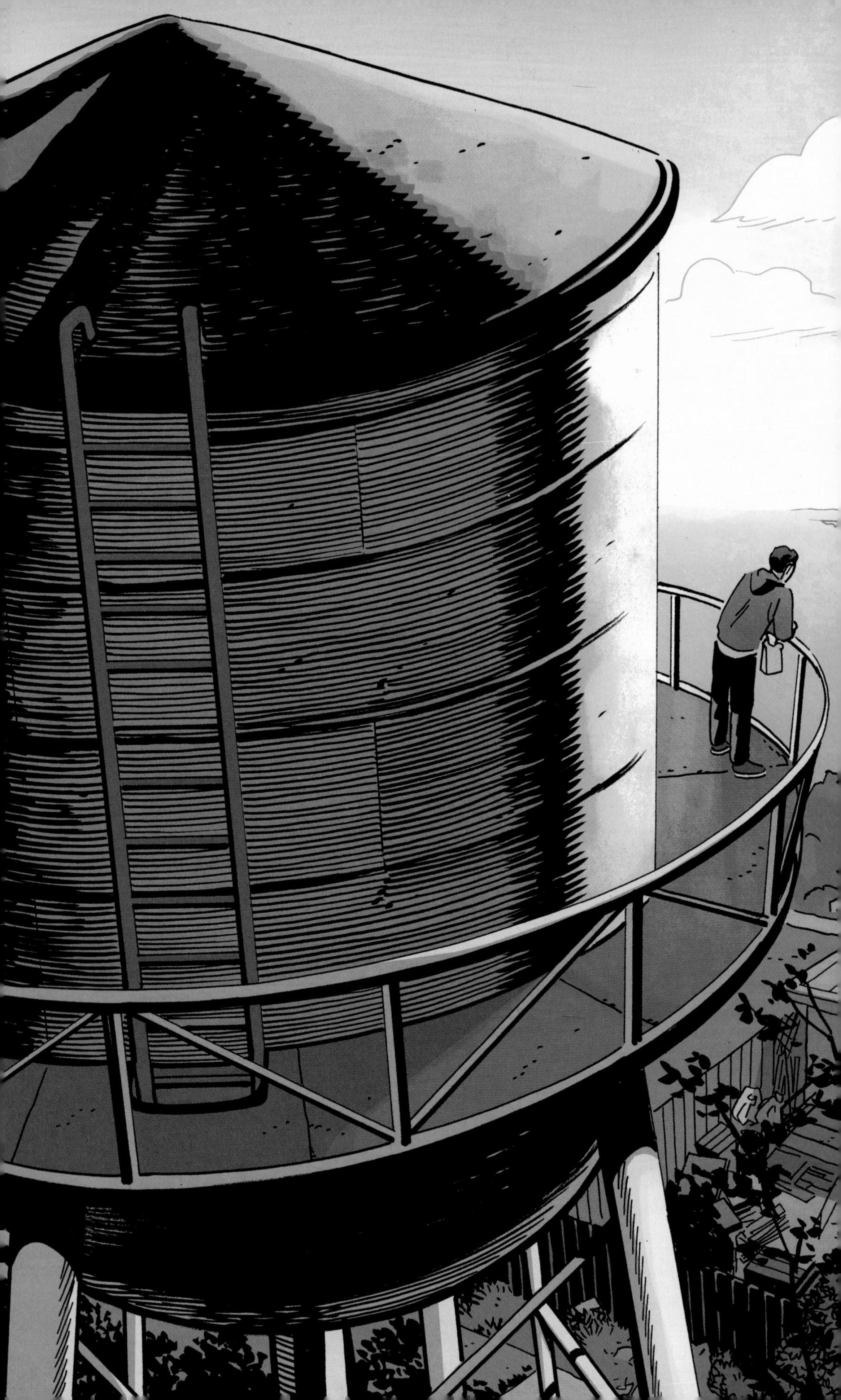

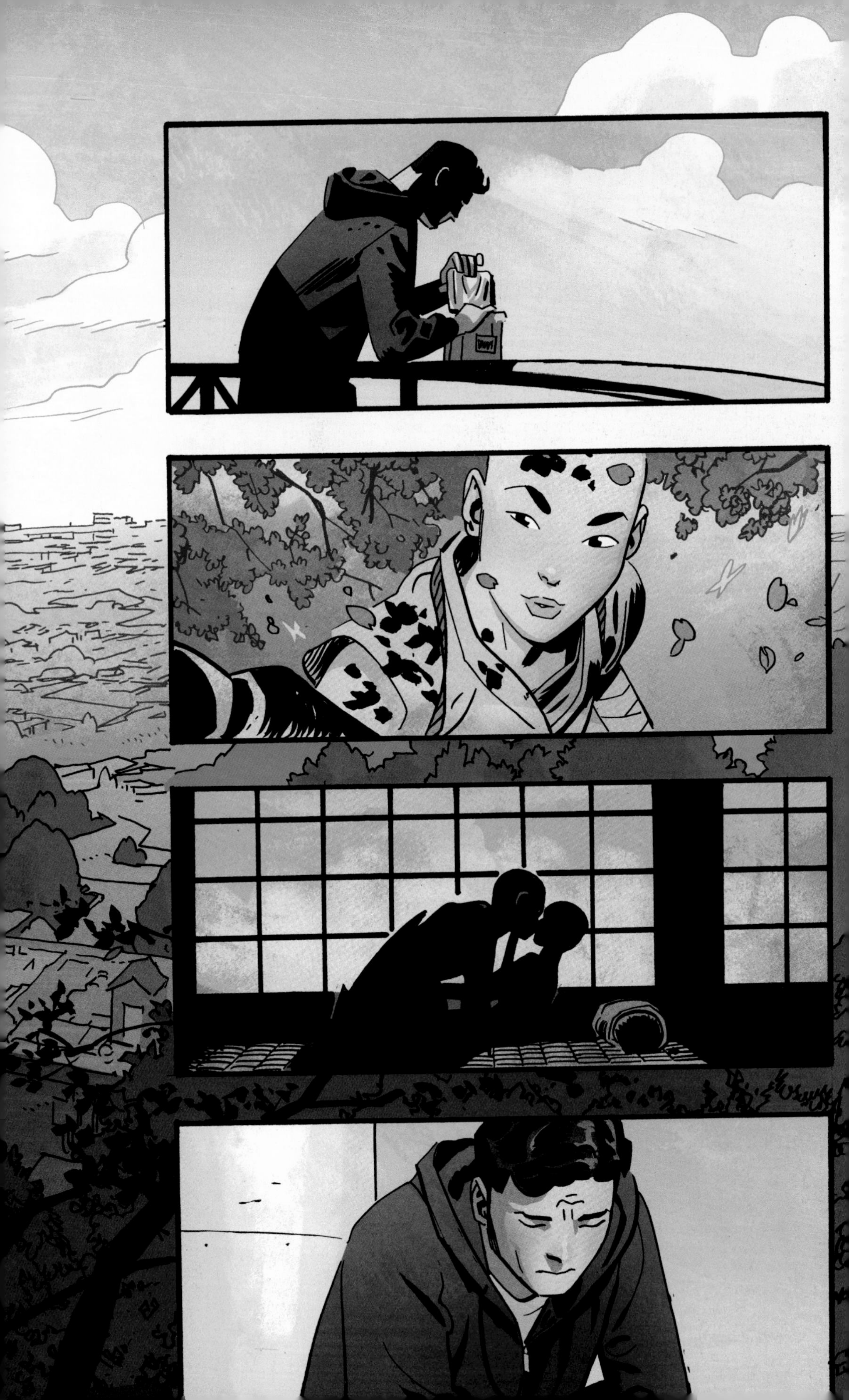

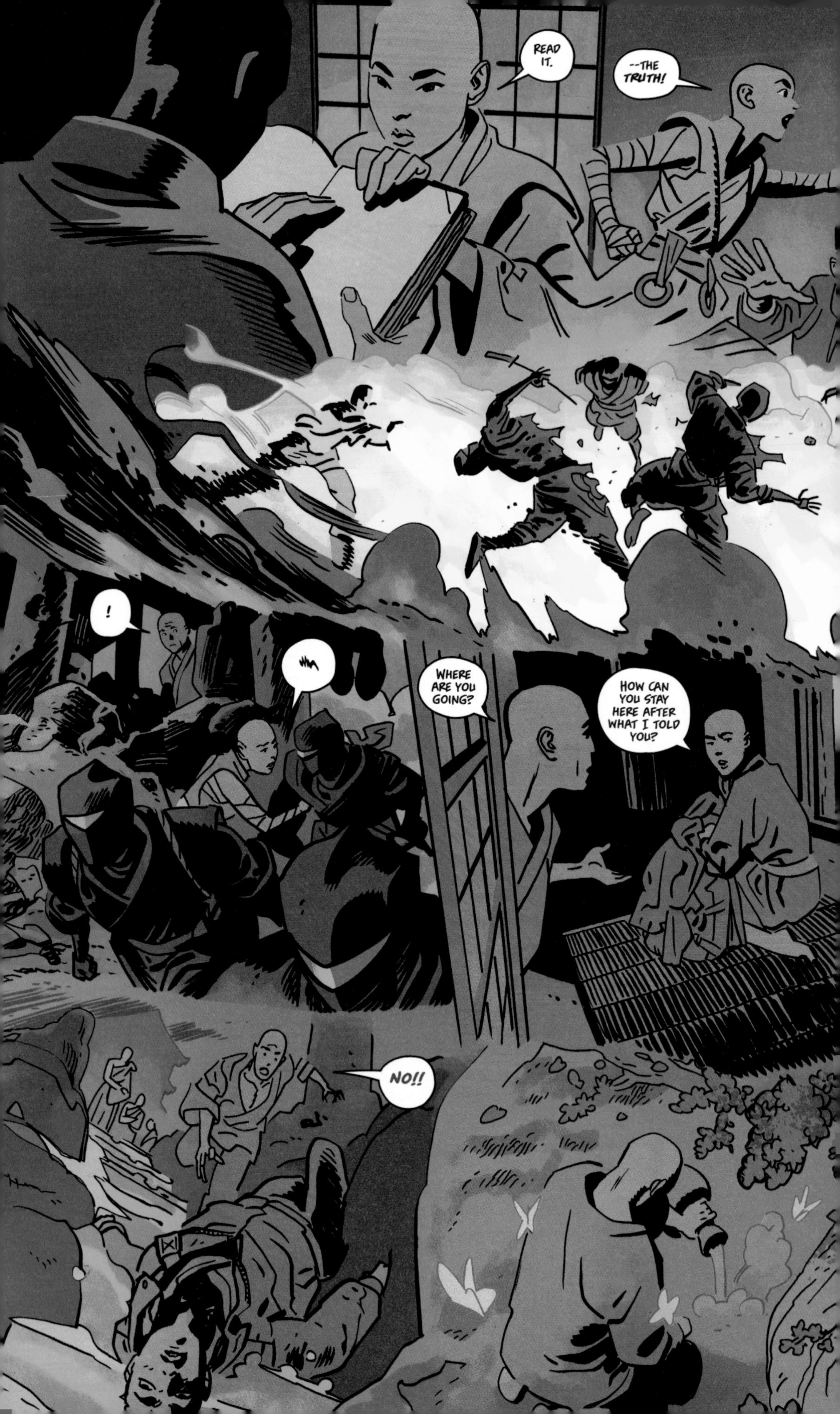
READ IT.
--THE TRUTH!
!
WHERE ARE YOU GOING?
HOW CAN YOU STAY HERE AFTER WHAT I TOLD YOU?
NO!!

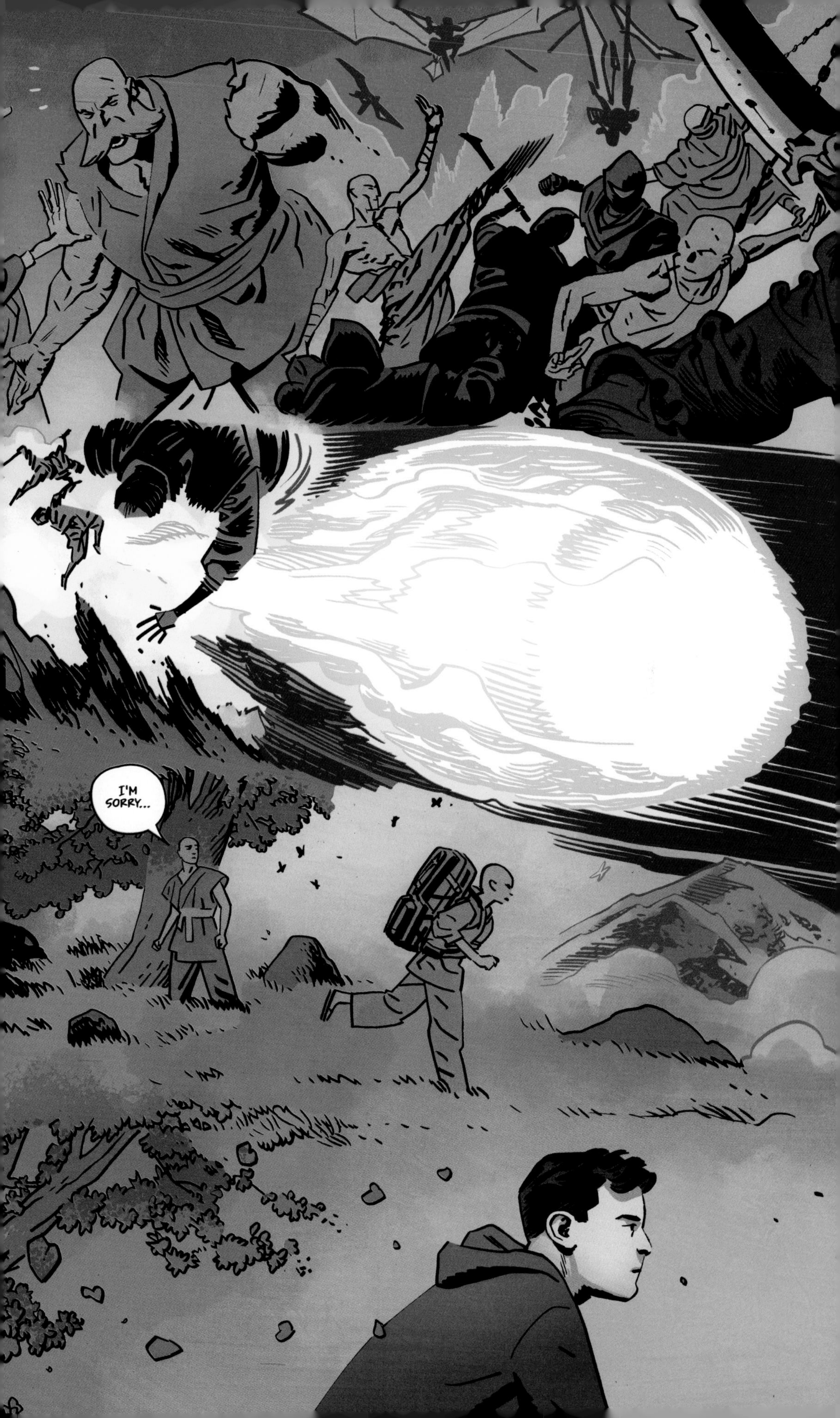
I'M SORRY...

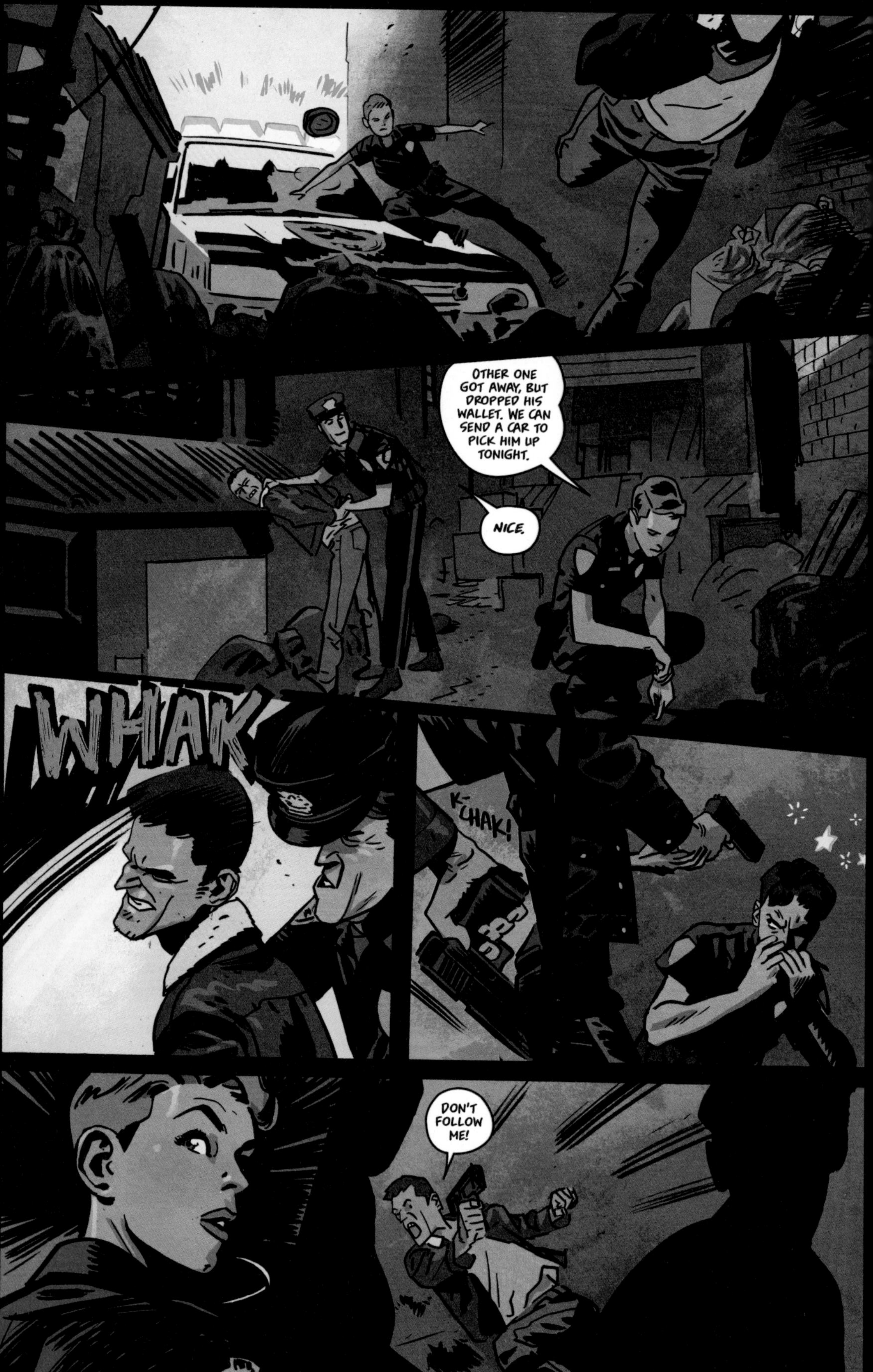
OTHER ONE GOT AWAY, BUT DROPPED HIS WALLET. WE CAN SEND A CAR TO PICK HIM UP TONIGHT.
NICE.
WHAK
K-CHAK!
DON'T FOLLOW ME!

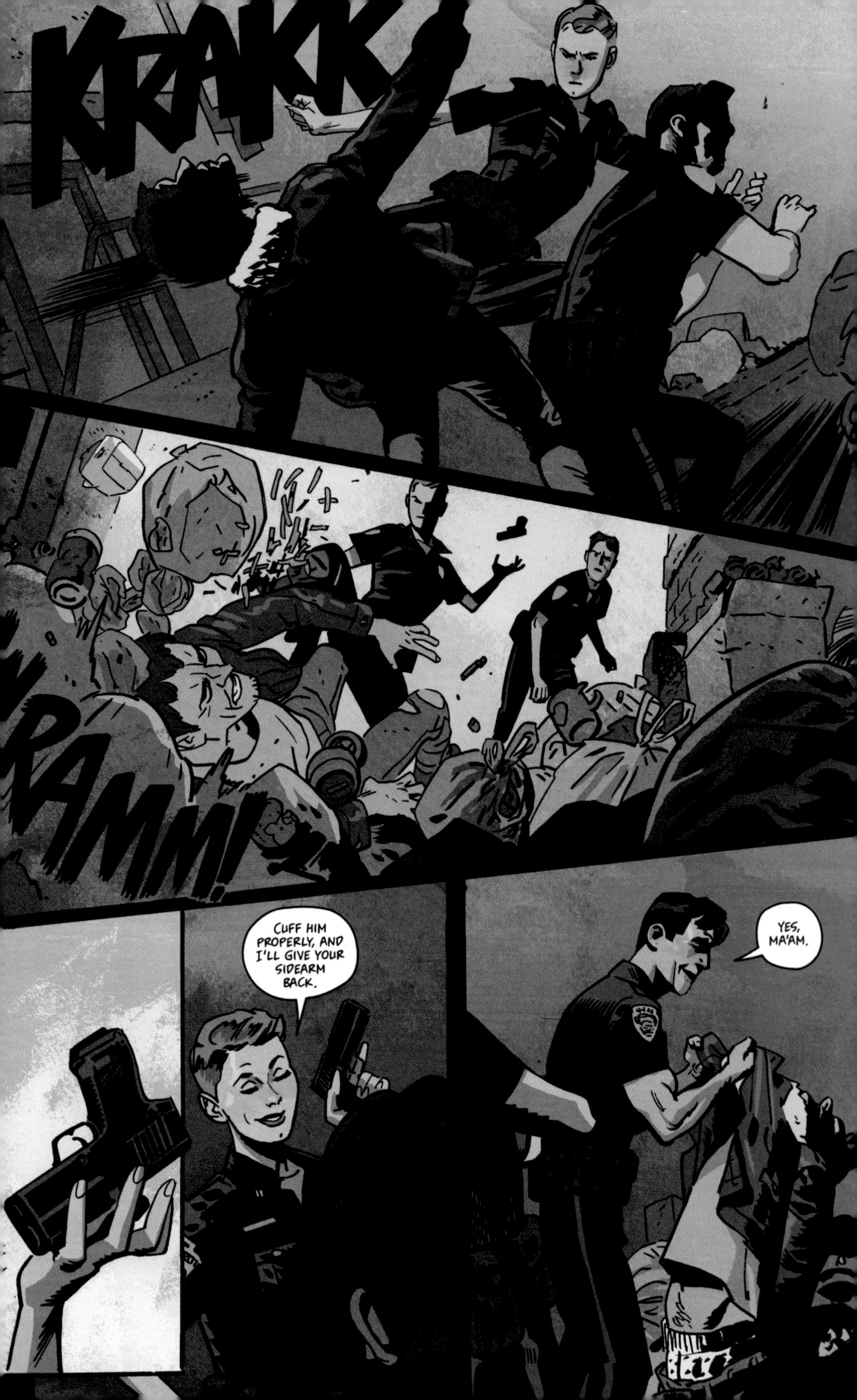
KRAKK
...RAMM!
CUFF HIM PROPERLY, AND I'LL GIVE YOUR SIDEARM BACK.
YES, MA'AM.

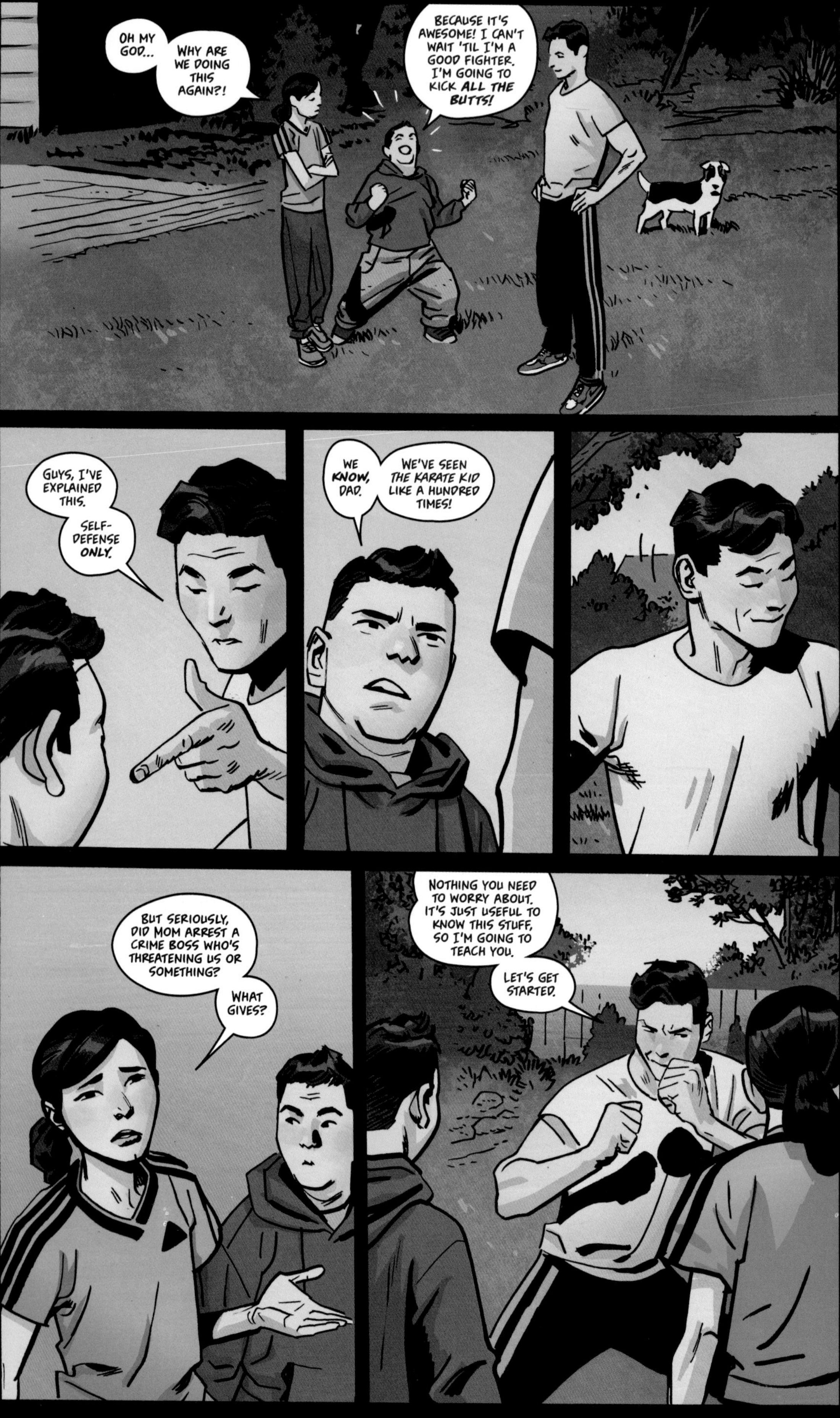
OH MY GOD...
WHY ARE WE DOING THIS AGAIN?!
BECAUSE IT'S AWESOME! I CAN'T WAIT 'TIL I'M A GOOD FIGHTER. I'M GOING TO KICK ALL THE BUTTS!
GUYS, I'VE EXPLAINED THIS.
SELF-DEFENSE ONLY.
WE KNOW, DAD.
WE'VE SEEN THE KARATE KID LIKE A HUNDRED TIMES!
BUT SERIOUSLY, DID MOM ARREST A CRIME BOSS WHO'S THREATENING US OR SOMETHING?
WHAT GIVES?
NOTHING YOU NEED TO WORRY ABOUT. IT'S JUST USEFUL TO KNOW THIS STUFF, SO I'M GOING TO TEACH YOU.
LET'S GET STARTED.

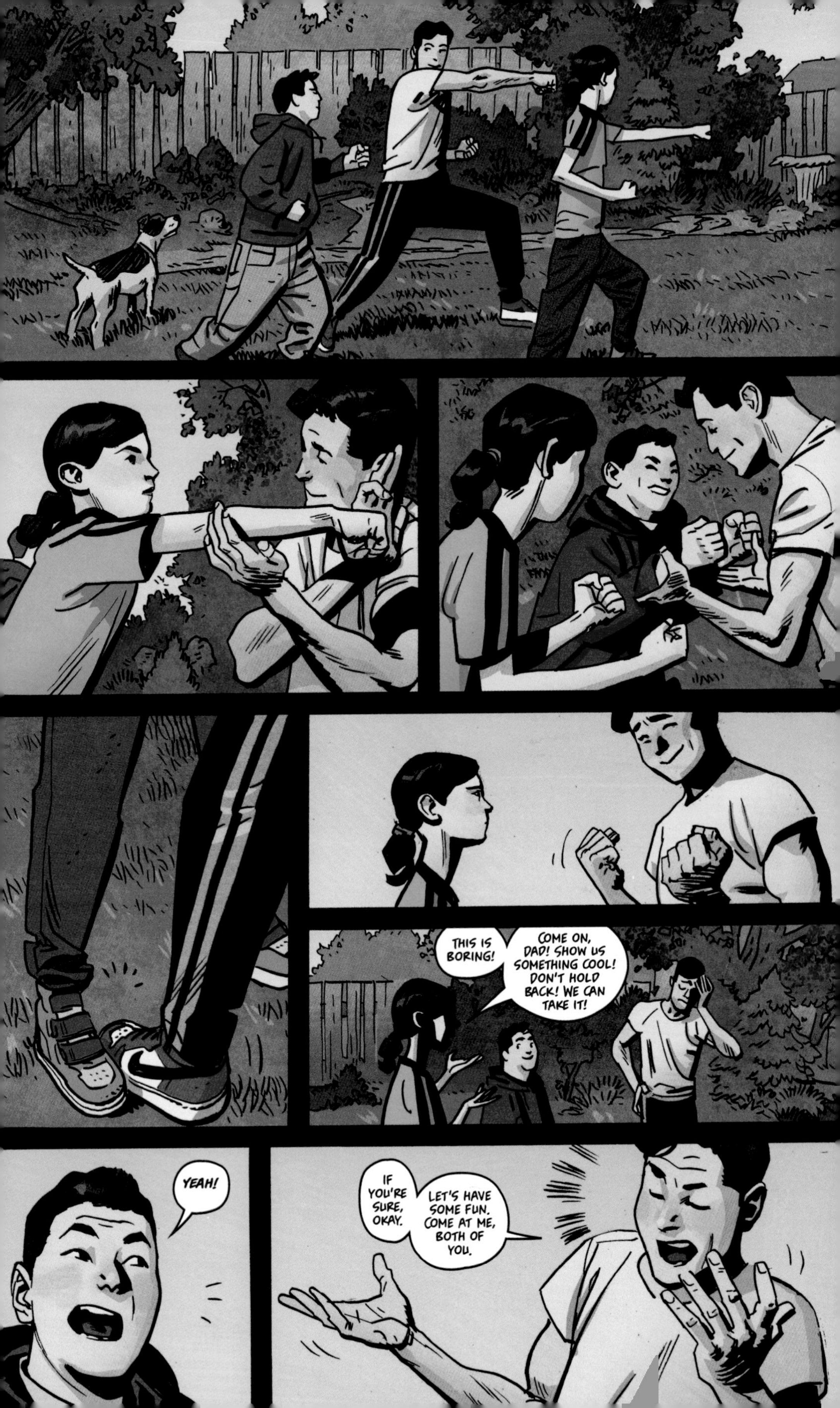

THIS IS BORING!
COME ON, DAD! SHOW US SOMETHING COOL! DON'T HOLD BACK! WE CAN TAKE IT!
YEAH!
IF YOU'RE SURE, OKAY.
LET'S HAVE SOME FUN. COME AT ME, BOTH OF YOU.

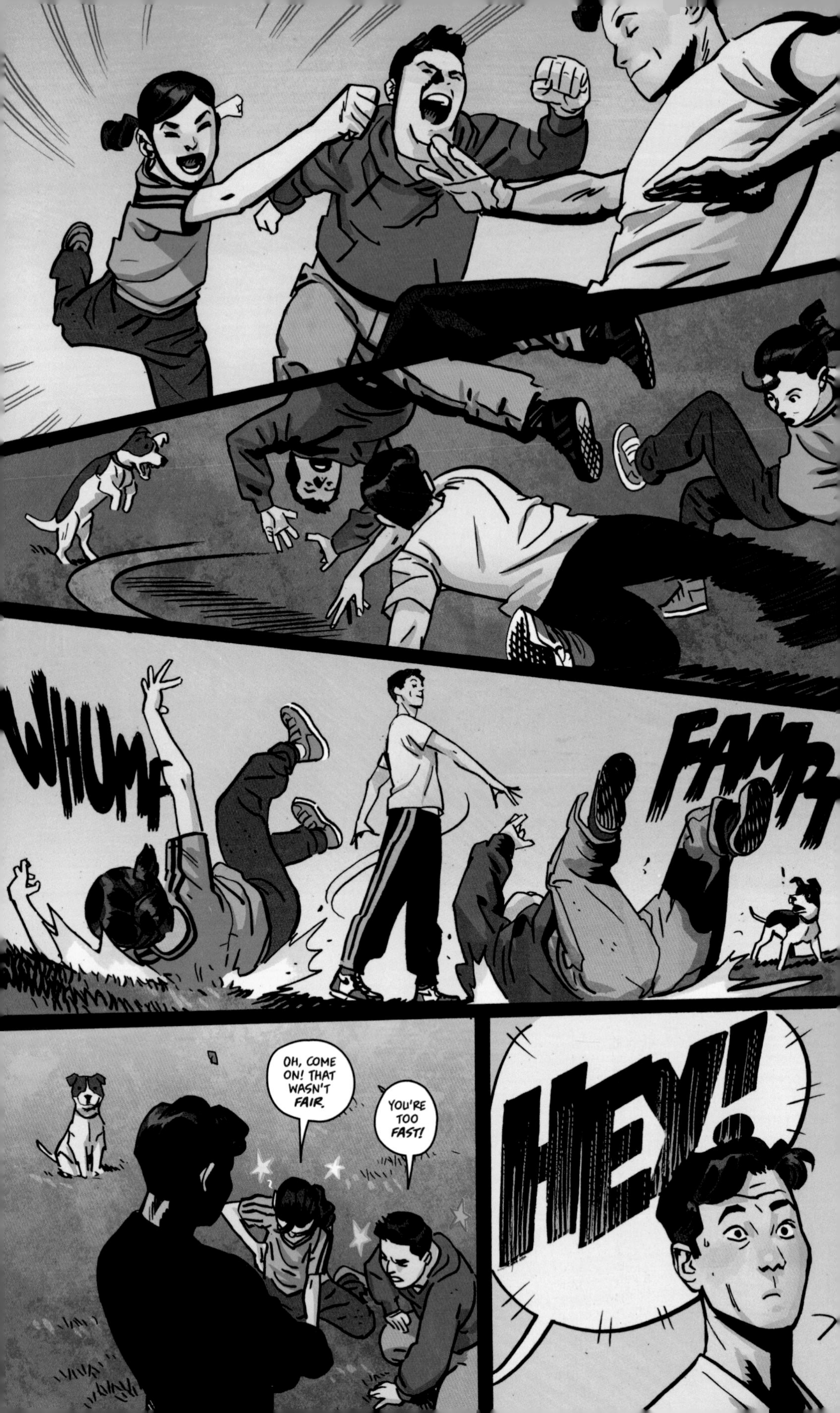
WHUMF
FAMP
OH, COME ON! THAT WASN'T FAIR.
YOU'RE TOO FAST!
HEY!

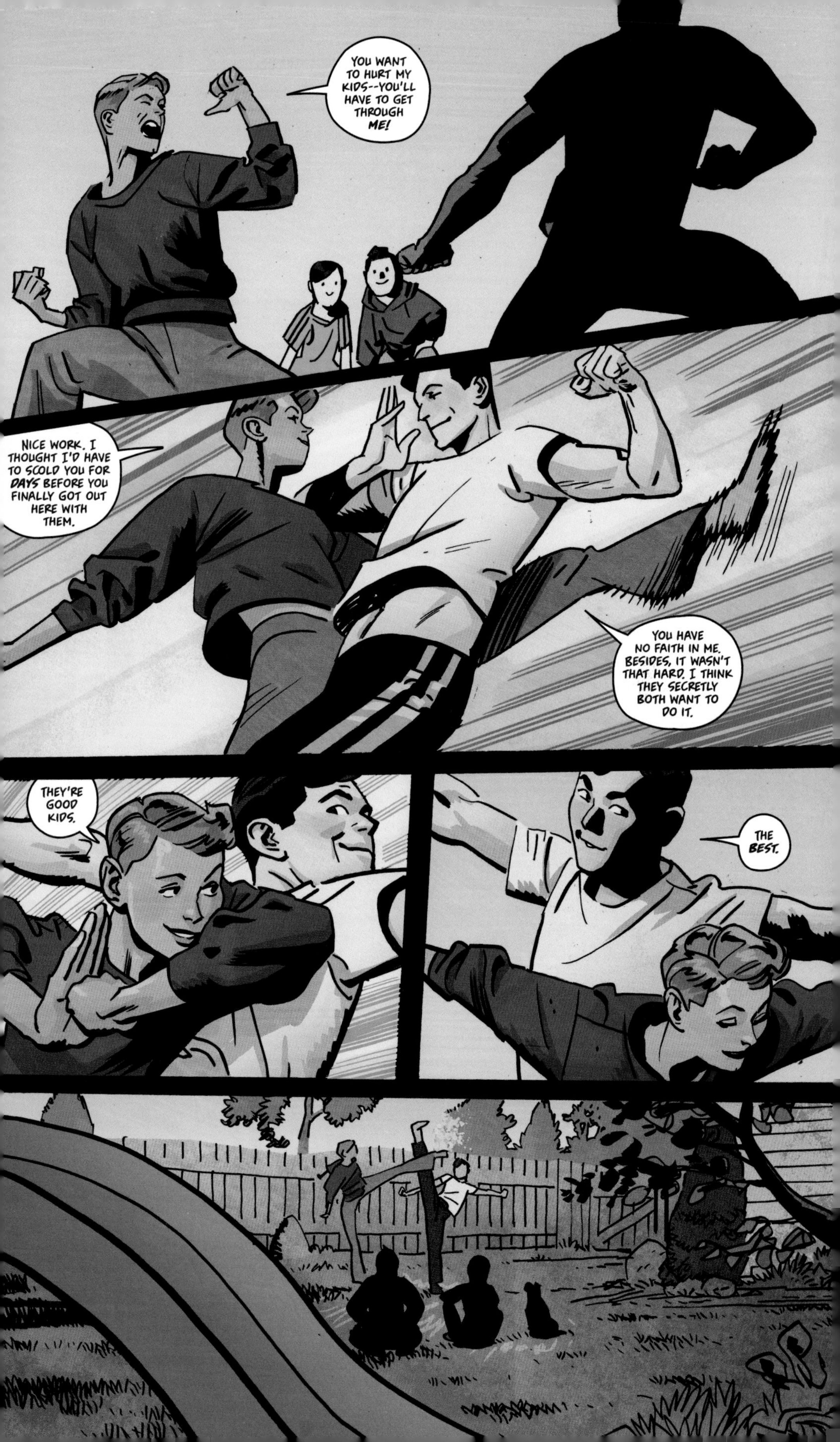
YOU WANT TO HURT MY KIDS--YOU'LL HAVE TO GET THROUGH ME!
NICE WORK. I THOUGHT I'D HAVE TO SCOLD YOU FOR DAYS BEFORE YOU FINALLY GOT OUT HERE WITH THEM.
YOU HAVE NO FAITH IN ME. BESIDES, IT WASN'T THAT HARD. I THINK THEY SECRETLY BOTH WANT TO DO IT.
THEY'RE GOOD KIDS.
THE BEST.

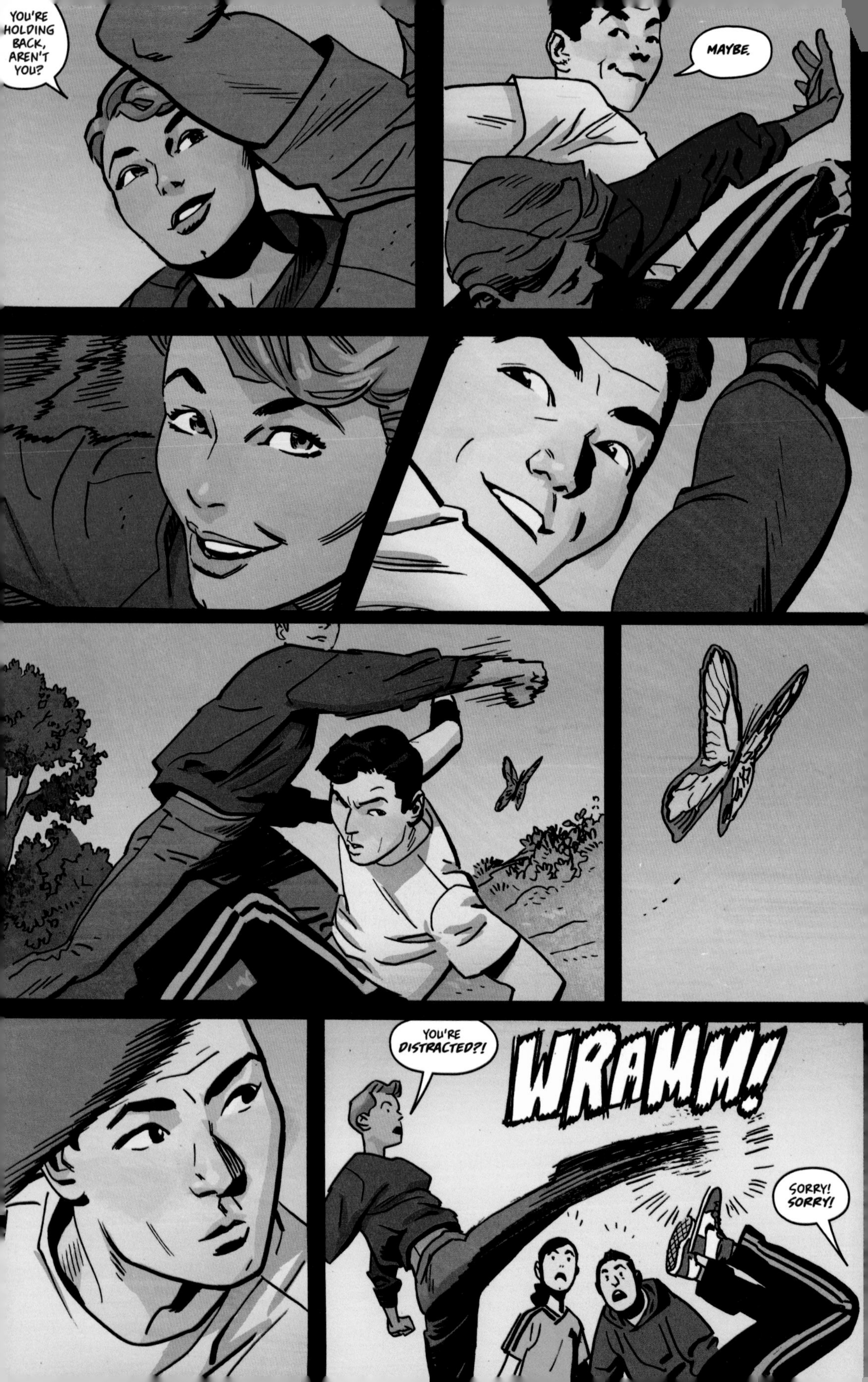
YOU'RE HOLDING BACK, AREN'T YOU?
MAYBE.
YOU'RE DISTRACTED?!
WRAMM!
SORRY! SORRY!

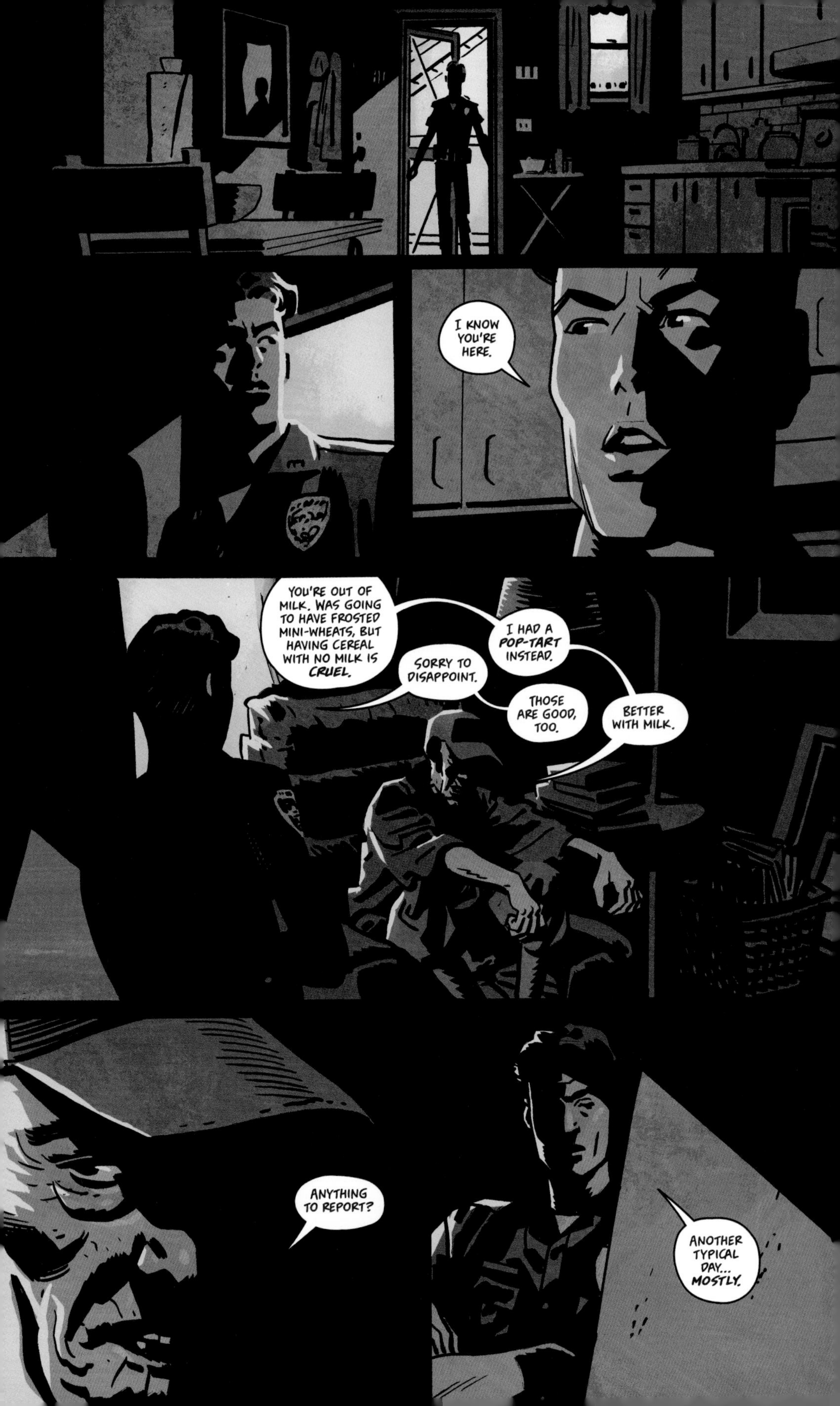
I KNOW YOU'RE HERE.
YOU'RE OUT OF MILK. WAS GOING TO HAVE FROSTED MINI-WHEATS, BUT HAVING CEREAL WITH NO MILK IS CRUEL.
SORRY TO DISAPPOINT.
I HAD A POP-TART INSTEAD.
THOSE ARE GOOD, TOO.
BETTER WITH MILK.
ANYTHING TO REPORT?
ANOTHER TYPICAL DAY... MOSTLY.

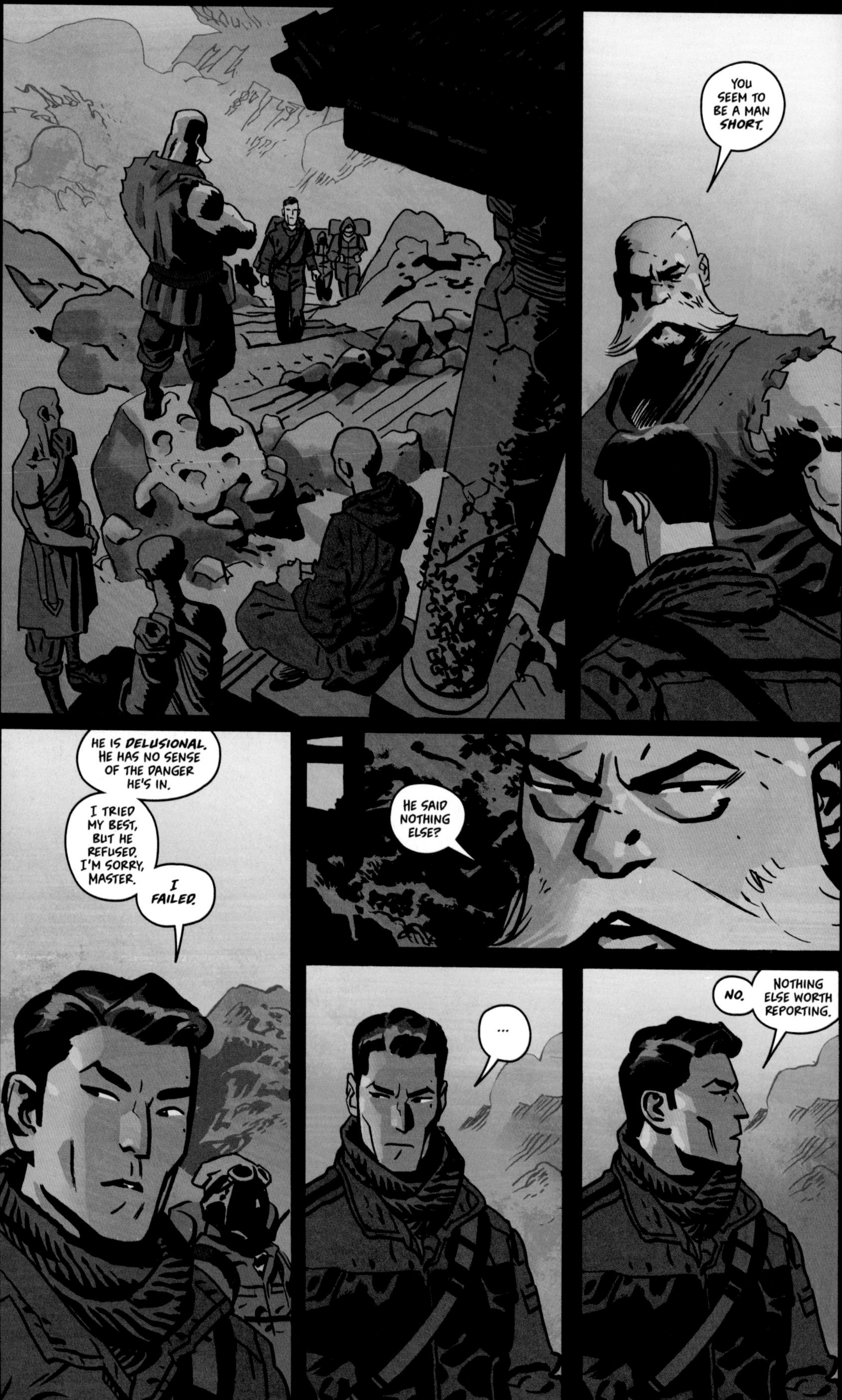
YOU SEEM TO BE A MAN SHORT.
HE IS DELUSIONAL. HE HAS NO SENSE OF THE DANGER HE'S IN.
I TRIED MY BEST, BUT HE REFUSED. I'M SORRY, MASTER.
I FAILED.
HE SAID NOTHING ELSE?
...
NO.
NOTHING ELSE WORTH REPORTING.

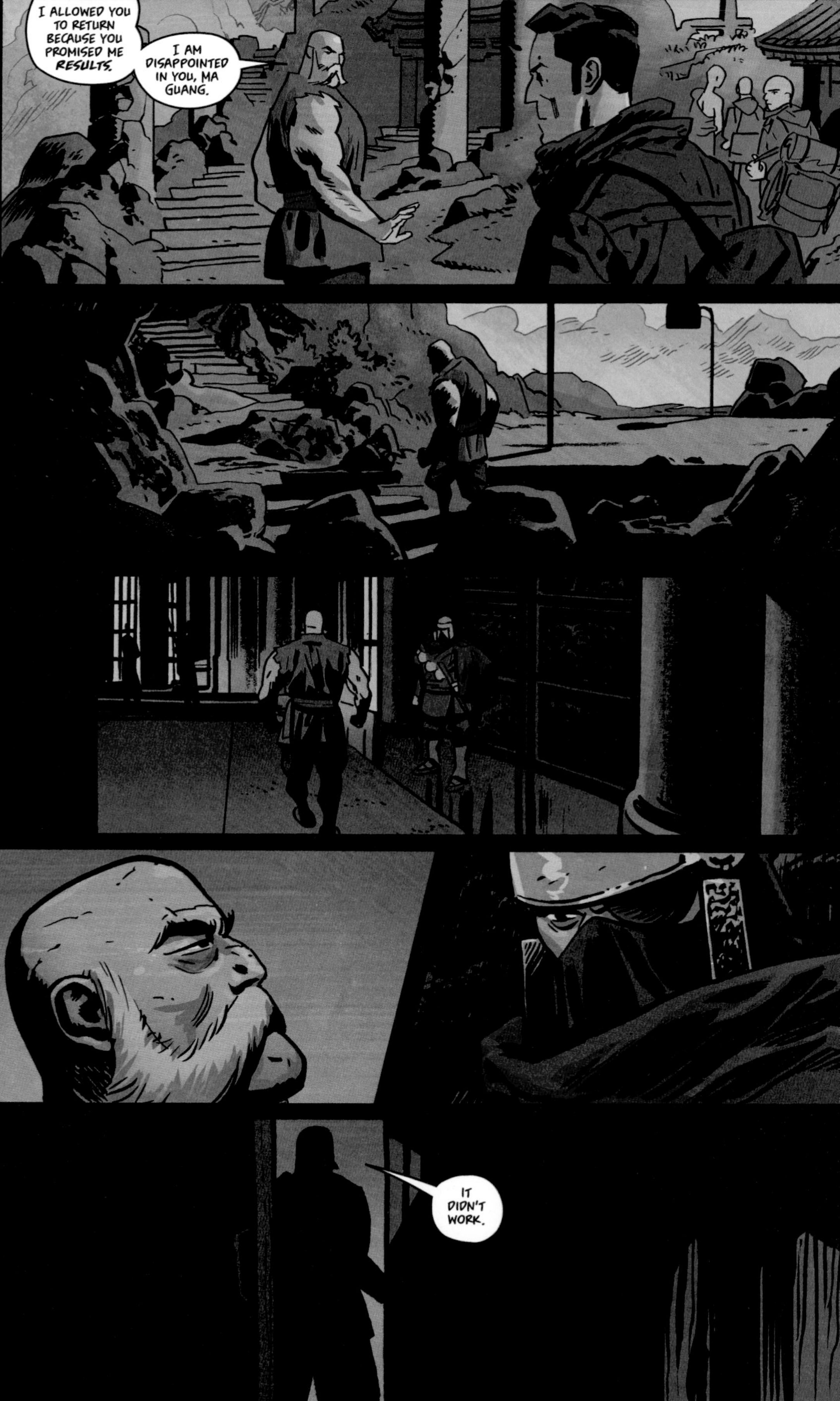

I ALLOWED YOU TO RETURN BECAUSE YOU PROMISED ME *RESULTS*.
I AM DISAPPOINTED IN YOU, MA GUANG.
IT DIDN'T WORK.

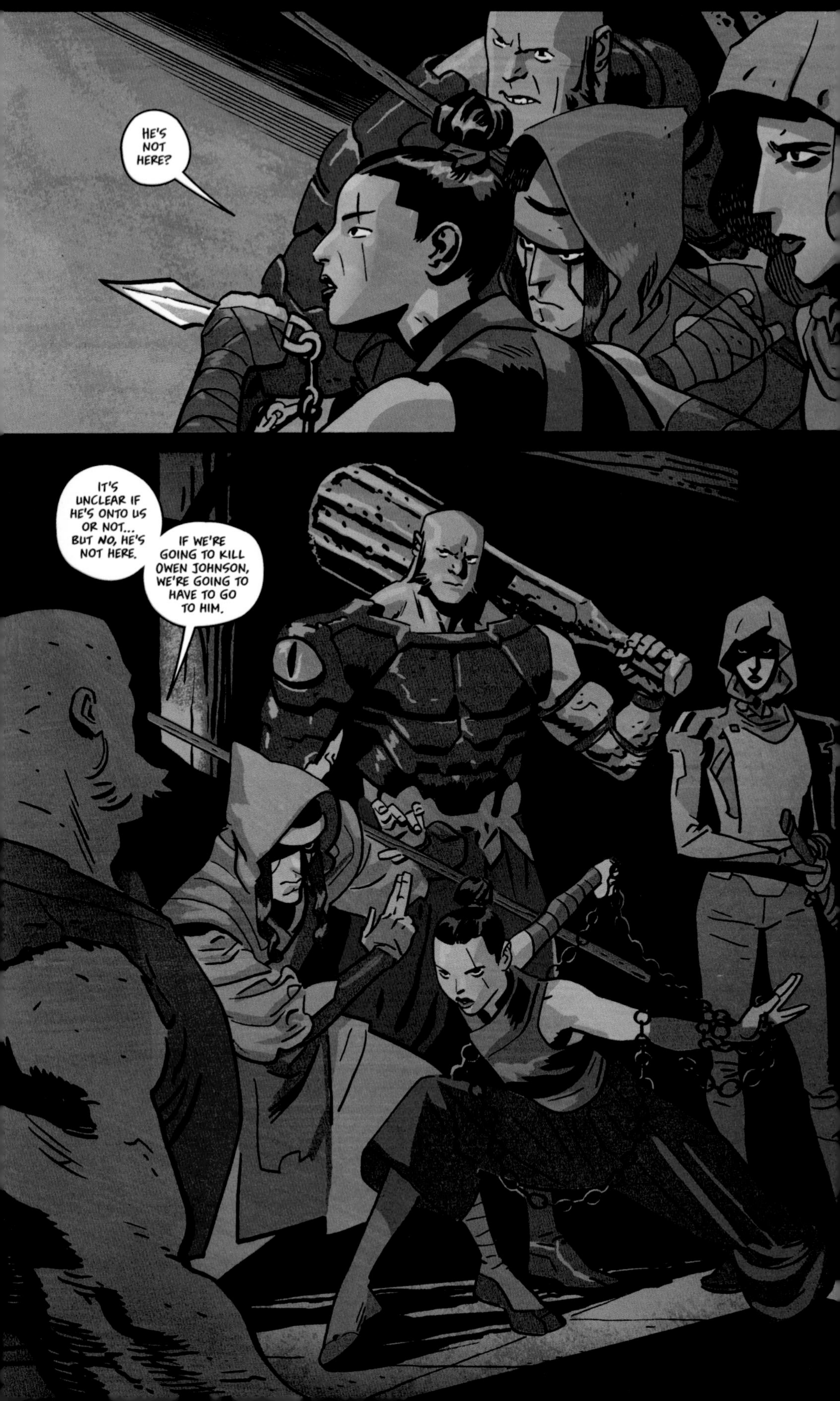
HE'S NOT HERE?
IT'S UNCLEAR IF HE'S ONTO US OR NOT... BUT NO, HE'S NOT HERE.
IF WE'RE GOING TO KILL OWEN JOHNSON, WE'RE GOING TO HAVE TO GO TO HIM.

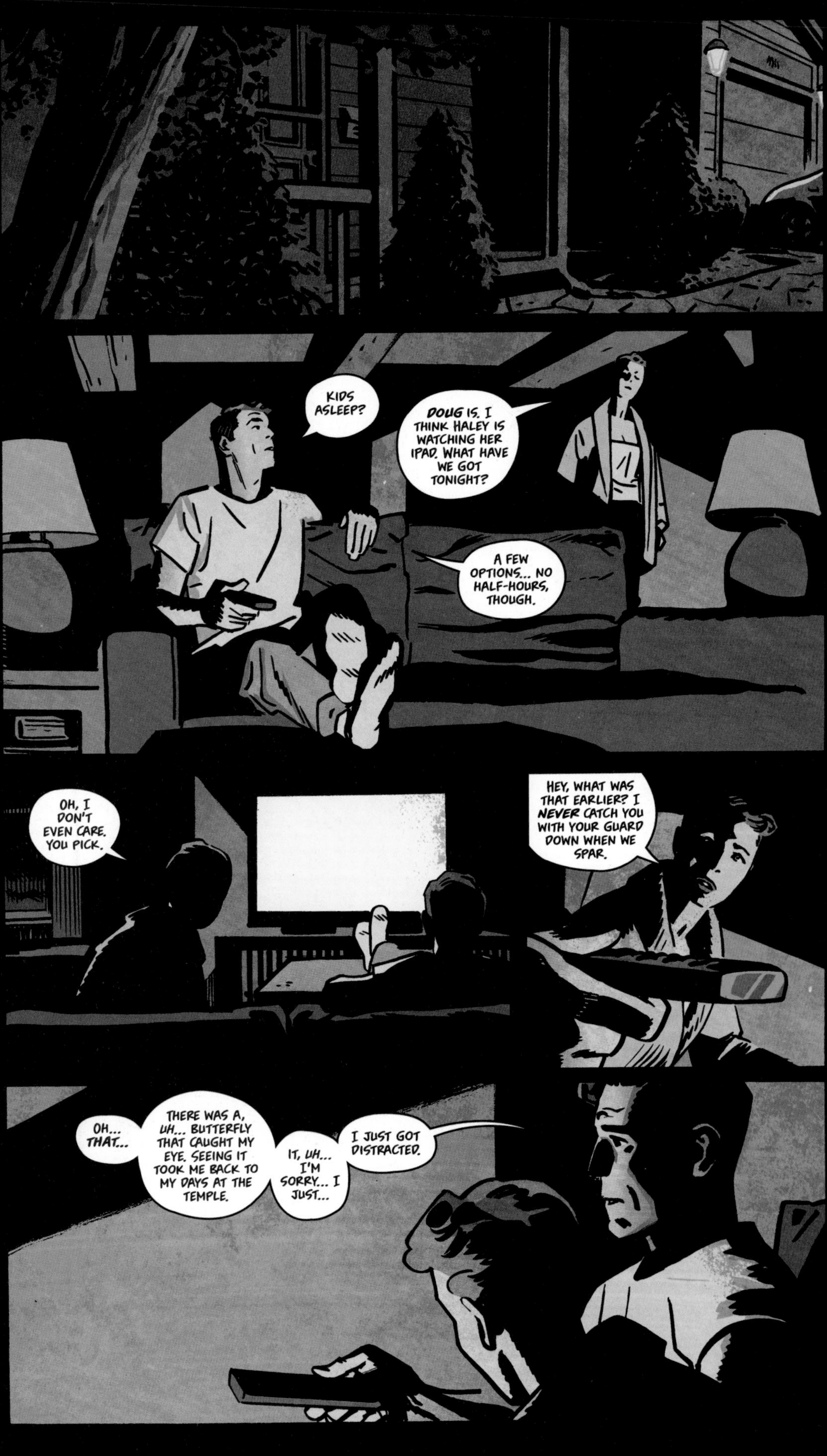
KIDS ASLEEP?
DOUG IS. I THINK HALEY IS WATCHING HER IPAD. WHAT HAVE WE GOT TONIGHT?
A FEW OPTIONS... NO HALF-HOURS, THOUGH.
OH, I DON'T EVEN CARE. YOU PICK.
HEY, WHAT WAS THAT EARLIER? I NEVER CATCH YOU WITH YOUR GUARD DOWN WHEN WE SPAR.
I JUST GOT DISTRACTED.
IT, UH... I'M SORRY... I JUST...
OH... THAT...
THERE WAS A, UH... BUTTERFLY THAT CAUGHT MY EYE. SEEING IT TOOK ME BACK TO MY DAYS AT THE TEMPLE.

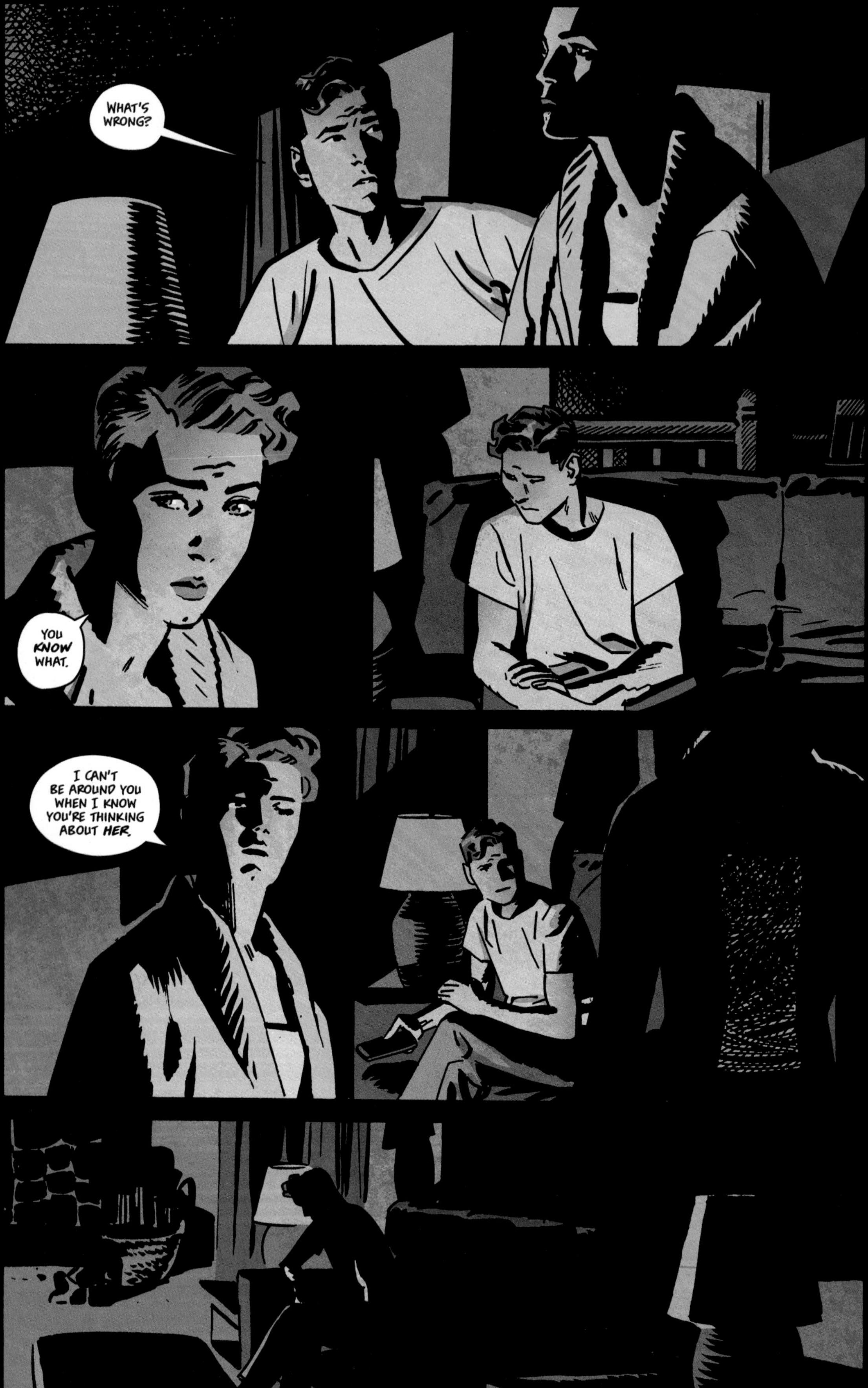
WHAT'S WRONG?
YOU KNOW WHAT.
I CAN'T BE AROUND YOU WHEN I KNOW YOU'RE THINKING ABOUT HER.

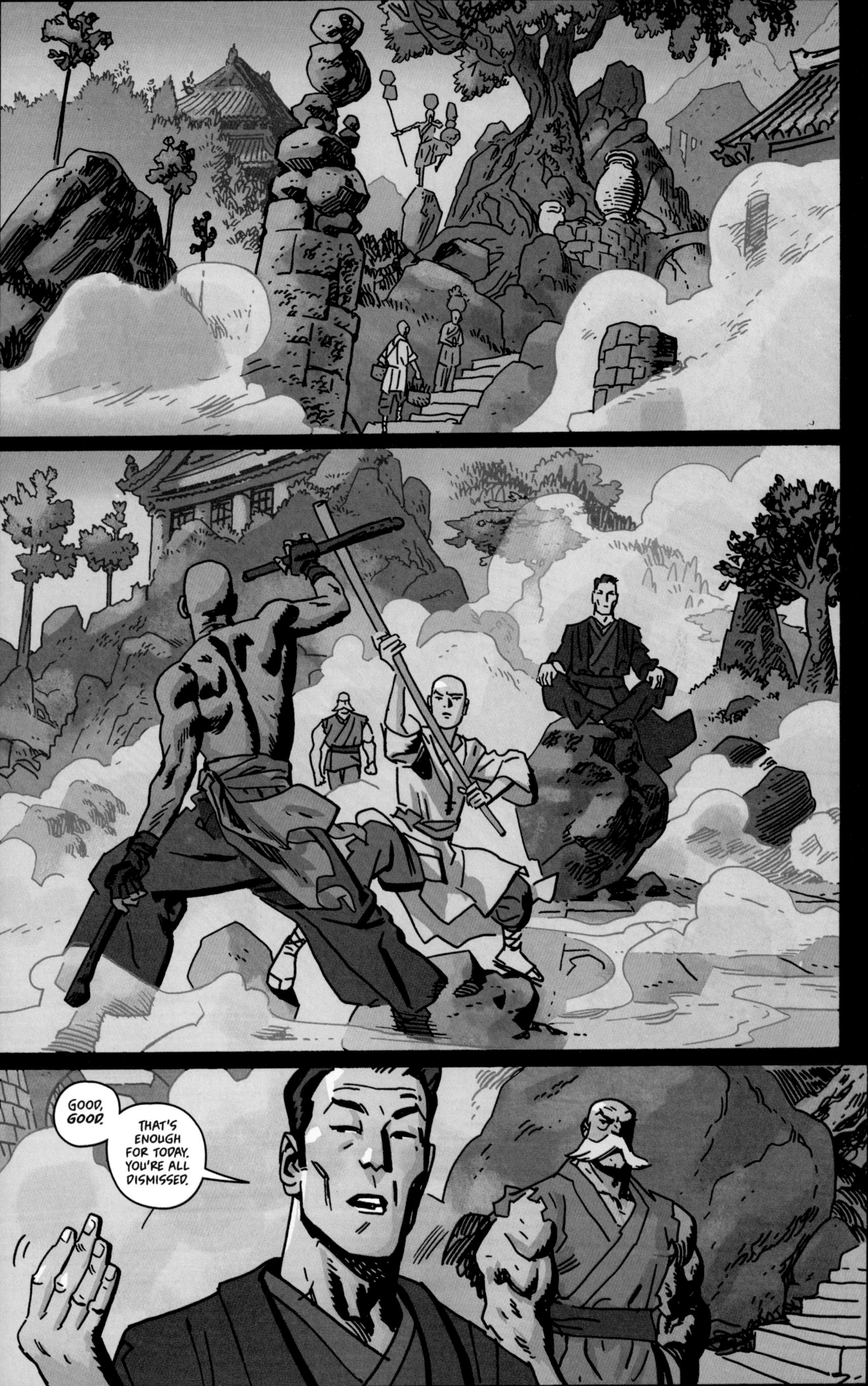
GOOD, GOOD.
THAT'S ENOUGH FOR TODAY. YOU'RE ALL DISMISSED.

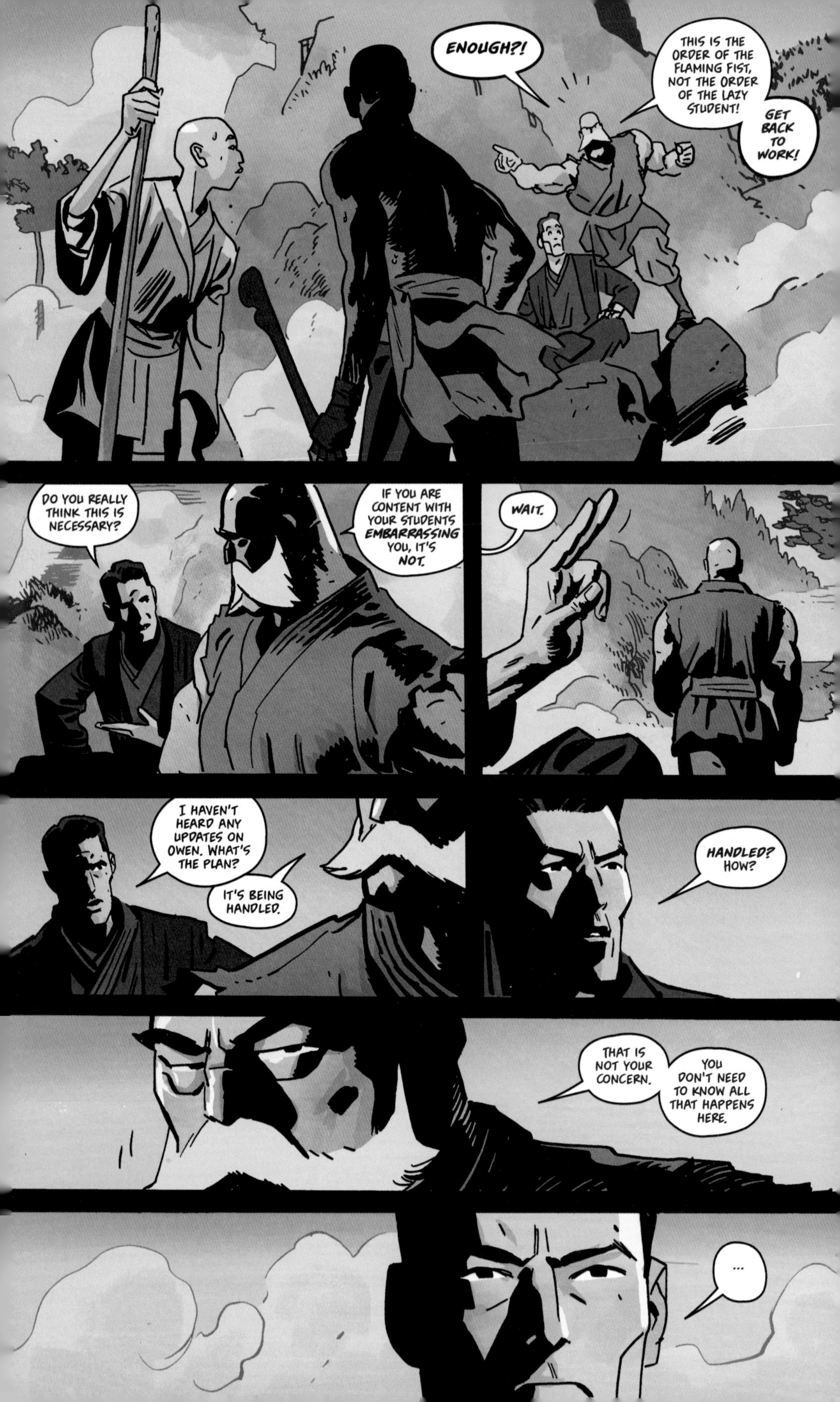
ENOUGH?!
THIS IS THE ORDER OF THE FLAMING FIST, NOT THE ORDER OF THE LAZY STUDENT!
GET BACK TO WORK!
DO YOU REALLY THINK THIS IS NECESSARY?
IF YOU ARE CONTENT WITH YOUR STUDENTS EMBARRASSING YOU, IT'S NOT.
WAIT.
I HAVEN'T HEARD ANY UPDATES ON OWEN. WHAT'S THE PLAN?
IT'S BEING HANDLED.
HANDLED? HOW?
THAT IS NOT YOUR CONCERN.
YOU DON'T NEED TO KNOW ALL THAT HAPPENS HERE.
...

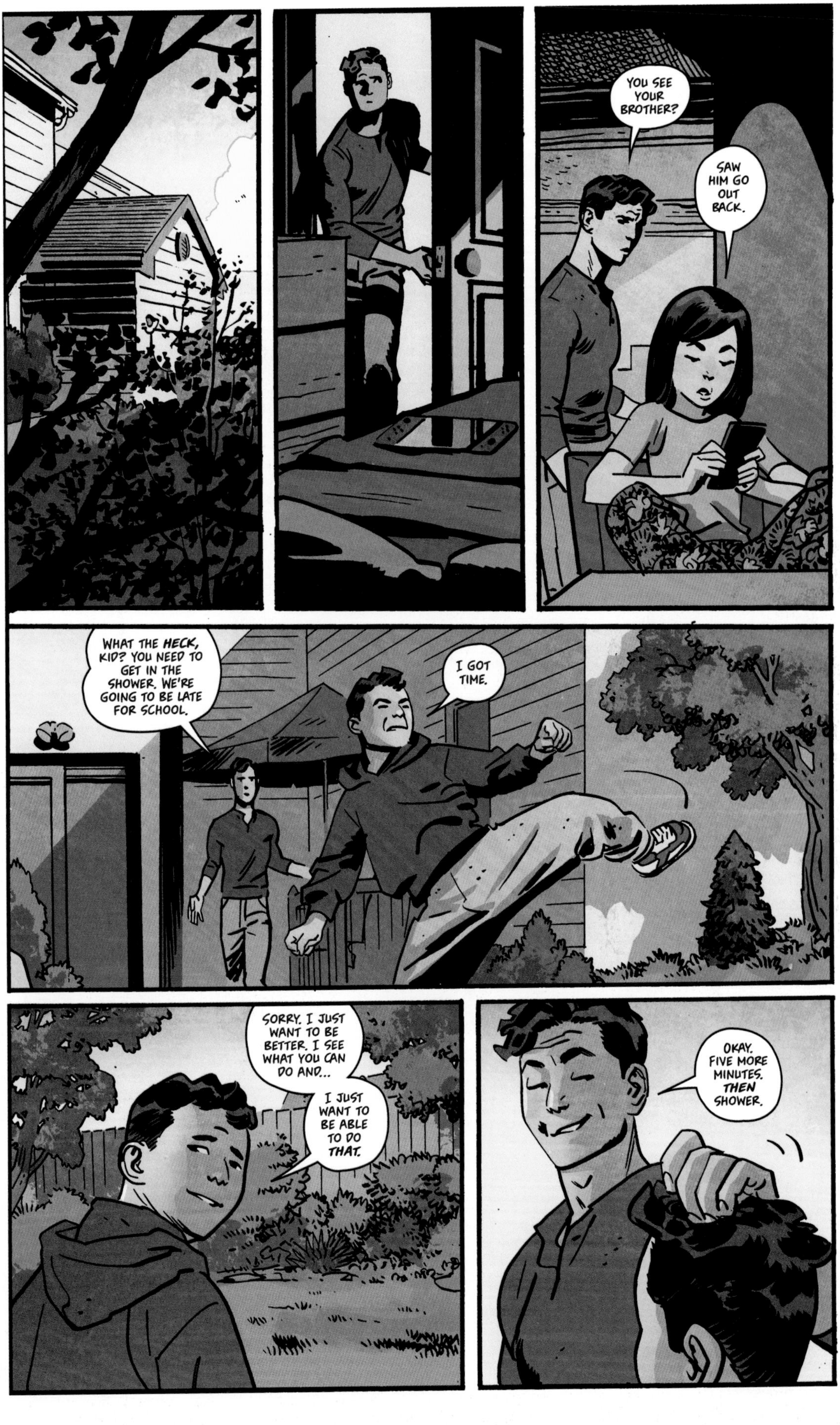
YOU SEE YOUR BROTHER?
SAW HIM GO OUT BACK.
WHAT THE HECK, KID? YOU NEED TO GET IN THE SHOWER. WE'RE GOING TO BE LATE FOR SCHOOL.
I GOT TIME.
SORRY. I JUST WANT TO BE BETTER. I SEE WHAT YOU CAN DO AND...
I JUST WANT TO BE ABLE TO DO THAT.
OKAY. FIVE MORE MINUTES. THEN SHOWER.

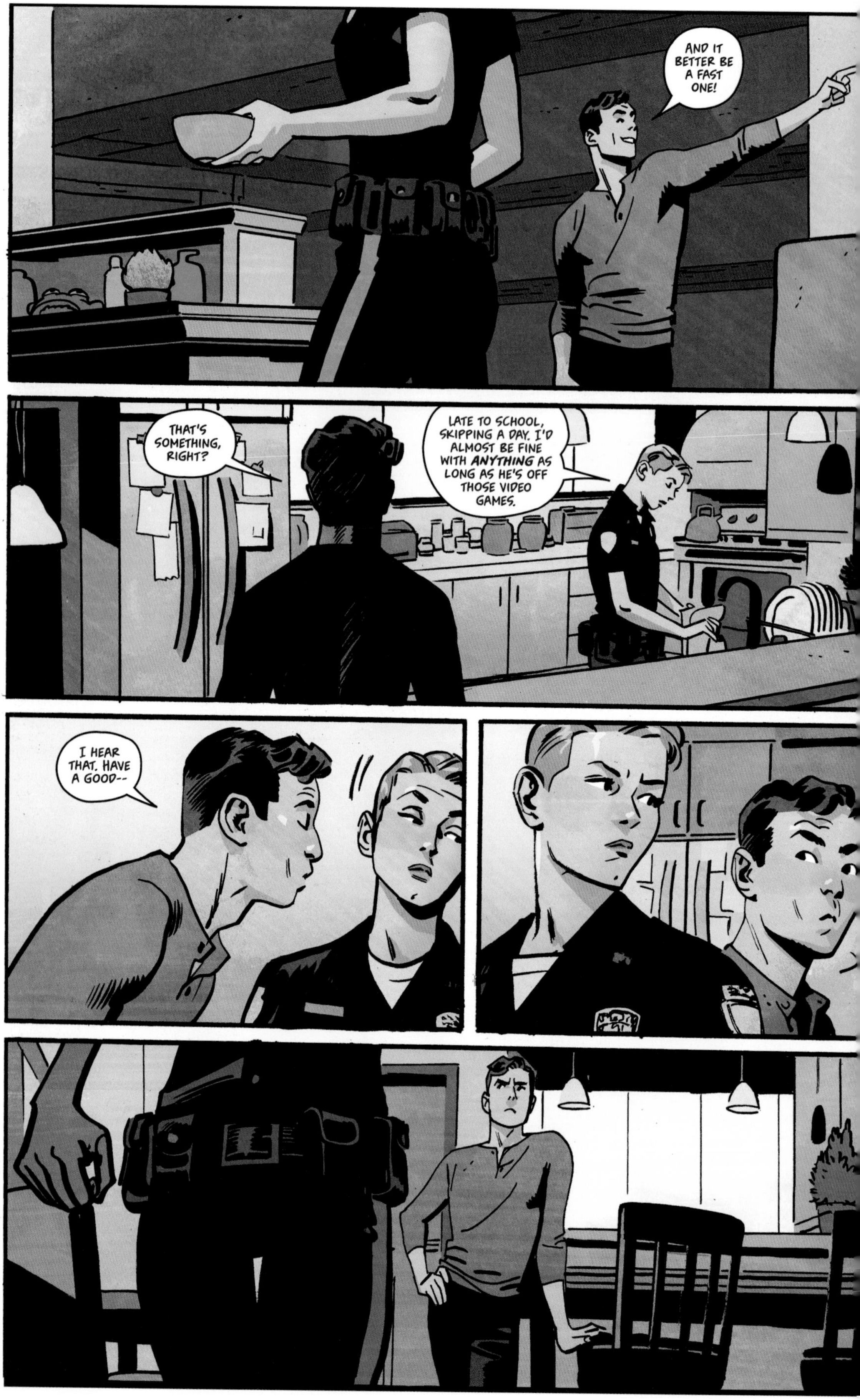
AND IT BETTER BE A FAST ONE!
THAT'S SOMETHING, RIGHT?
LATE TO SCHOOL, SKIPPING A DAY. I'D ALMOST BE FINE WITH ANYTHING AS LONG AS HE'S OFF THOSE VIDEO GAMES.
I HEAR THAT. HAVE A GOOD--

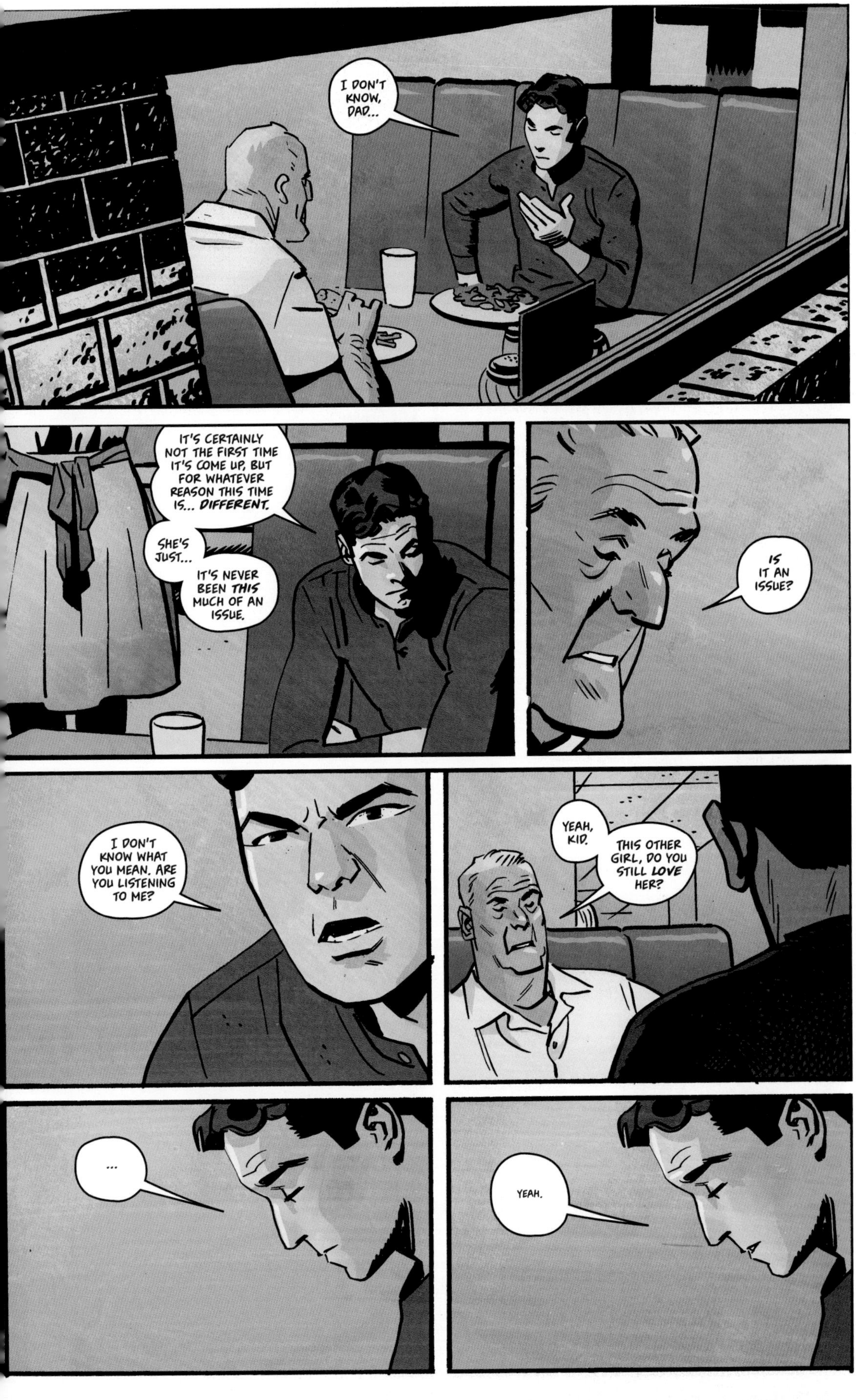
I DON'T KNOW, DAD...
IT'S CERTAINLY NOT THE FIRST TIME IT'S COME UP, BUT FOR WHATEVER REASON THIS TIME IS... DIFFERENT.
SHE'S JUST...
IT'S NEVER BEEN THIS MUCH OF AN ISSUE.
IS IT AN ISSUE?
I DON'T KNOW WHAT YOU MEAN. ARE YOU LISTENING TO ME?
YEAH, KID.
THIS OTHER GIRL, DO YOU STILL LOVE HER?
...
YEAH.

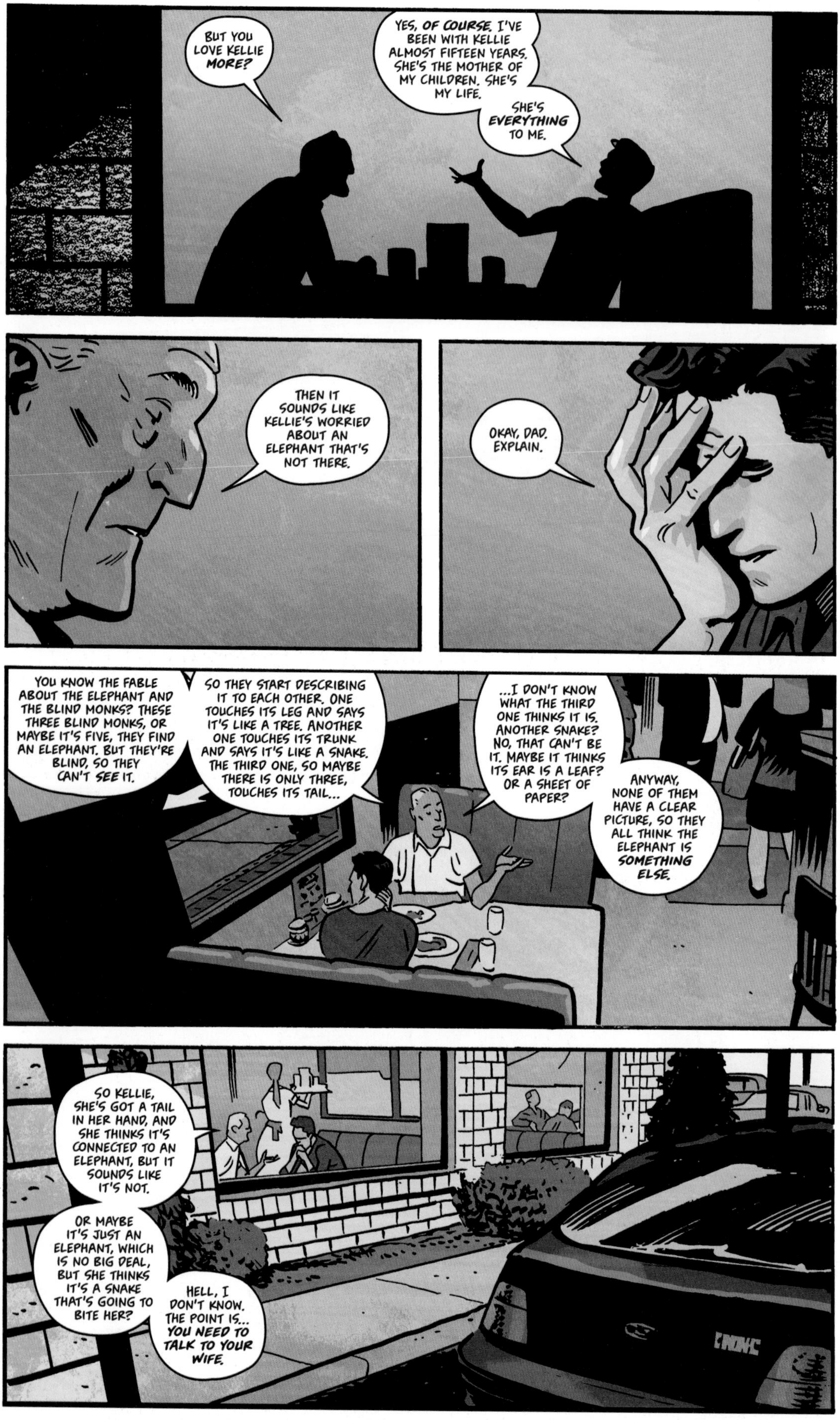
BUT YOU LOVE KELLIE MORE?
YES, OF COURSE. I'VE BEEN WITH KELLIE ALMOST FIFTEEN YEARS. SHE'S THE MOTHER OF MY CHILDREN. SHE'S MY LIFE.
SHE'S EVERYTHING TO ME.
THEN IT SOUNDS LIKE KELLIE'S WORRIED ABOUT AN ELEPHANT THAT'S NOT THERE.
OKAY, DAD. EXPLAIN.
YOU KNOW THE FABLE ABOUT THE ELEPHANT AND THE BLIND MONKS? THESE THREE BLIND MONKS, OR MAYBE IT'S FIVE, THEY FIND AN ELEPHANT. BUT THEY'RE BLIND, SO THEY CAN'T SEE IT.
SO THEY START DESCRIBING IT TO EACH OTHER. ONE TOUCHES ITS LEG AND SAYS IT'S LIKE A TREE. ANOTHER ONE TOUCHES ITS TRUNK AND SAYS IT'S LIKE A SNAKE. THE THIRD ONE, SO MAYBE THERE IS ONLY THREE, TOUCHES ITS TAIL...
...I DON'T KNOW WHAT THE THIRD ONE THINKS IT IS. ANOTHER SNAKE? NO, THAT CAN'T BE IT. MAYBE IT THINKS ITS EAR IS A LEAF? OR A SHEET OF PAPER?
ANYWAY, NONE OF THEM HAVE A CLEAR PICTURE, SO THEY ALL THINK THE ELEPHANT IS SOMETHING ELSE.
SO KELLIE, SHE'S GOT A TAIL IN HER HAND, AND SHE THINKS IT'S CONNECTED TO AN ELEPHANT, BUT IT SOUNDS LIKE IT'S NOT.
OR MAYBE IT'S JUST AN ELEPHANT, WHICH IS NO BIG DEAL, BUT SHE THINKS IT'S A SNAKE THAT'S GOING TO BITE HER?
HELL, I DON'T KNOW. THE POINT IS... YOU NEED TO TALK TO YOUR WIFE.

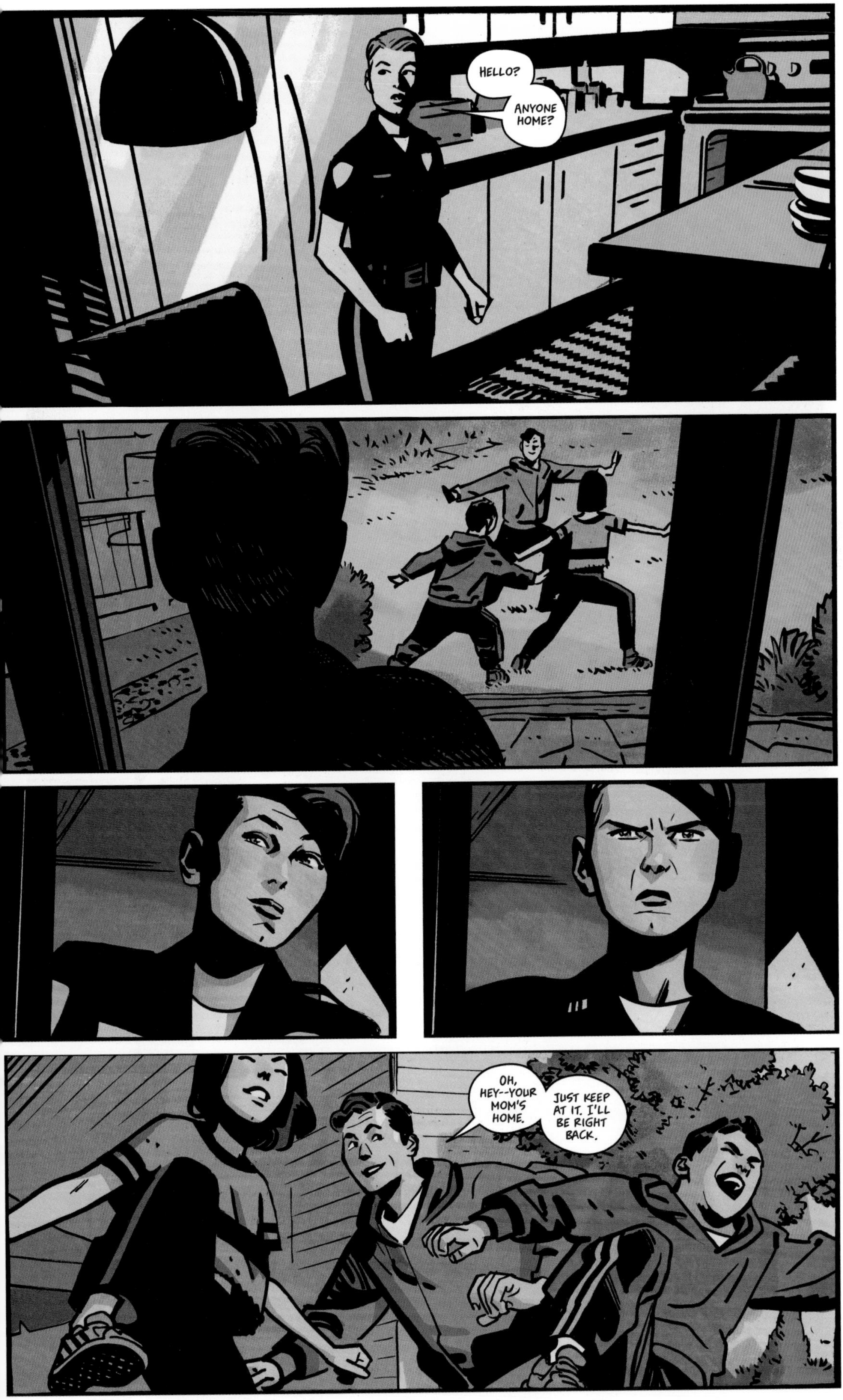
HELLO?
ANYONE HOME?
OH, HEY--YOUR MOM'S HOME.
JUST KEEP AT IT. I'LL BE RIGHT BACK.

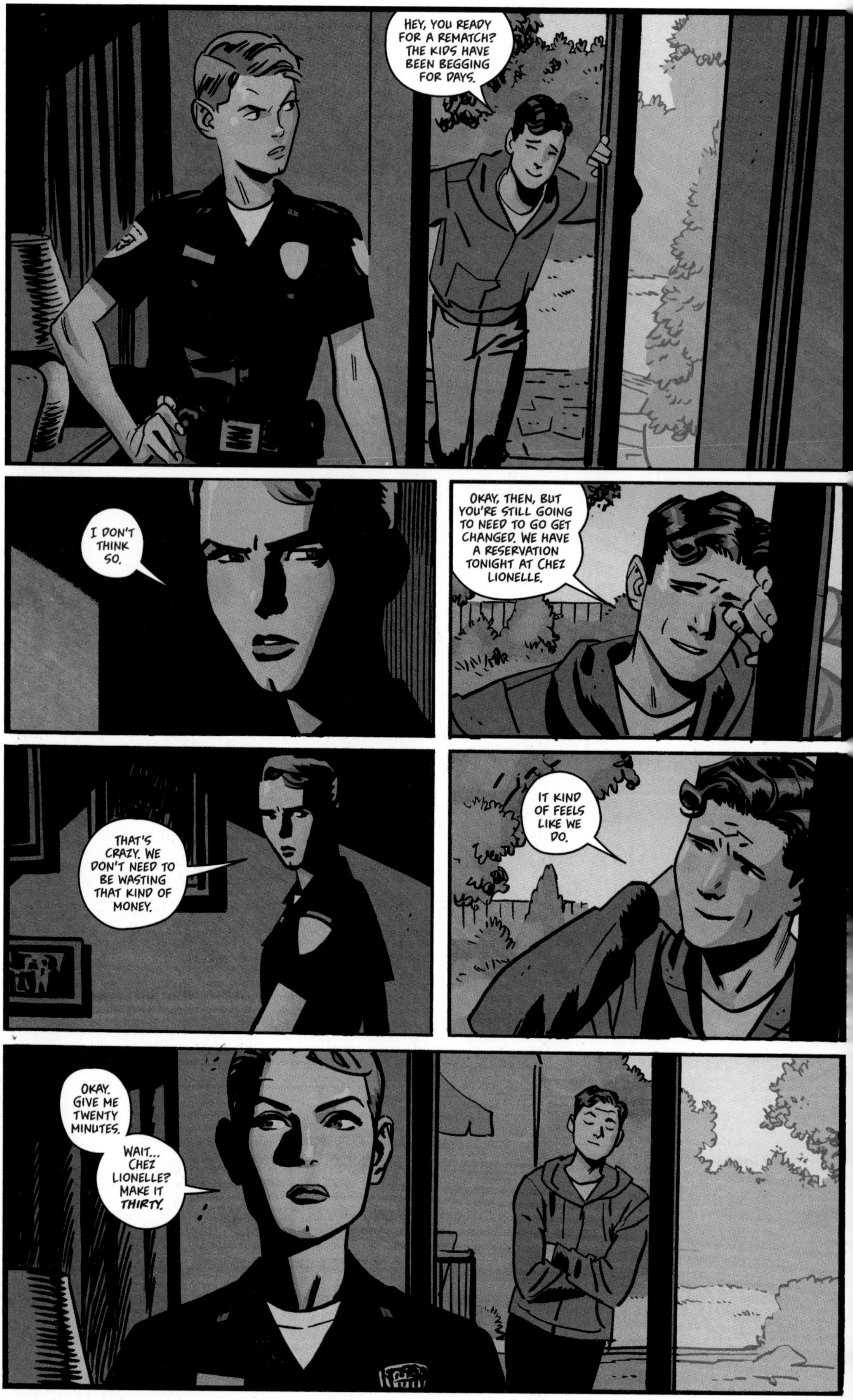

HEY, YOU READY FOR A REMATCH? THE KIDS HAVE BEEN BEGGING FOR DAYS.
I DON'T THINK SO.
OKAY, THEN, BUT YOU'RE STILL GOING TO NEED TO GO GET CHANGED. WE HAVE A RESERVATION TONIGHT AT CHEZ LIONELLE.
THAT'S CRAZY. WE DON'T NEED TO BE WASTING THAT KIND OF MONEY.
IT KIND OF FEELS LIKE WE DO.
OKAY. GIVE ME TWENTY MINUTES.
WAIT... CHEZ LIONELLE? MAKE IT THIRTY.

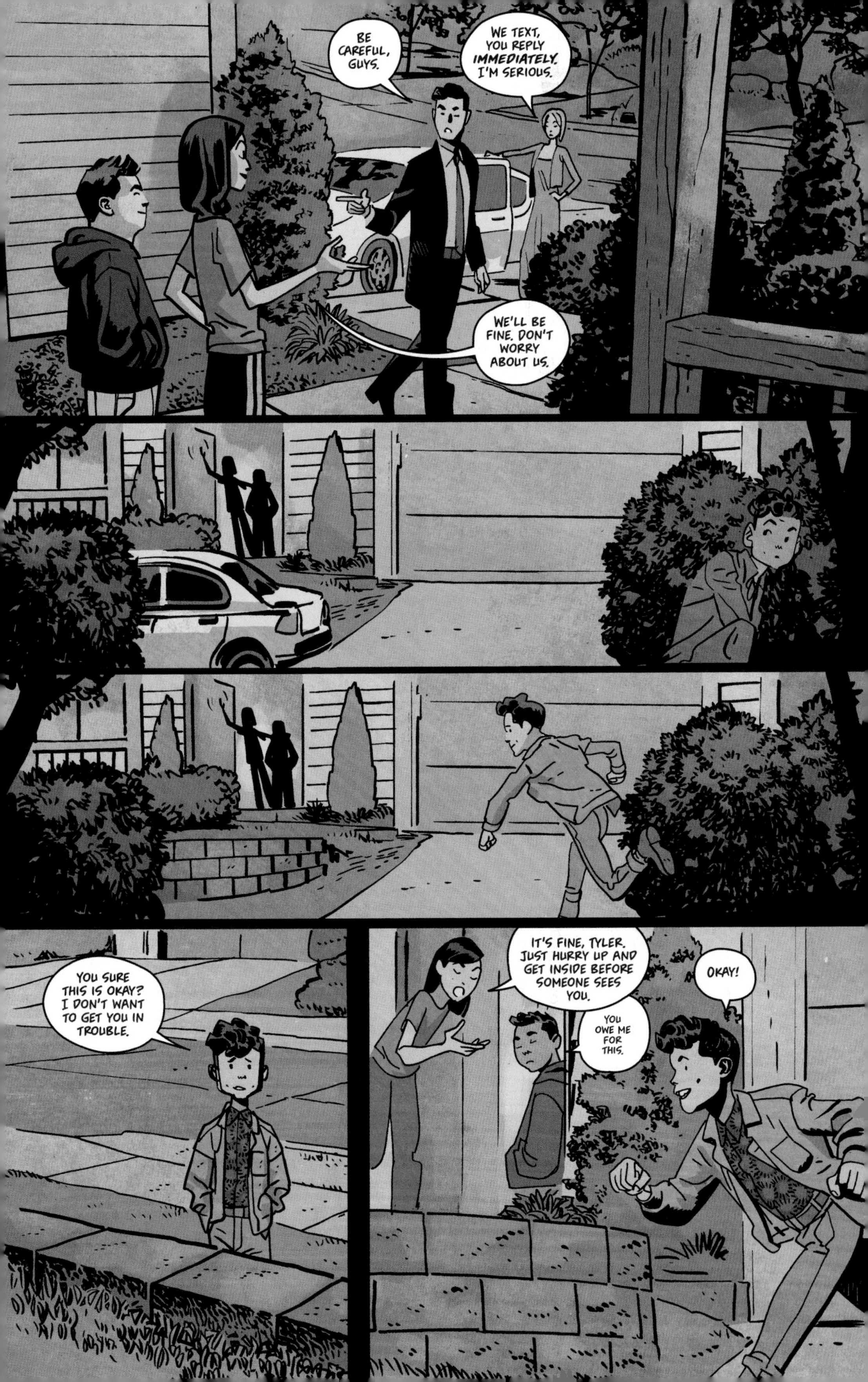
BE CAREFUL, GUYS.
WE TEXT, YOU REPLY IMMEDIATELY. I'M SERIOUS.
WE'LL BE FINE. DON'T WORRY ABOUT US.
YOU SURE THIS IS OKAY? I DON'T WANT TO GET YOU IN TROUBLE.
IT'S FINE, TYLER. JUST HURRY UP AND GET INSIDE BEFORE SOMEONE SEES YOU.
YOU OWE ME FOR THIS.
OKAY!

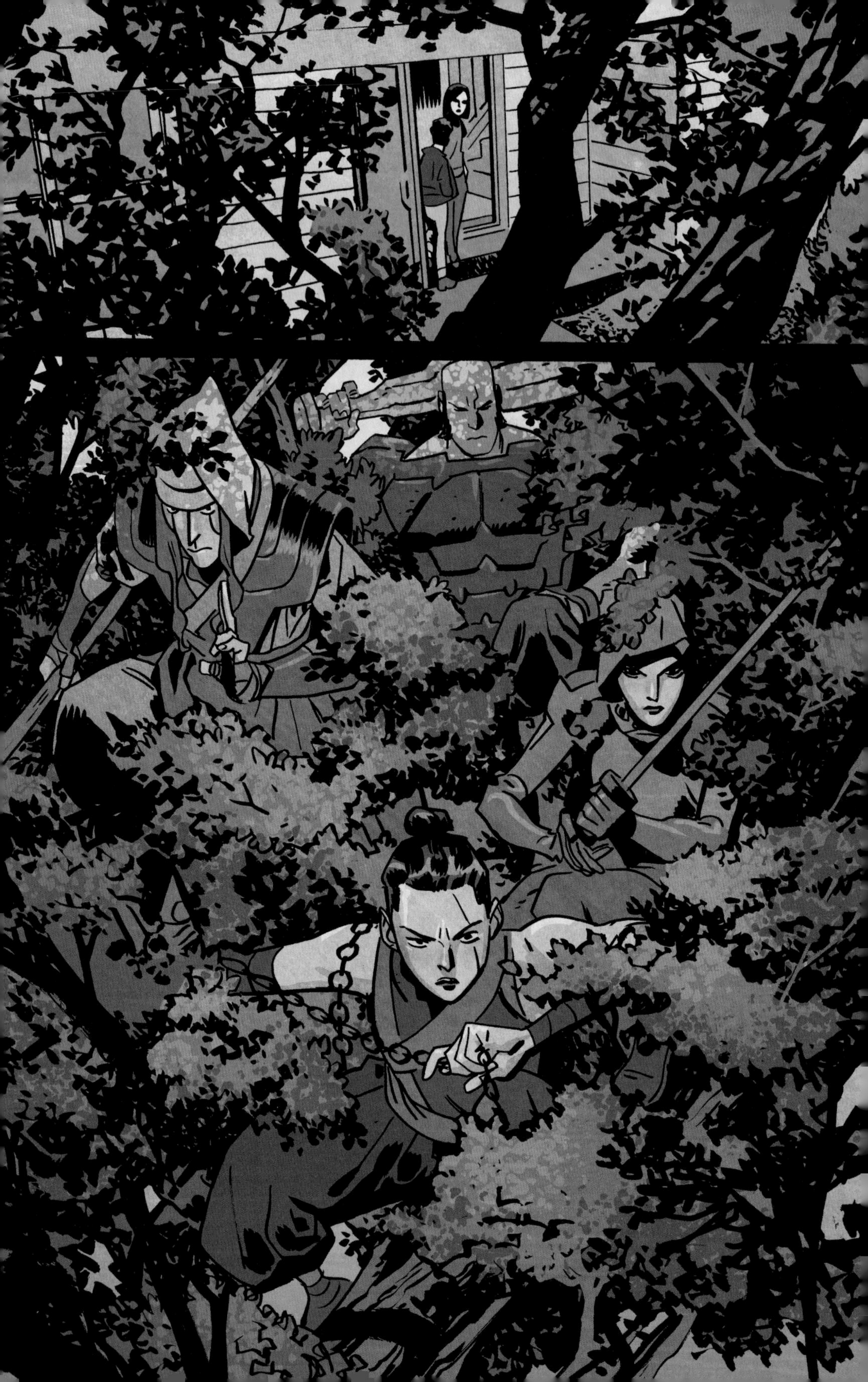

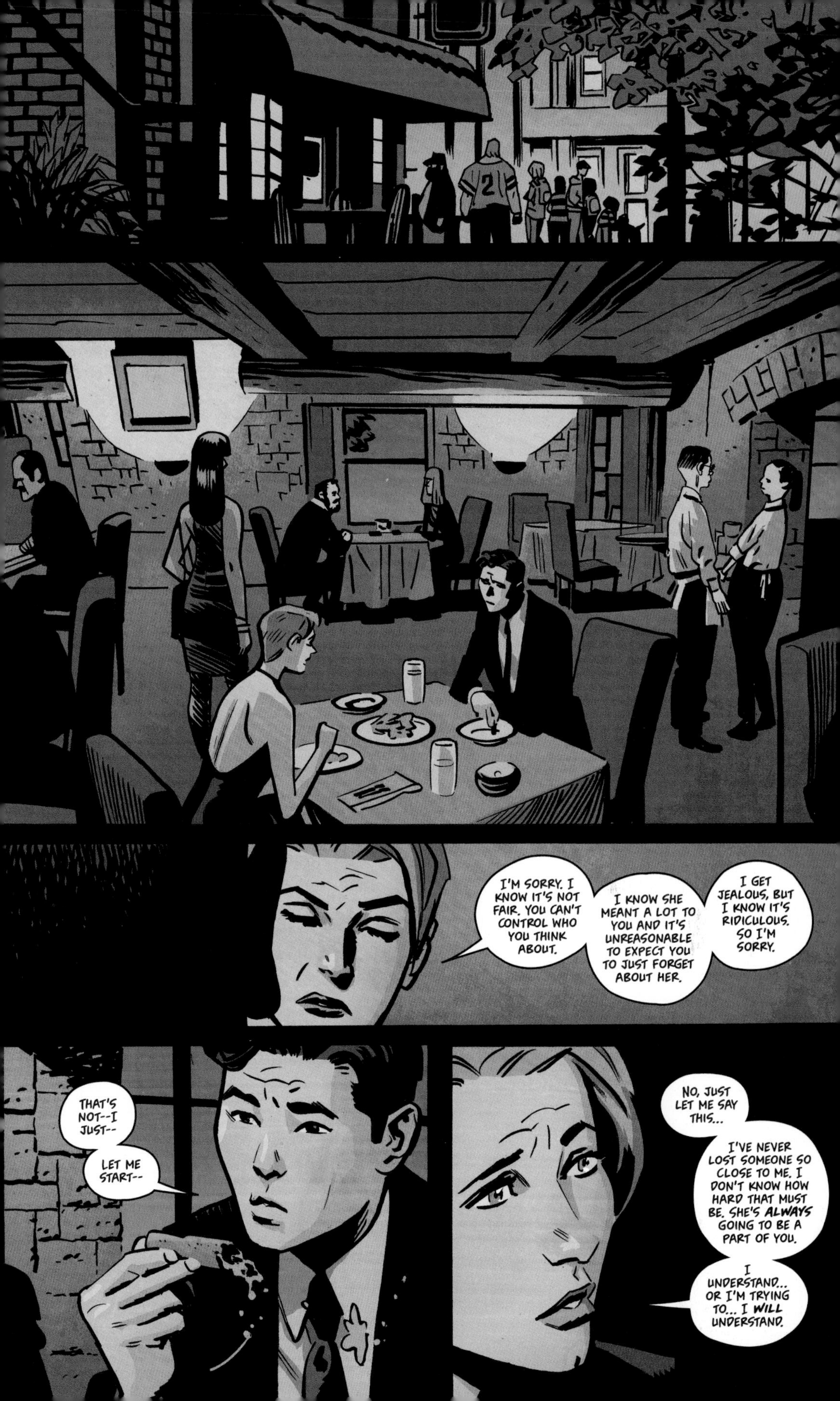
I'M SORRY. I KNOW IT'S NOT FAIR. YOU CAN'T CONTROL WHO YOU THINK ABOUT.
I KNOW SHE MEANT A LOT TO YOU AND IT'S UNREASONABLE TO EXPECT YOU TO JUST FORGET ABOUT HER.
I GET JEALOUS, BUT I KNOW IT'S RIDICULOUS. SO I'M SORRY.
THAT'S NOT--I JUST--
LET ME START--
NO, JUST LET ME SAY THIS...
I'VE NEVER LOST SOMEONE SO CLOSE TO ME. I DON'T KNOW HOW HARD THAT MUST BE. SHE'S **ALWAYS** GOING TO BE A PART OF YOU.
I UNDERSTAND... OR I'M TRYING TO... I **WILL** UNDERSTAND.

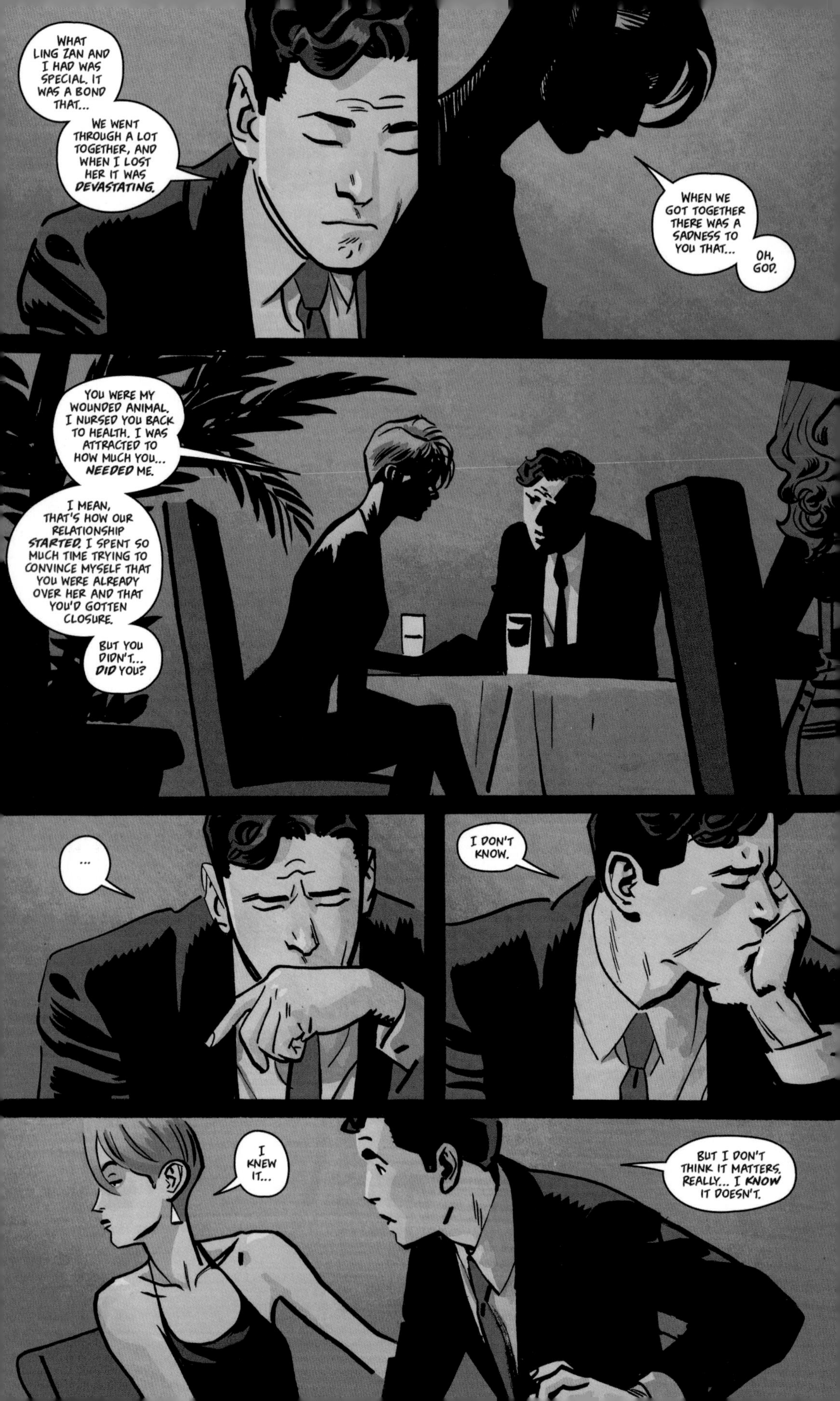
WHAT LING ZAN AND I HAD WAS SPECIAL. IT WAS A BOND THAT...
WE WENT THROUGH A LOT TOGETHER, AND WHEN I LOST HER IT WAS DEVASTATING.
WHEN WE GOT TOGETHER THERE WAS A SADNESS TO YOU THAT...
OH, GOD.
YOU WERE MY WOUNDED ANIMAL. I NURSED YOU BACK TO HEALTH. I WAS ATTRACTED TO HOW MUCH YOU... NEEDED ME.
I MEAN, THAT'S HOW OUR RELATIONSHIP STARTED. I SPENT SO MUCH TIME TRYING TO CONVINCE MYSELF THAT YOU WERE ALREADY OVER HER AND THAT YOU'D GOTTEN CLOSURE.
BUT YOU DIDN'T... DID YOU?
...
I DON'T KNOW.
I KNEW IT...
BUT I DON'T THINK IT MATTERS, REALLY... I KNOW IT DOESN'T.

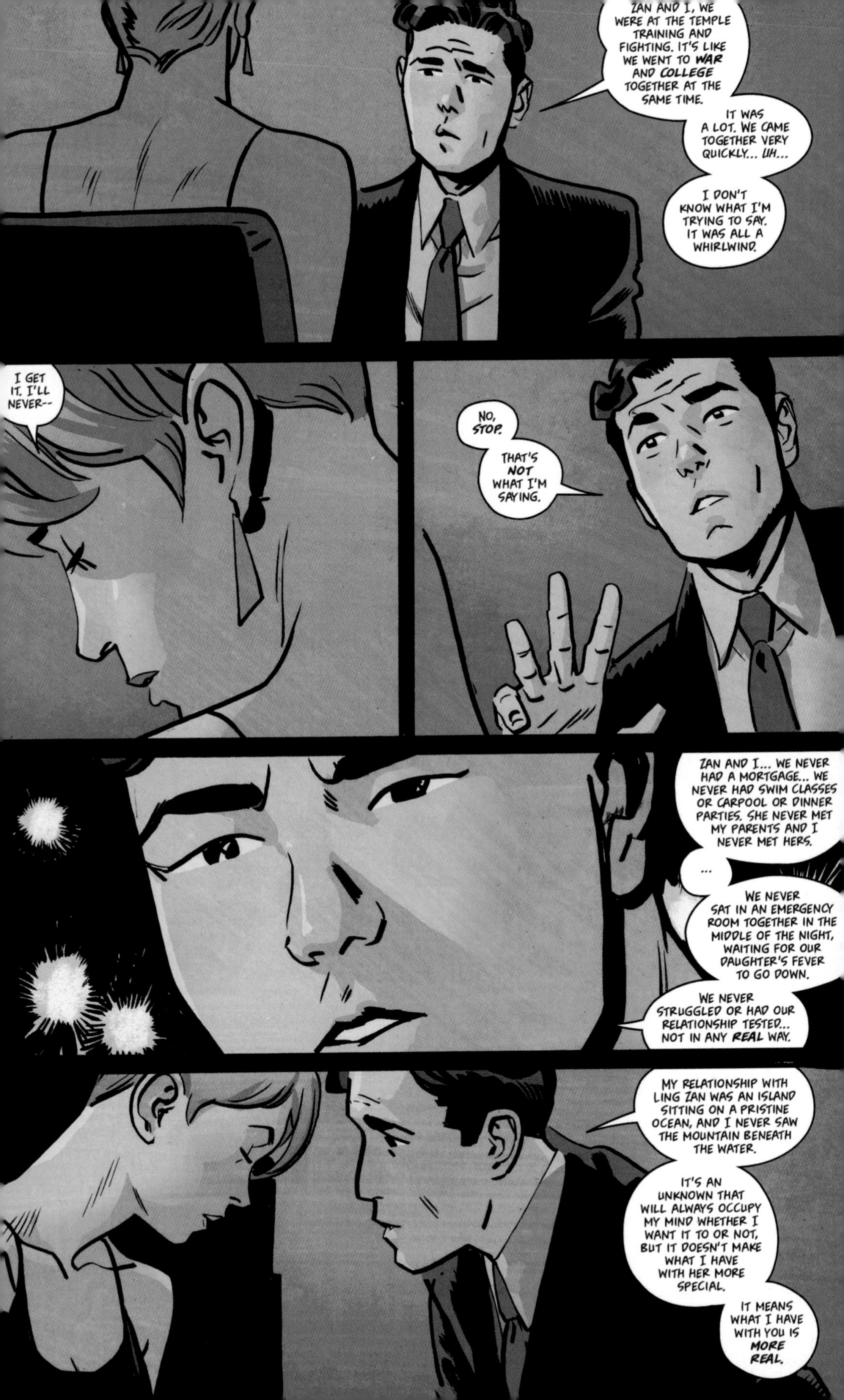

ZAN AND I, WE WERE AT THE TEMPLE TRAINING AND FIGHTING. IT'S LIKE WE WENT TO WAR AND COLLEGE TOGETHER AT THE SAME TIME.
IT WAS A LOT. WE CAME TOGETHER VERY QUICKLY... UH...
I DON'T KNOW WHAT I'M TRYING TO SAY. IT WAS ALL A WHIRLWIND.
I GET IT. I'LL NEVER--
NO, STOP.
THAT'S NOT WHAT I'M SAYING.
ZAN AND I... WE NEVER HAD A MORTGAGE... WE NEVER HAD SWIM CLASSES OR CARPOOL OR DINNER PARTIES. SHE NEVER MET MY PARENTS AND I NEVER MET HERS.
...
WE NEVER SAT IN AN EMERGENCY ROOM TOGETHER IN THE MIDDLE OF THE NIGHT, WAITING FOR OUR DAUGHTER'S FEVER TO GO DOWN.
WE NEVER STRUGGLED OR HAD OUR RELATIONSHIP TESTED... NOT IN ANY REAL WAY.
MY RELATIONSHIP WITH LING ZAN WAS AN ISLAND SITTING ON A PRISTINE OCEAN, AND I NEVER SAW THE MOUNTAIN BENEATH THE WATER.
IT'S AN UNKNOWN THAT WILL ALWAYS OCCUPY MY MIND WHETHER I WANT IT TO OR NOT, BUT IT DOESN'T MAKE WHAT I HAVE WITH HER MORE SPECIAL.
IT MEANS WHAT I HAVE WITH YOU IS MORE REAL.

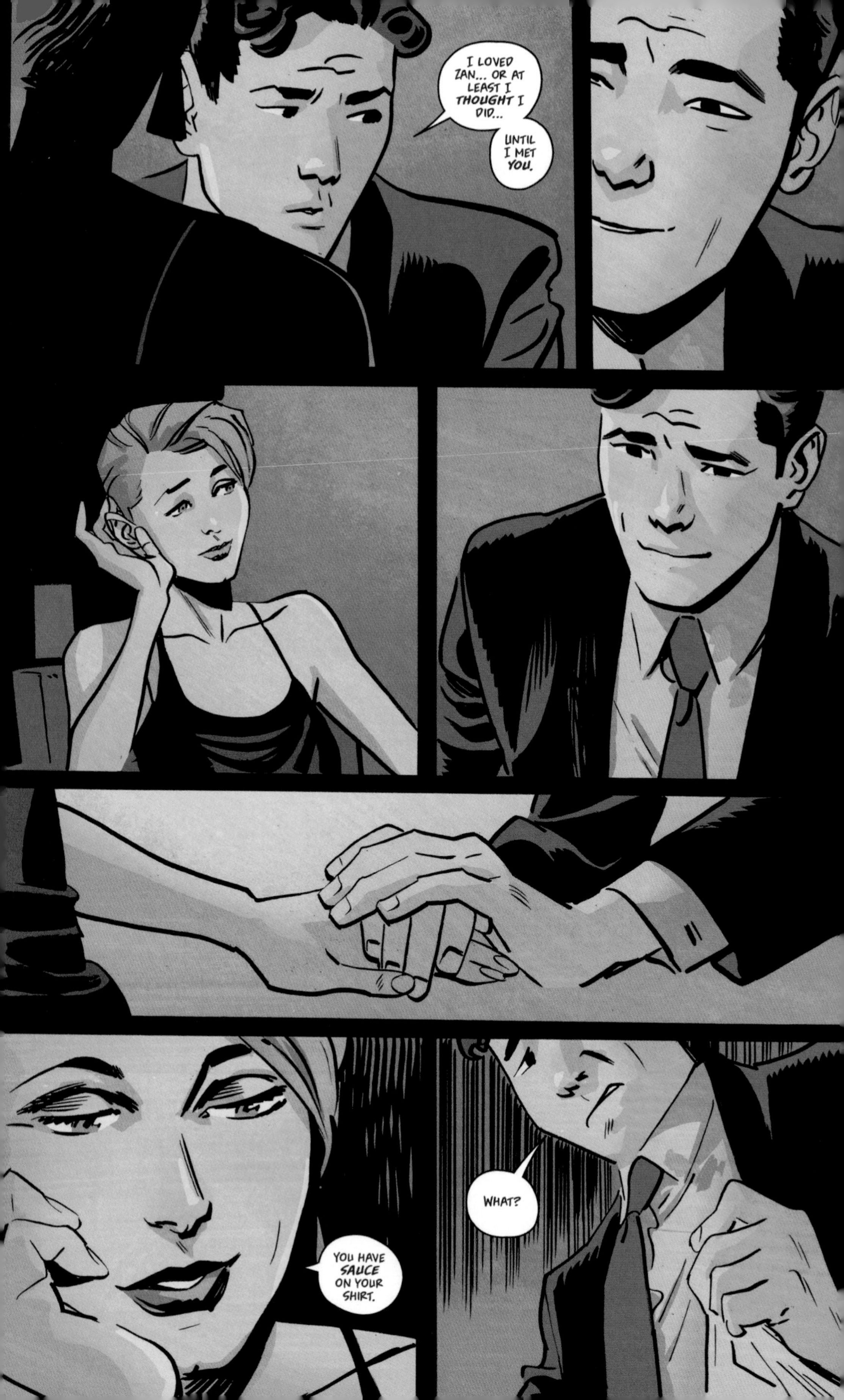
I LOVED ZAN... OR AT LEAST I THOUGHT I DID...
UNTIL I MET YOU.
YOU HAVE SAUCE ON YOUR SHIRT.
WHAT?

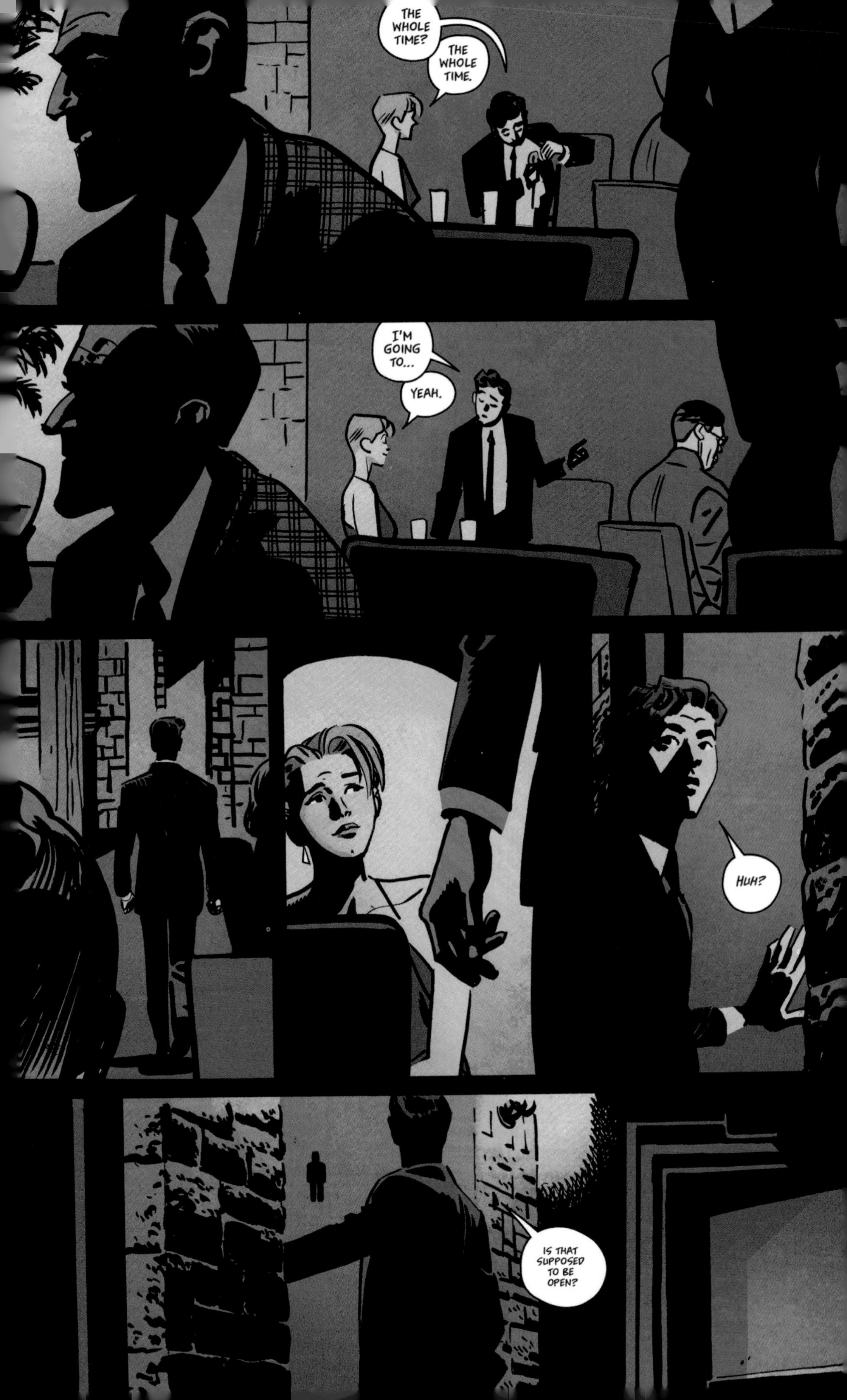
THE WHOLE TIME?
THE WHOLE TIME.
I'M GOING TO...
YEAH.
HUH?
IS THAT SUPPOSED TO BE OPEN?

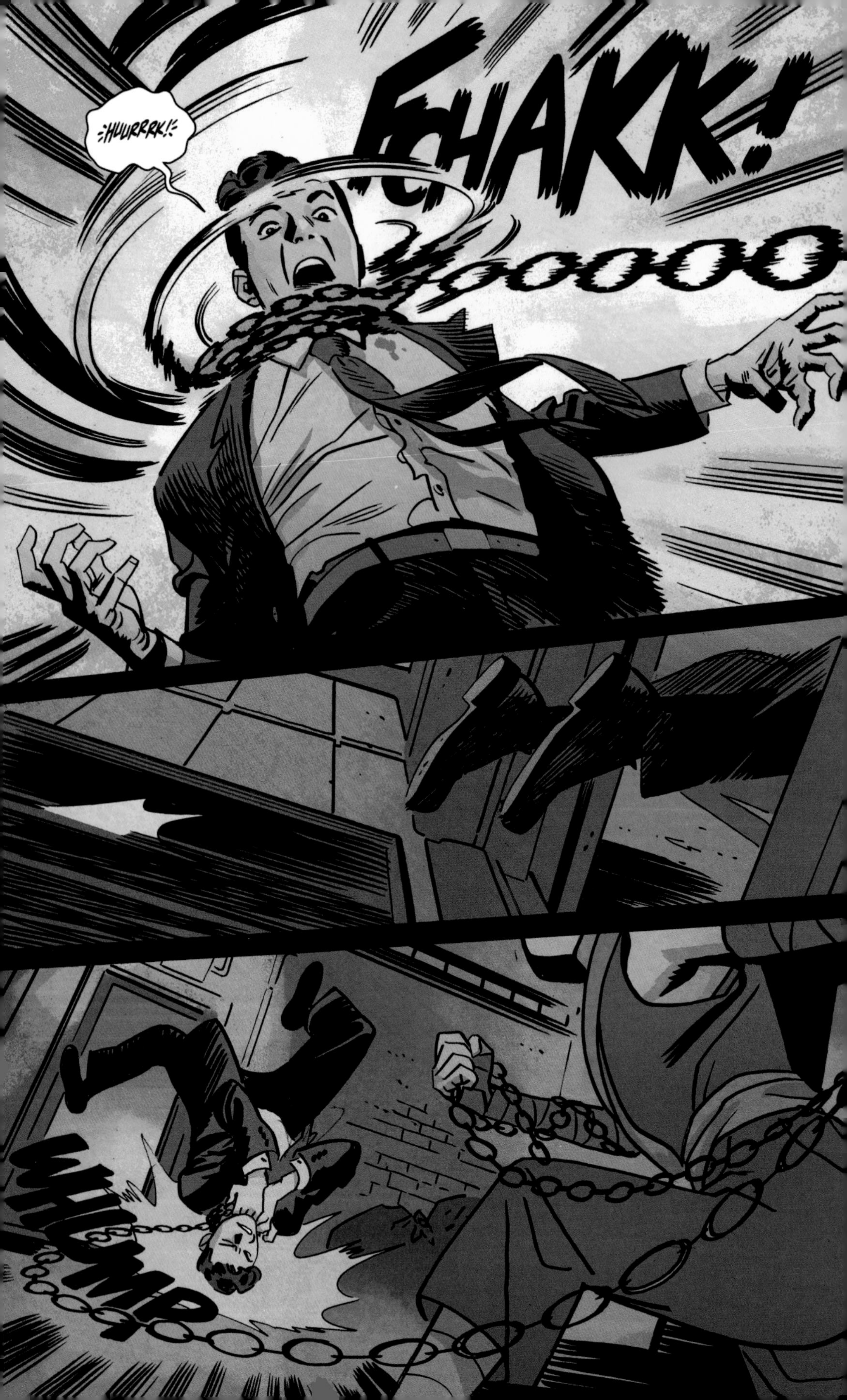

HUURRRK!
FCHAKK!
Yooooooo
WHUMP

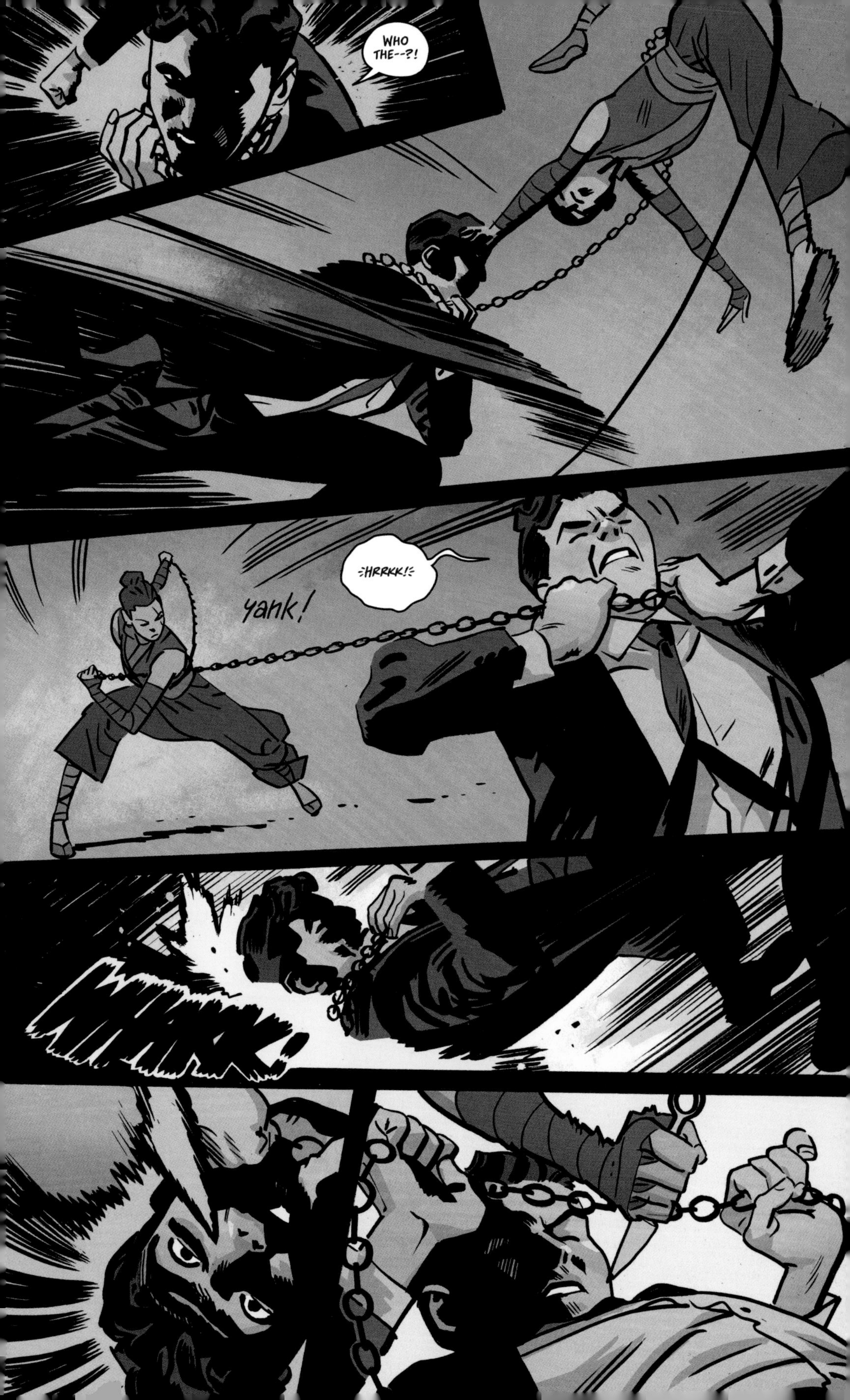
WHO THE--?!
HRRKK!
yank!
WHAK!

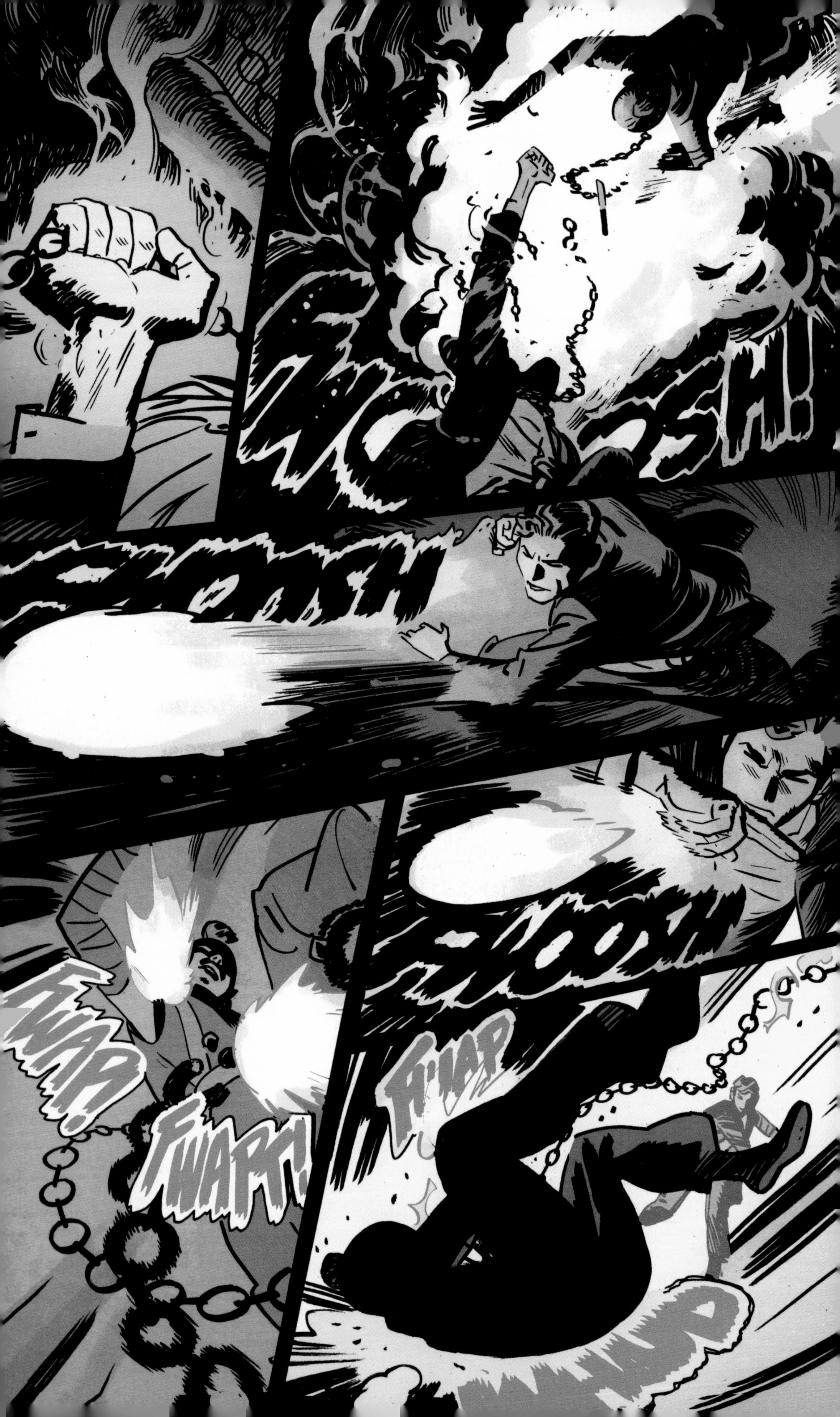
FWAP!
FWAPP!

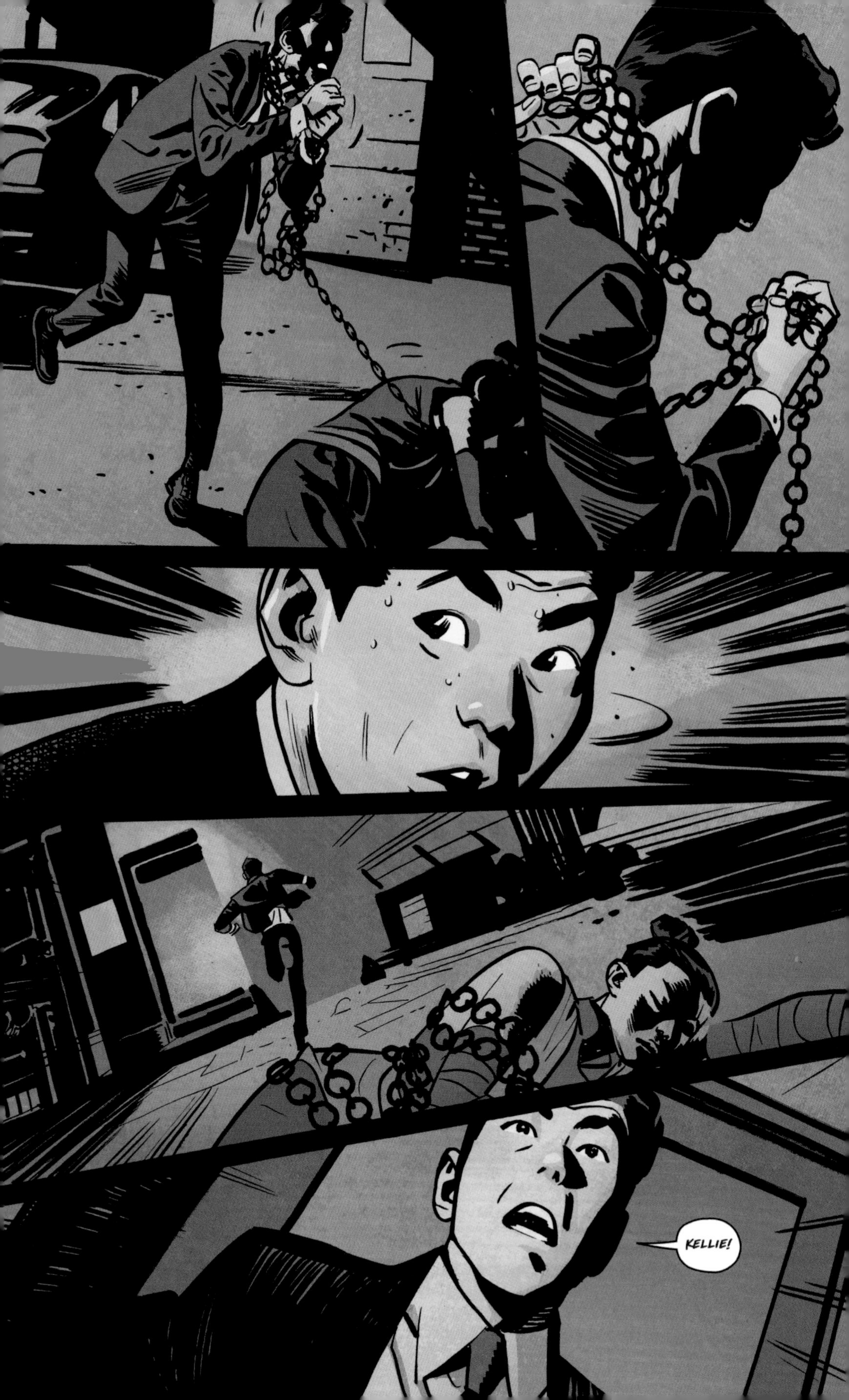
KELLIE!

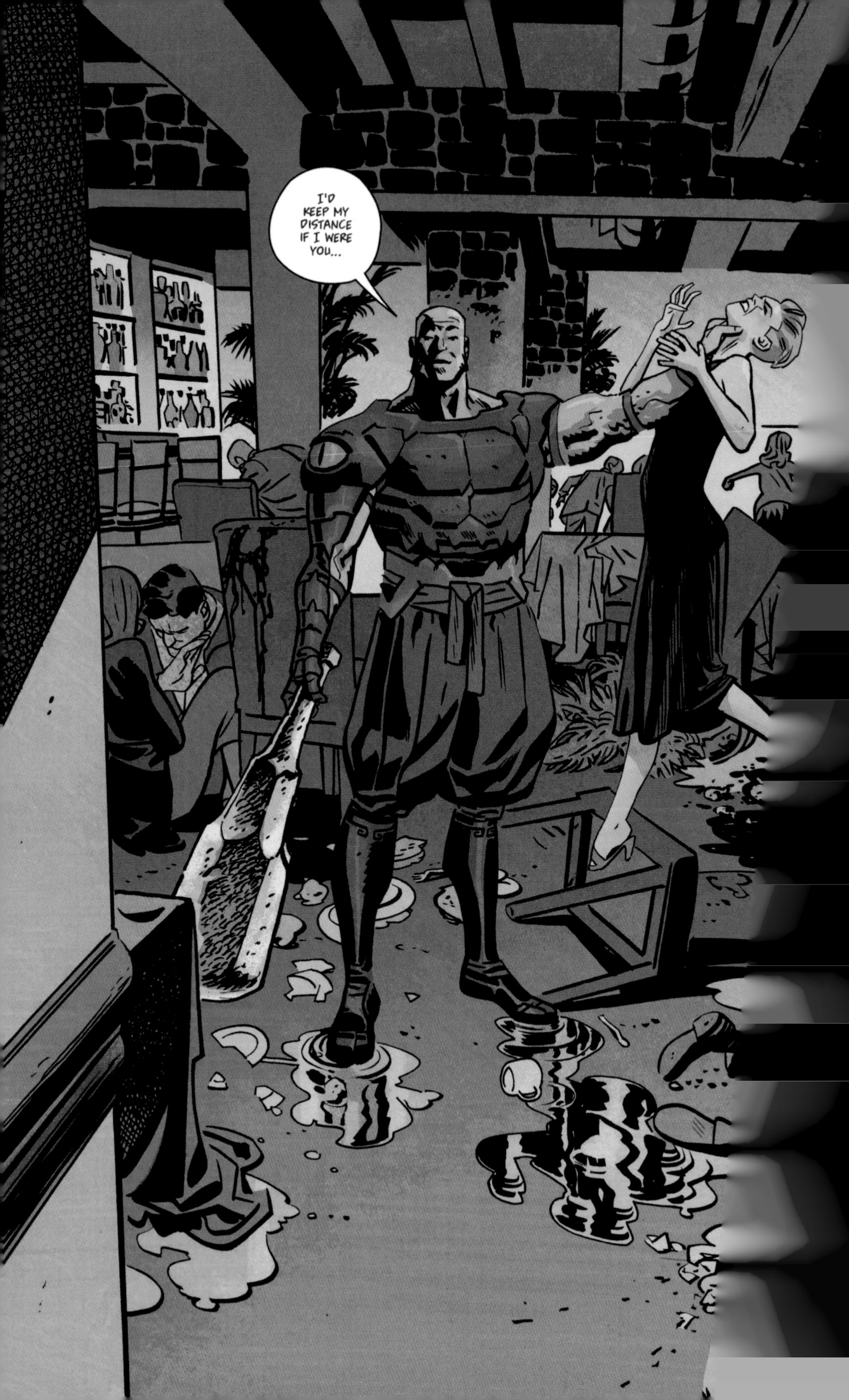
I'D KEEP MY DISTANCE IF I WERE YOU...

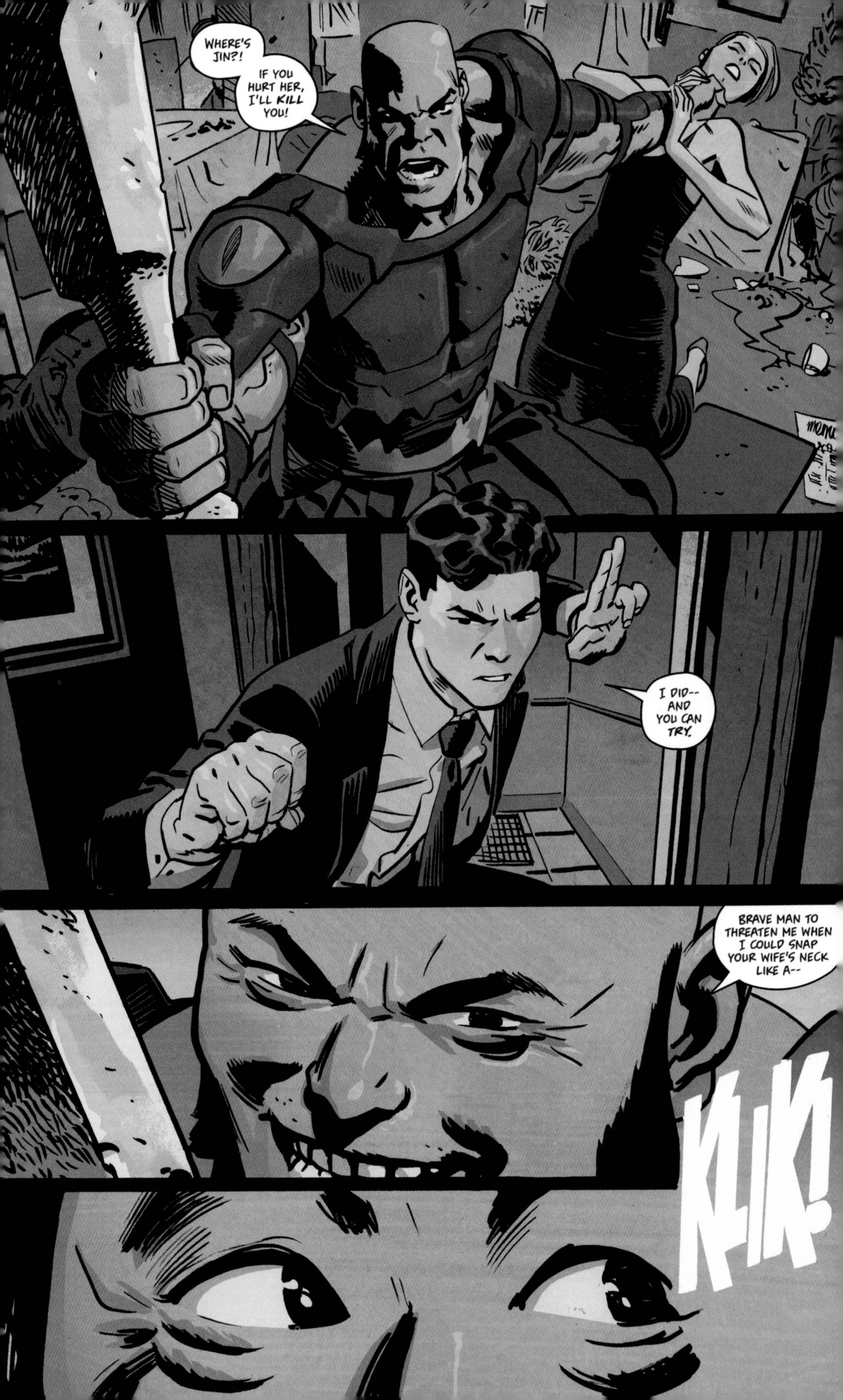
WHERE'S JIN?!
IF YOU HURT HER, I'LL KILL YOU!
I DID-- AND YOU CAN TRY.
BRAVE MAN TO THREATEN ME WHEN I COULD SNAP YOUR WIFE'S NECK LIKE A--
KLIK!

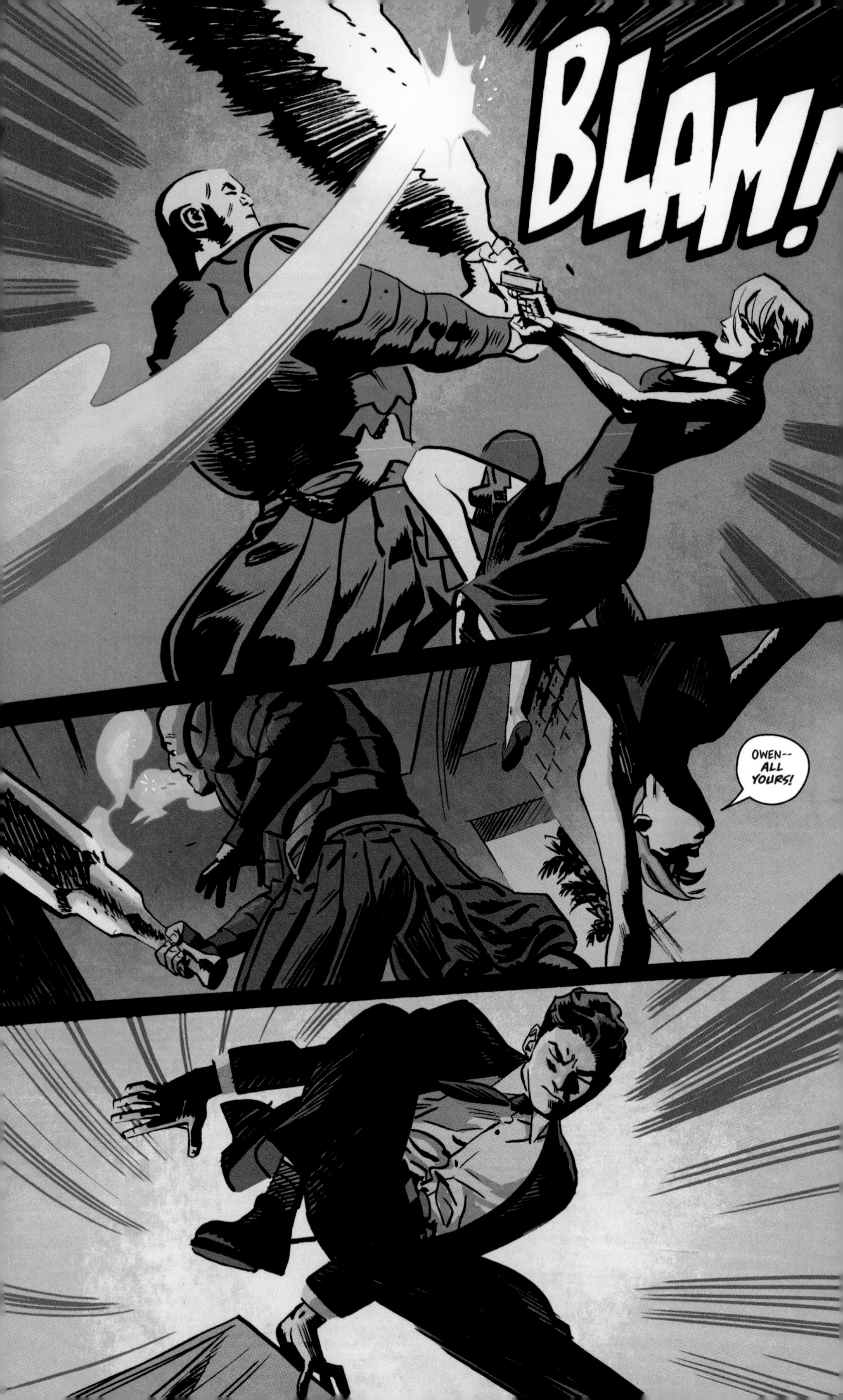
BLAM!
OWEN-- ALL YOURS!

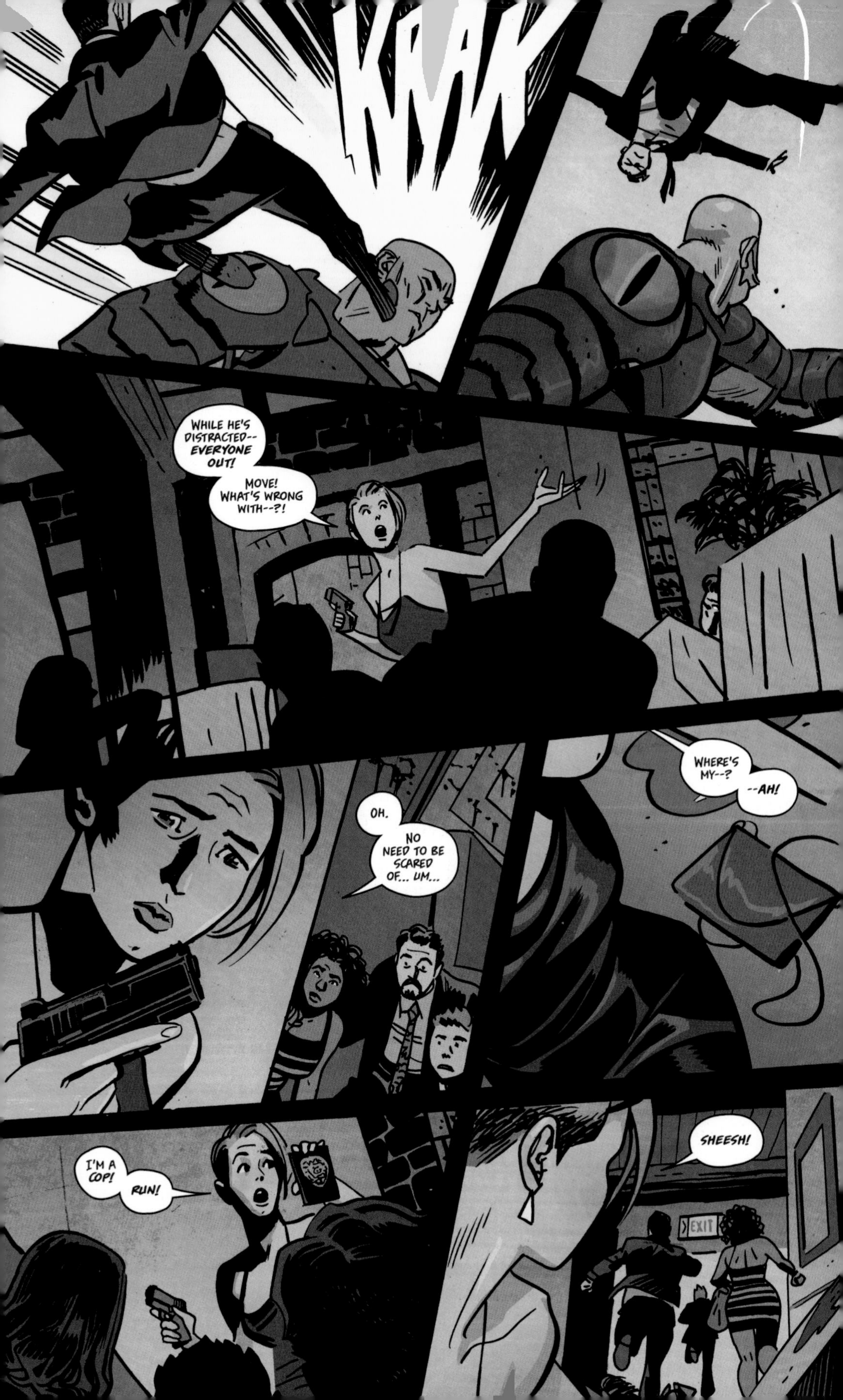

KRAK
WHILE HE'S DISTRACTED-- EVERYONE OUT!
MOVE! WHAT'S WRONG WITH--?!
OH.
NO NEED TO BE SCARED OF... UM...
WHERE'S MY--?
--AH!
I'M A COP!
RUN!
SHEESH!
EXIT

WROKK!

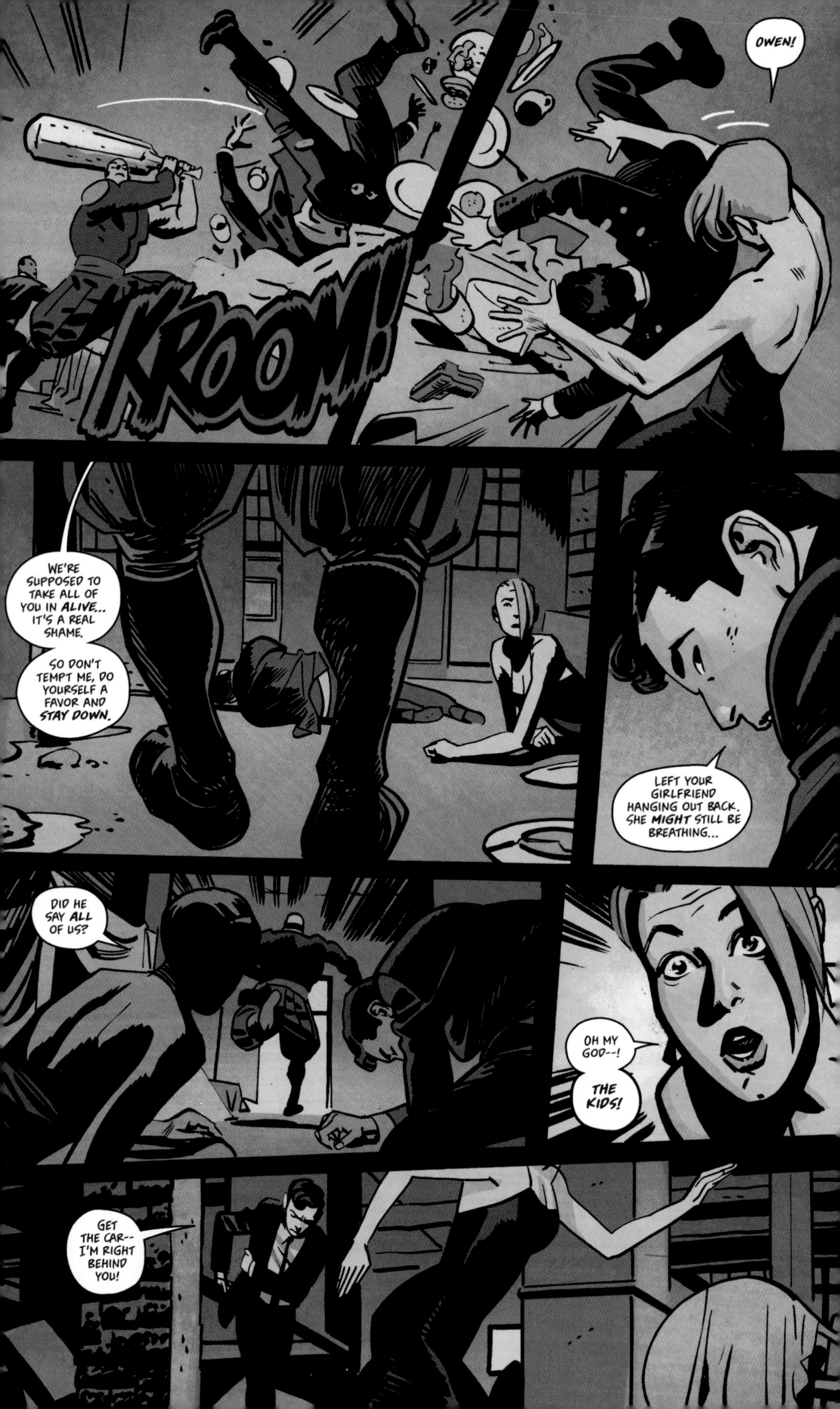
OWEN!
KROOM!
WE'RE SUPPOSED TO TAKE ALL OF YOU IN ALIVE... IT'S A REAL SHAME.
SO DON'T TEMPT ME, DO YOURSELF A FAVOR AND STAY DOWN.
LEFT YOUR GIRLFRIEND HANGING OUT BACK. SHE MIGHT STILL BE BREATHING...
DID HE SAY ALL OF US?
OH MY GOD--!
THE KIDS!
GET THE CAR-- I'M RIGHT BEHIND YOU!

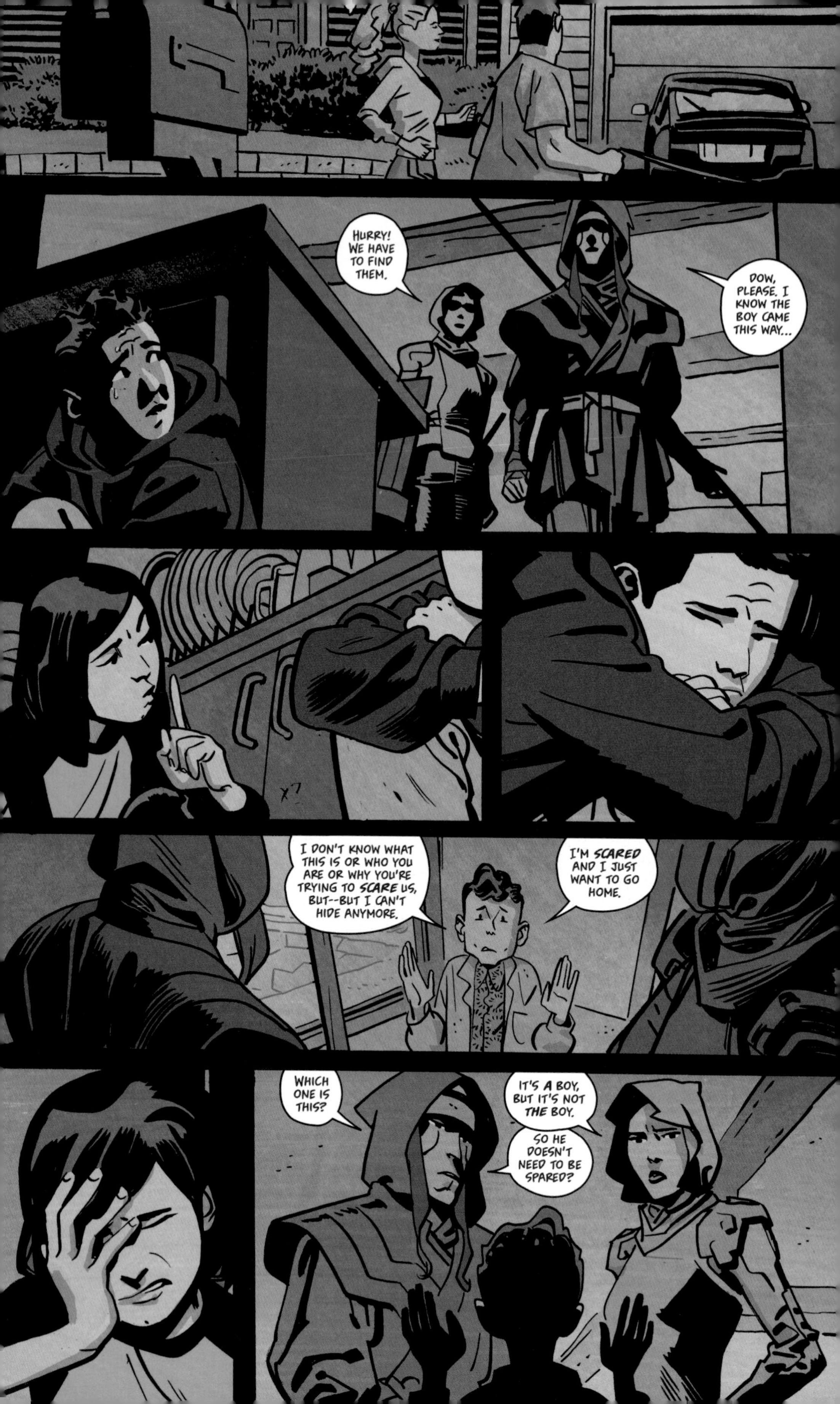
HURRY! WE HAVE TO FIND THEM.
DOW, PLEASE. I KNOW THE BOY CAME THIS WAY...
I DON'T KNOW WHAT THIS IS OR WHO YOU ARE OR WHY YOU'RE TRYING TO SCARE US, BUT--BUT I CAN'T HIDE ANYMORE.
I'M SCARED AND I JUST WANT TO GO HOME.
WHICH ONE IS THIS?
IT'S A BOY, BUT IT'S NOT THE BOY.
SO HE DOESN'T NEED TO BE SPARED?

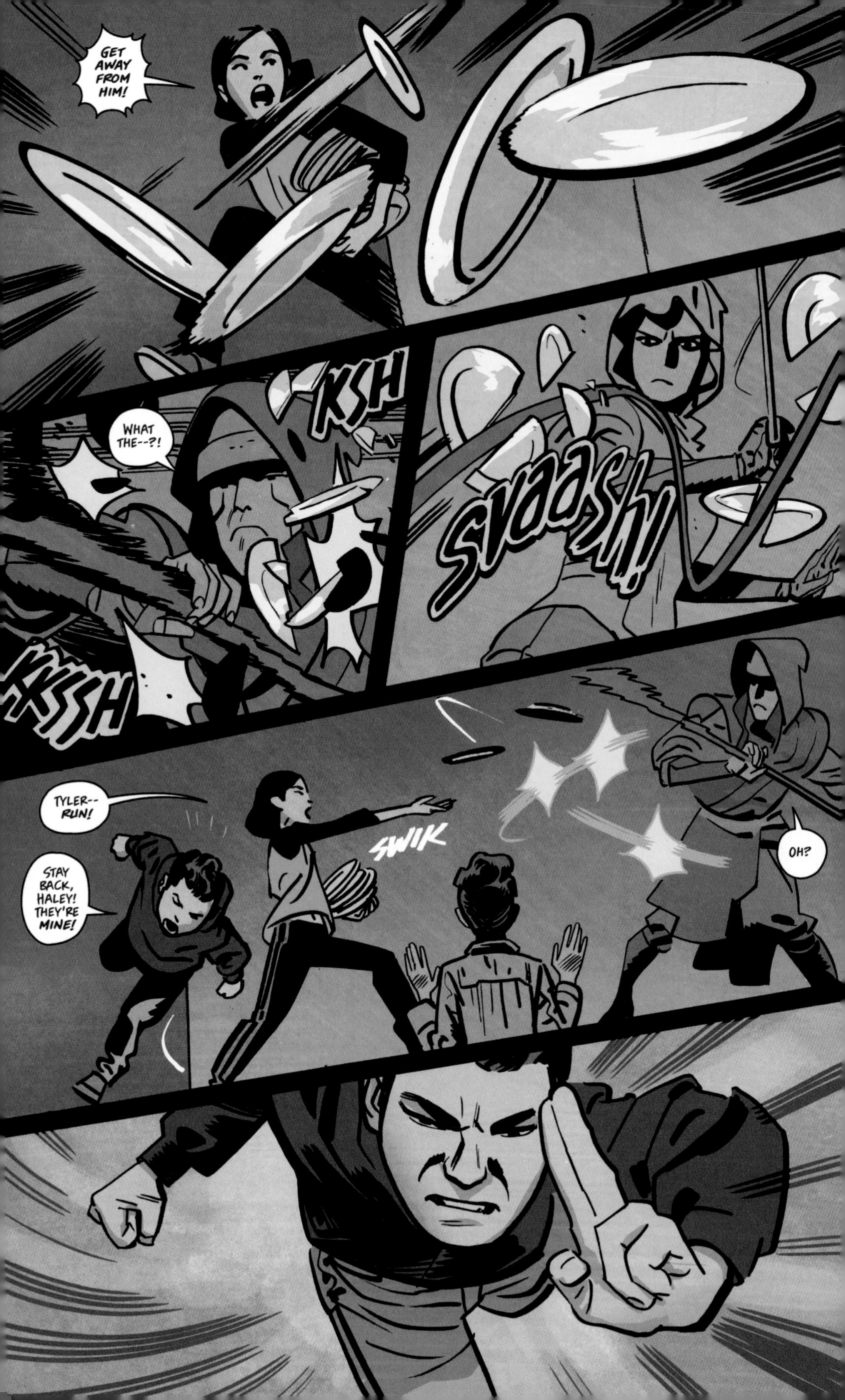
GET AWAY FROM HIM!
WHAT THE--?!
KSH
KKSSH
SVAASH!
TYLER-- RUN!
SWIK
OH?
STAY BACK, HALEY! THEY'RE MINE!

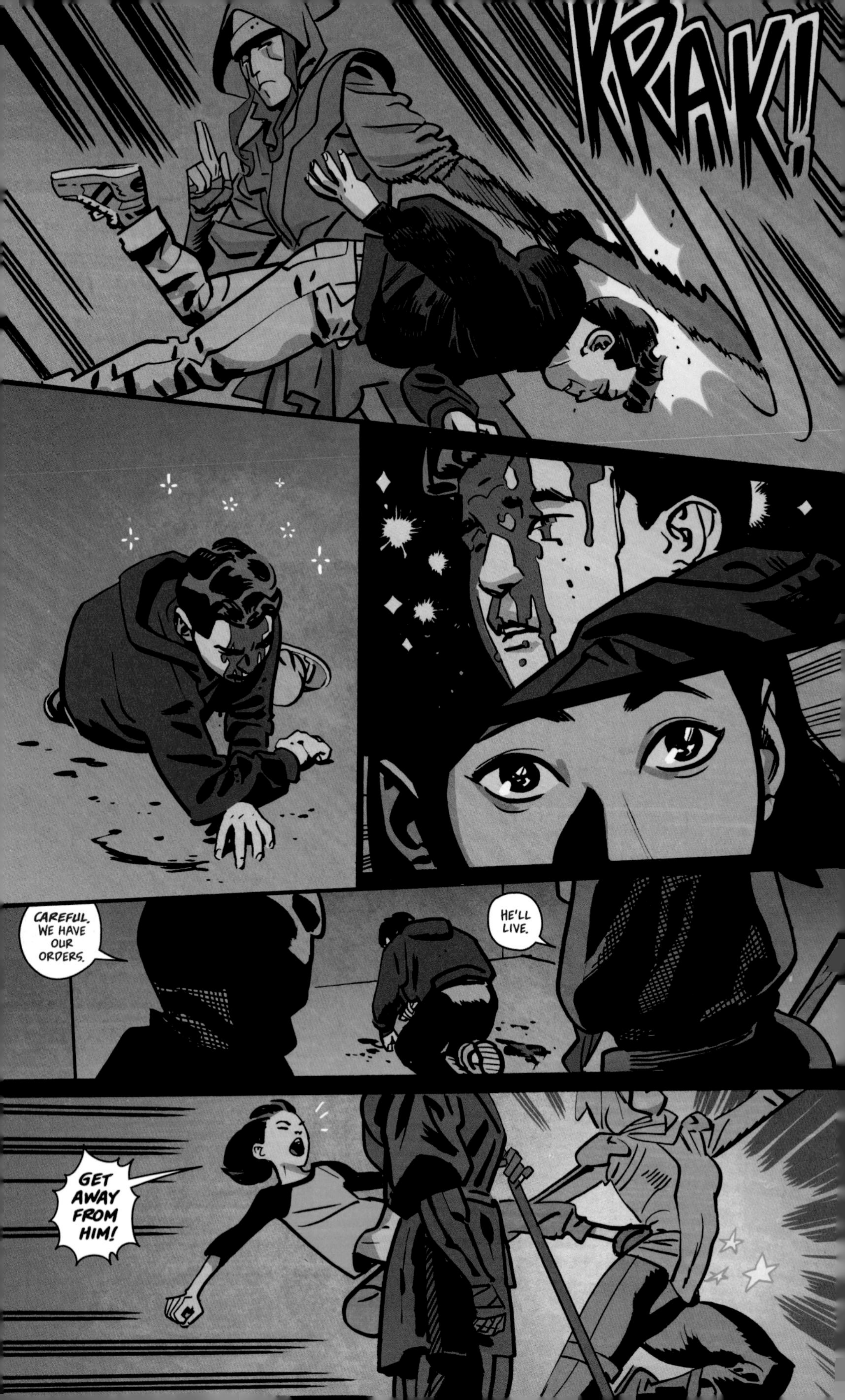
KRAK!!
CAREFUL. WE HAVE OUR ORDERS.
HE'LL LIVE.
GET AWAY FROM HIM!

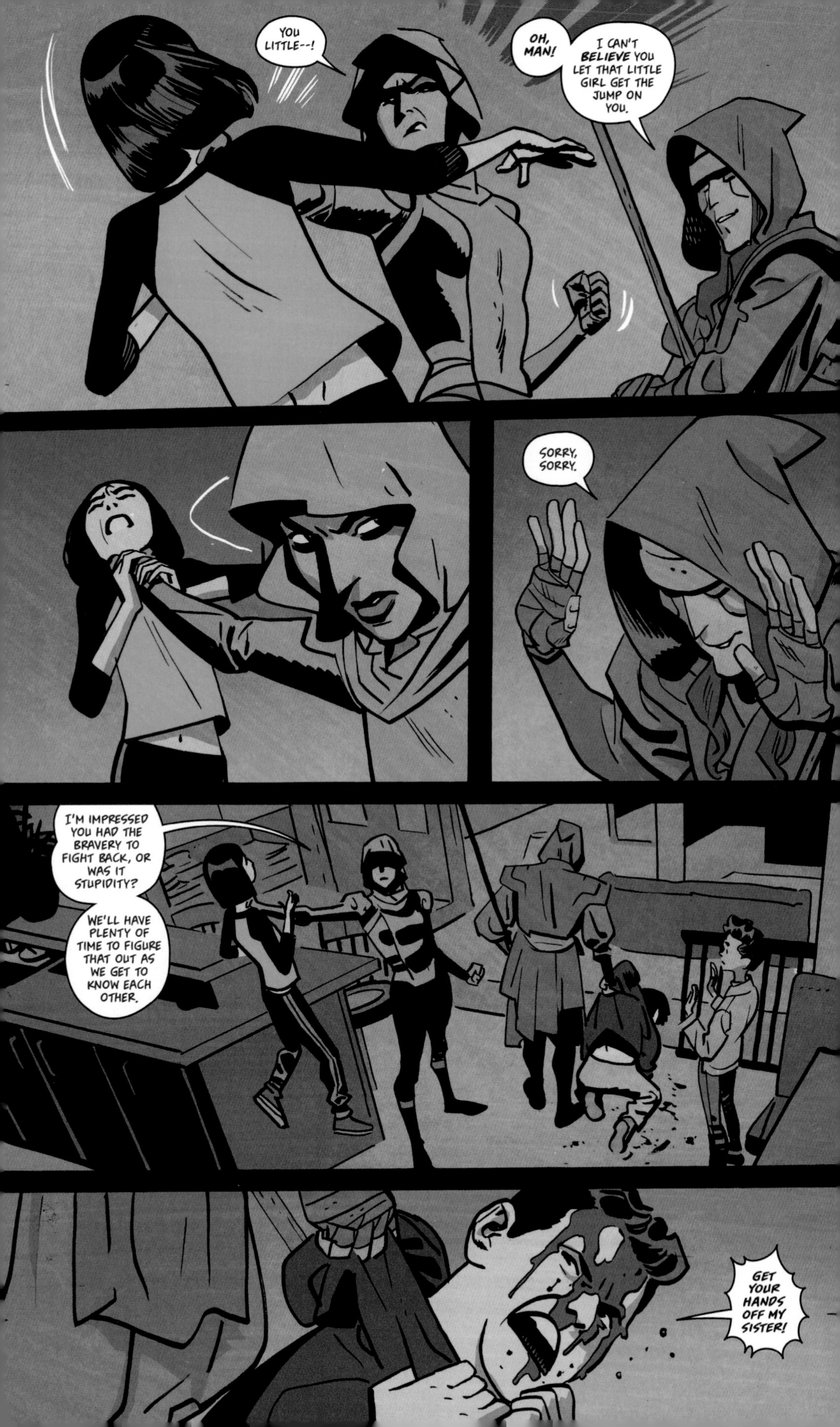
YOU LITTLE--!
OH, MAN!
I CAN'T BELIEVE YOU LET THAT LITTLE GIRL GET THE JUMP ON YOU.
SORRY, SORRY.
I'M IMPRESSED YOU HAD THE BRAVERY TO FIGHT BACK, OR WAS IT STUPIDITY?
WE'LL HAVE PLENTY OF TIME TO FIGURE THAT OUT AS WE GET TO KNOW EACH OTHER.
GET YOUR HANDS OFF MY SISTER!

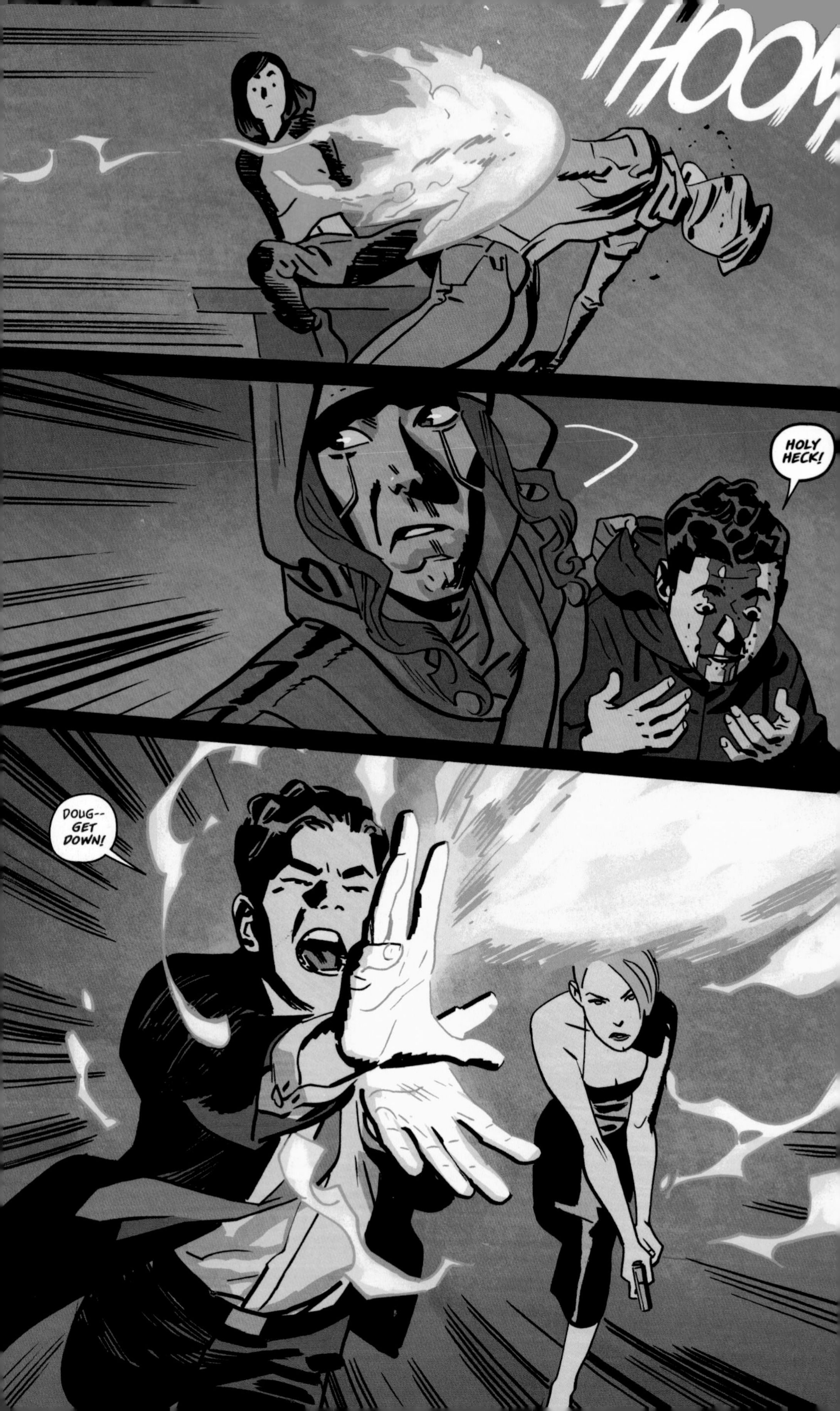
THOOM
HOLY HECK!
DOUG-- GET DOWN!

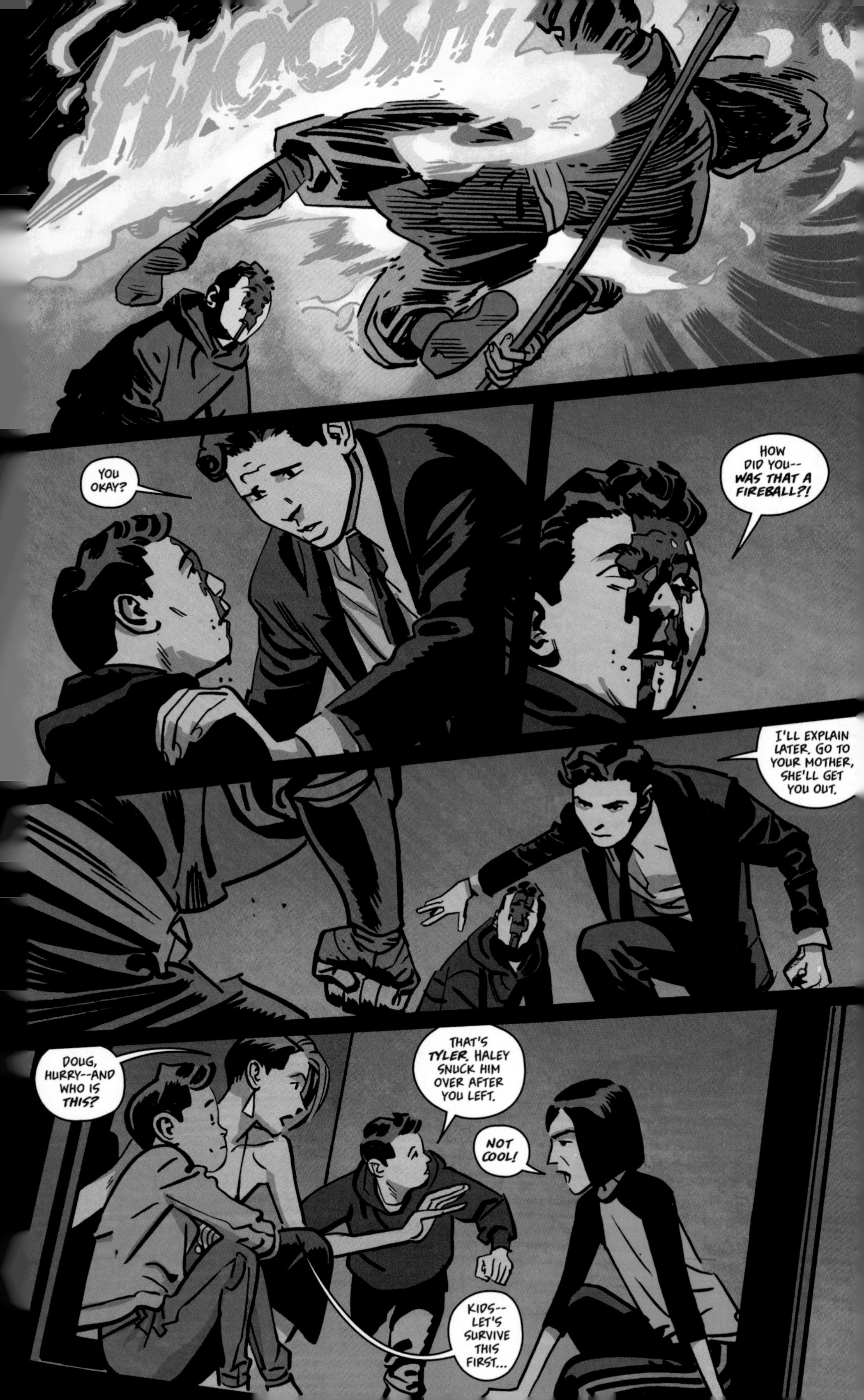
FWOOSH!
YOU OKAY?
HOW DID YOU-- WAS THAT A FIREBALL?!
I'LL EXPLAIN LATER. GO TO YOUR MOTHER, SHE'LL GET YOU OUT.
DOUG, HURRY--AND WHO IS THIS?
THAT'S TYLER. HALEY SNUCK HIM OVER AFTER YOU LEFT.
NOT COOL!
KIDS-- LET'S SURVIVE THIS FIRST...

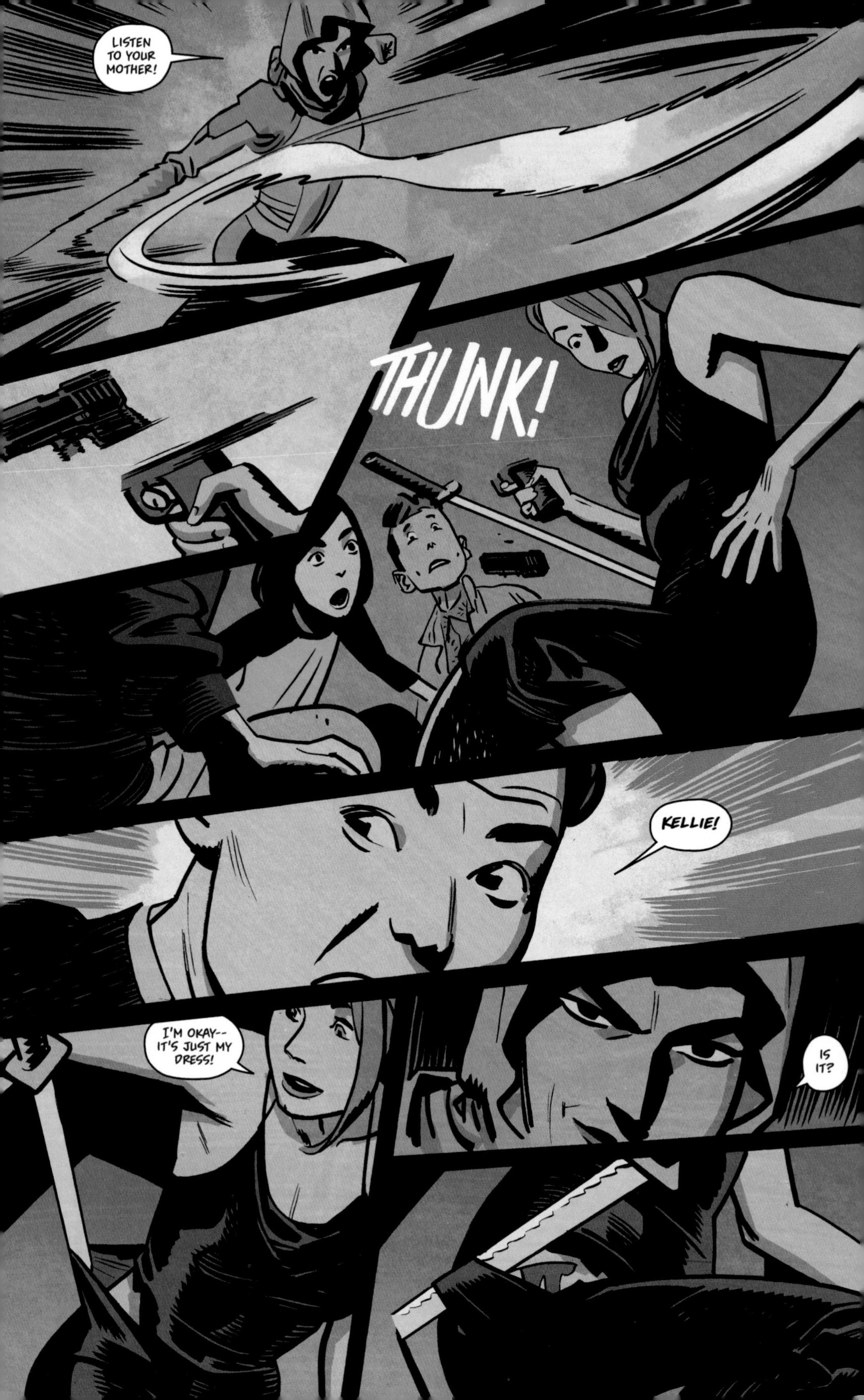
LISTEN TO YOUR MOTHER!
THUNK!
KELLIE!
I'M OKAY-- IT'S JUST MY DRESS!
IS IT?

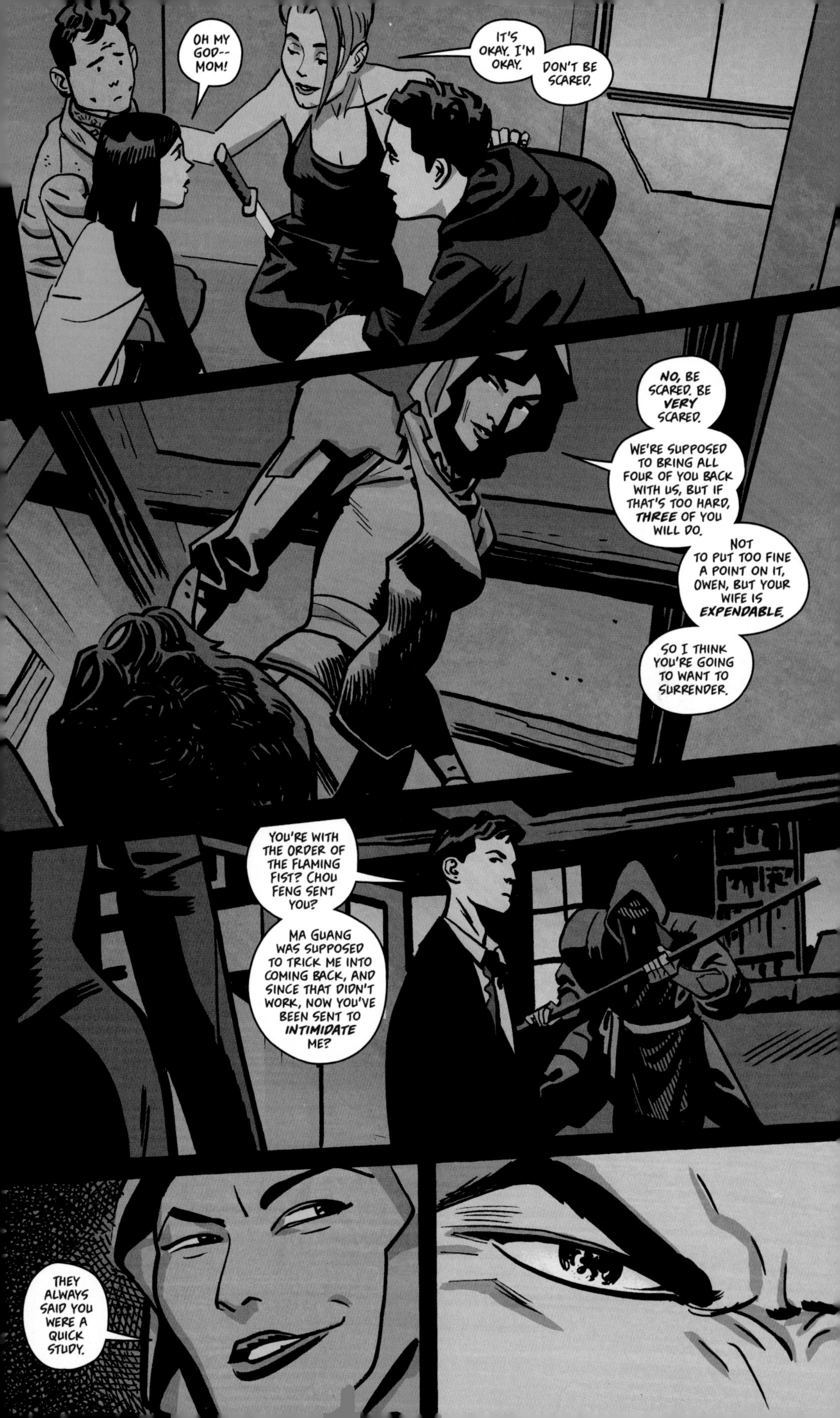
OH MY GOD-- MOM!
IT'S OKAY. I'M OKAY.
DON'T BE SCARED.
NO, BE SCARED. BE VERY SCARED.
WE'RE SUPPOSED TO BRING ALL FOUR OF YOU BACK WITH US, BUT IF THAT'S TOO HARD, THREE OF YOU WILL DO.
NOT TO PUT TOO FINE A POINT ON IT, OWEN, BUT YOUR WIFE IS EXPENDABLE.
SO I THINK YOU'RE GOING TO WANT TO SURRENDER.
. . .
YOU'RE WITH THE ORDER OF THE FLAMING FIST? CHOU FENG SENT YOU?
MA GUANG WAS SUPPOSED TO TRICK ME INTO COMING BACK, AND SINCE THAT DIDN'T WORK, NOW YOU'VE BEEN SENT TO INTIMIDATE ME?
THEY ALWAYS SAID YOU WERE A QUICK STUDY.

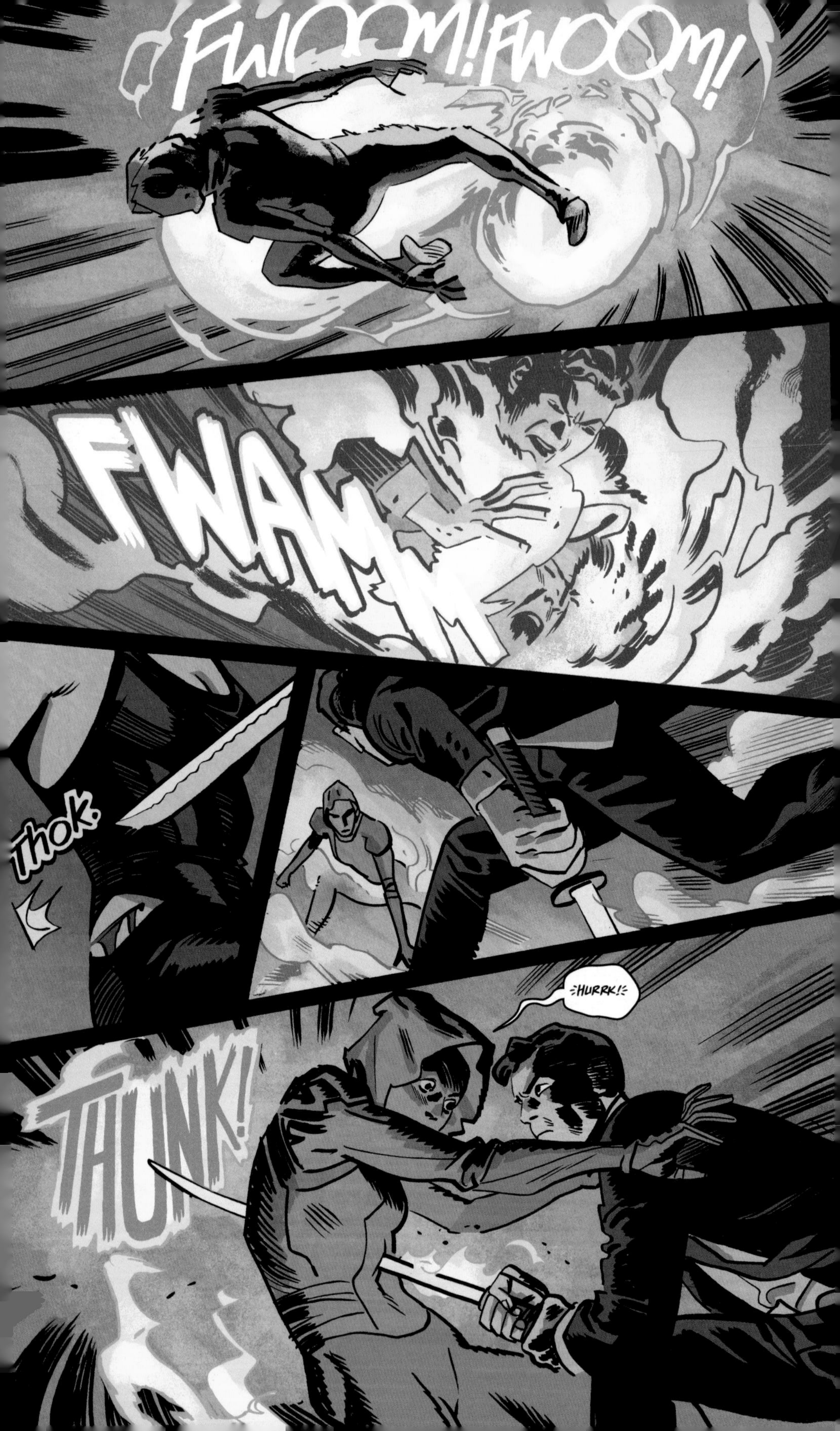
FWOOOM! FWOOOM!
FWAM
thok.
HURRK!
THUNK!

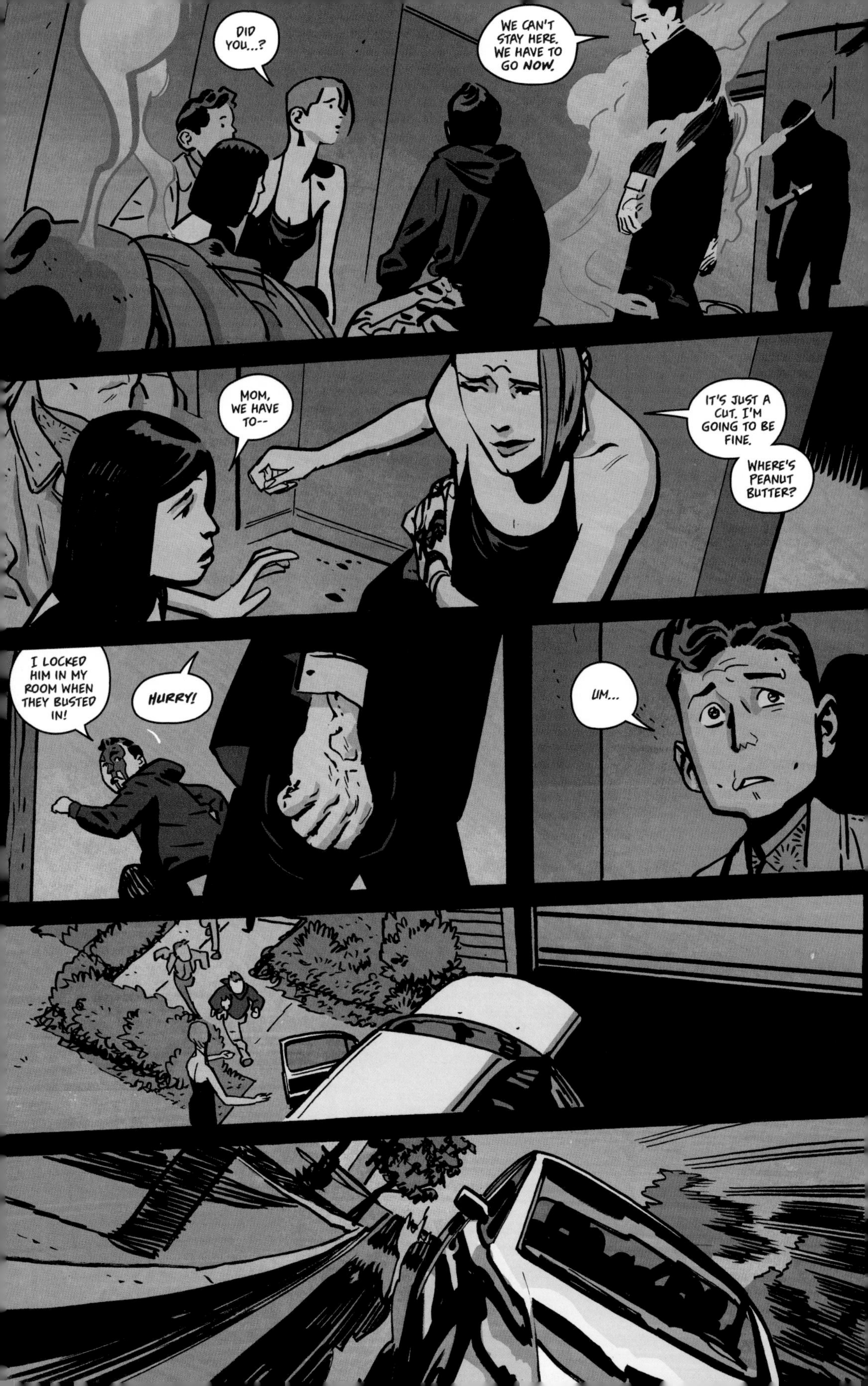
DID YOU...?
WE CAN'T STAY HERE. WE HAVE TO GO NOW.
MOM, WE HAVE TO--
IT'S JUST A CUT. I'M GOING TO BE FINE.
WHERE'S PEANUT BUTTER?
I LOCKED HIM IN MY ROOM WHEN THEY BUSTED IN!
HURRY!
UM...

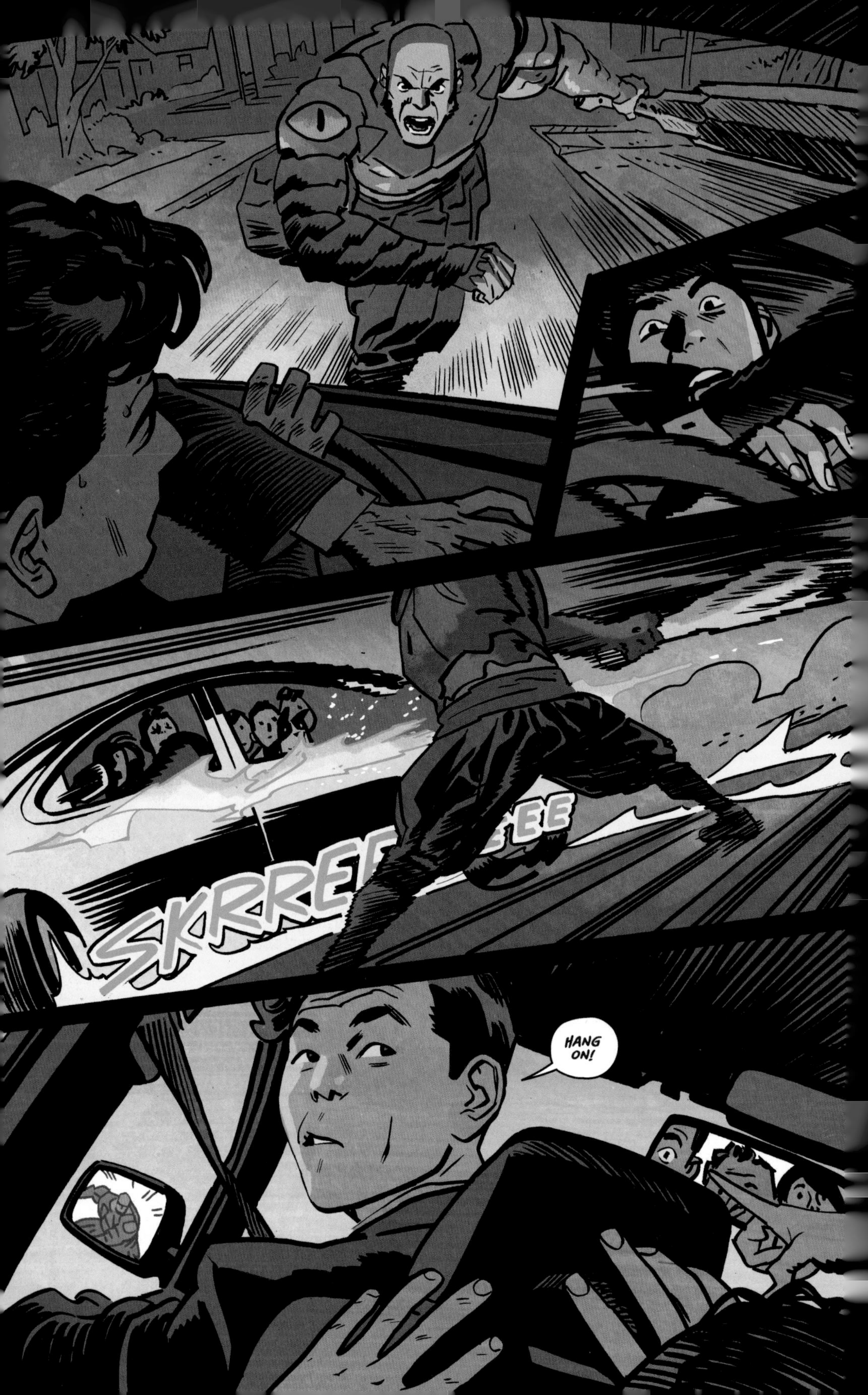
SKRREEEEEE
HANG ON!

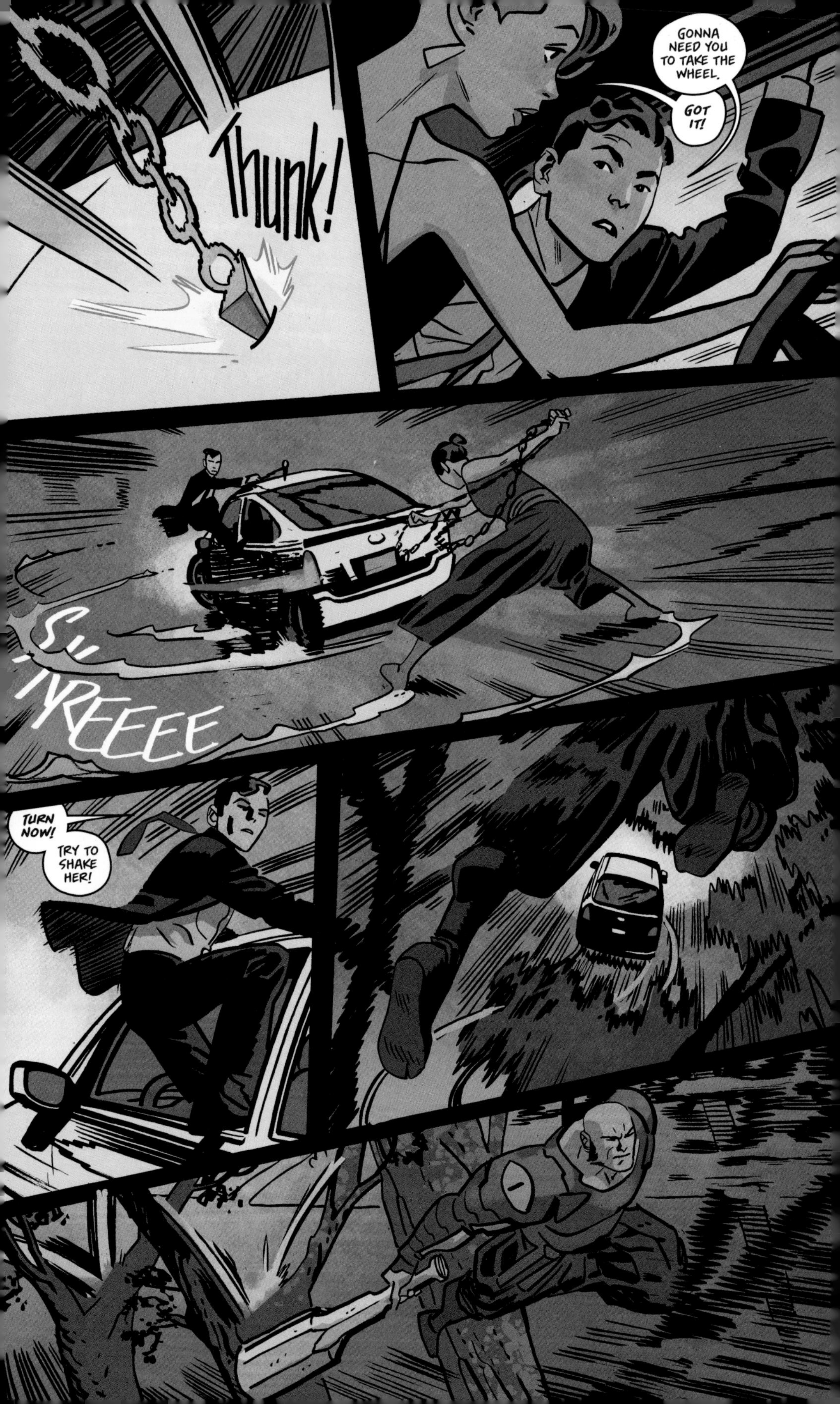
Thunk!
GONNA NEED YOU TO TAKE THE WHEEL.
GOT IT!
SKREEEE
TURN NOW!
TRY TO SHAKE HER!

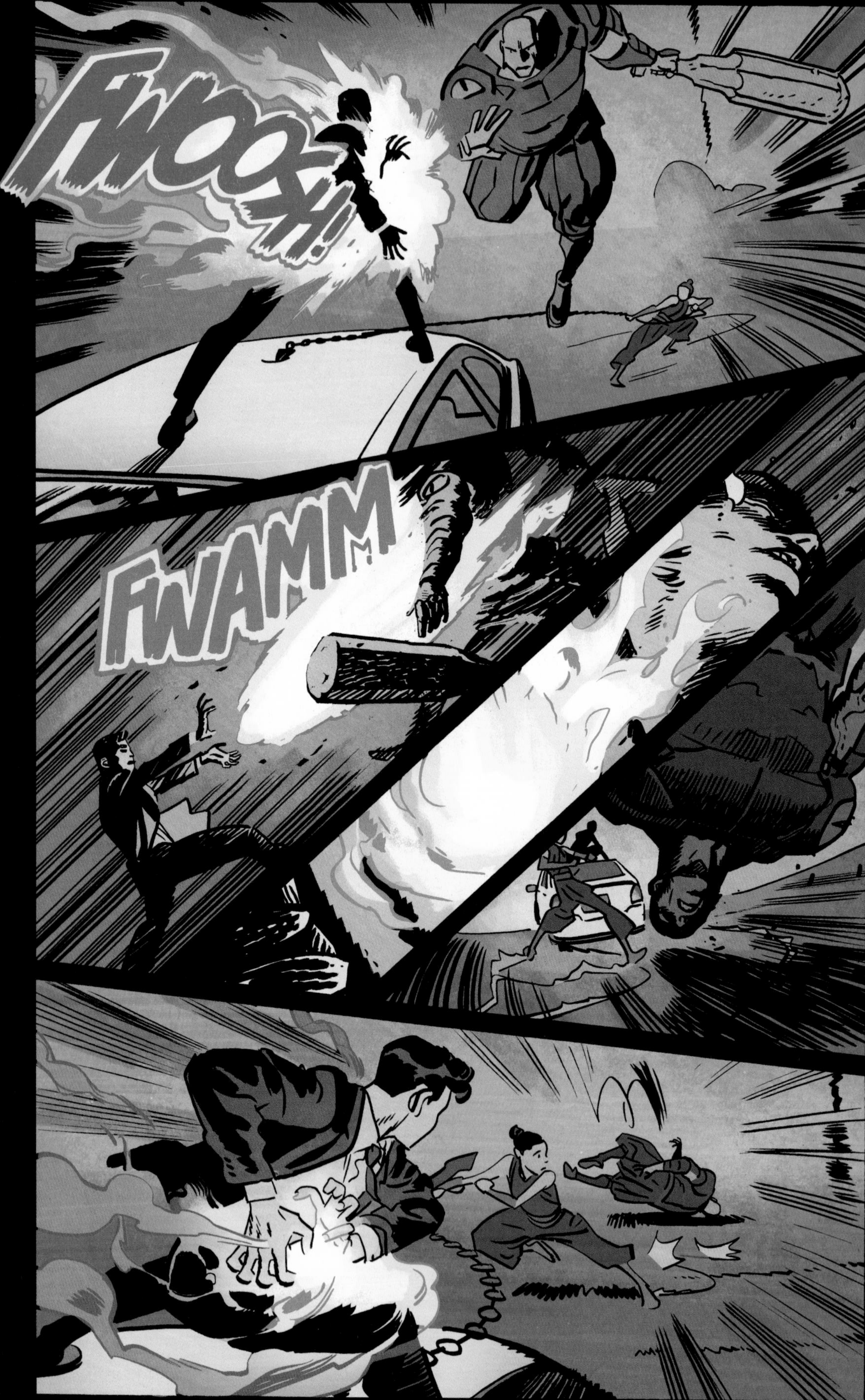
FWOOSH!
FWAMM

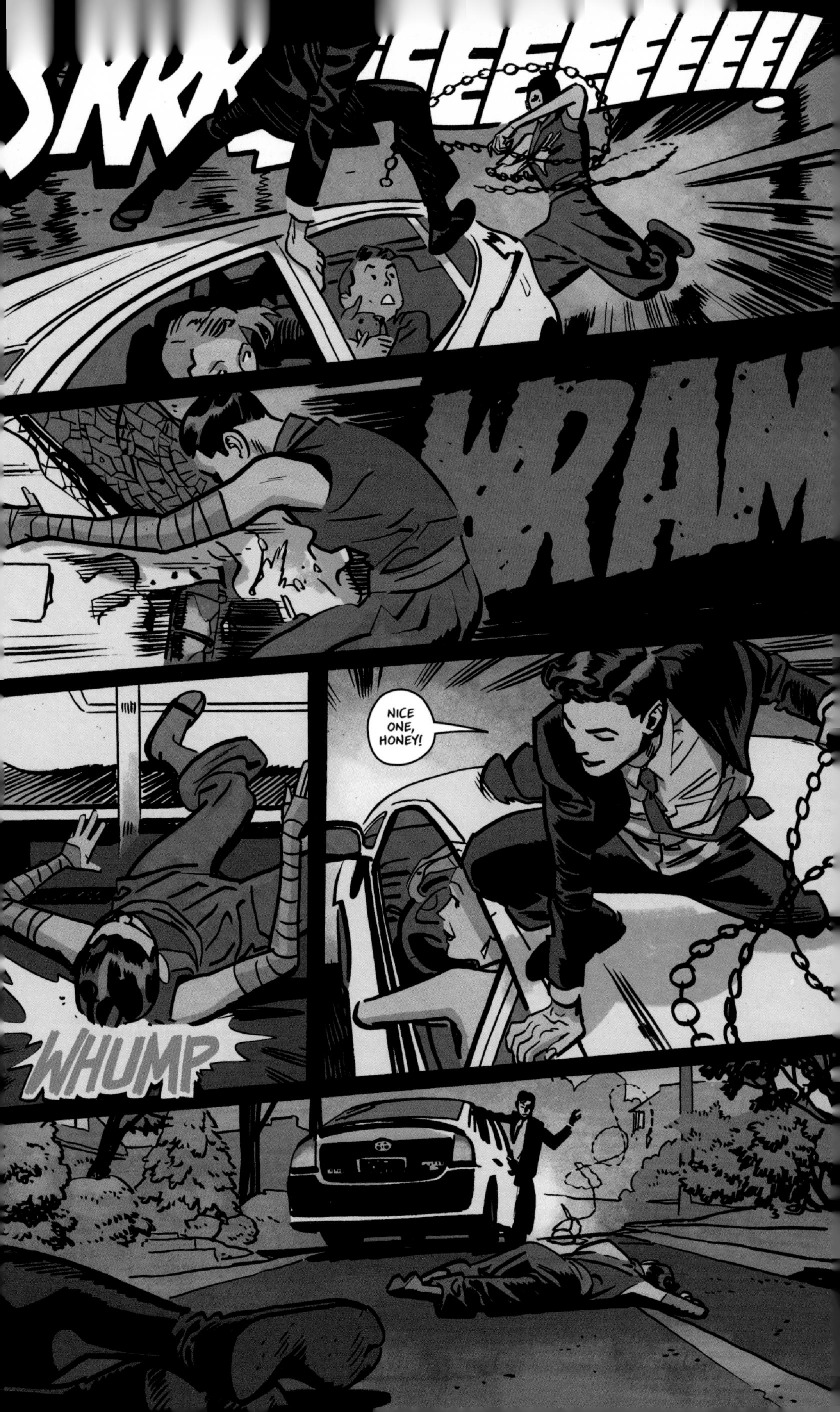
SKKKEEEEEEEEEE!
KRAM
WHUMP
NICE ONE, HONEY!

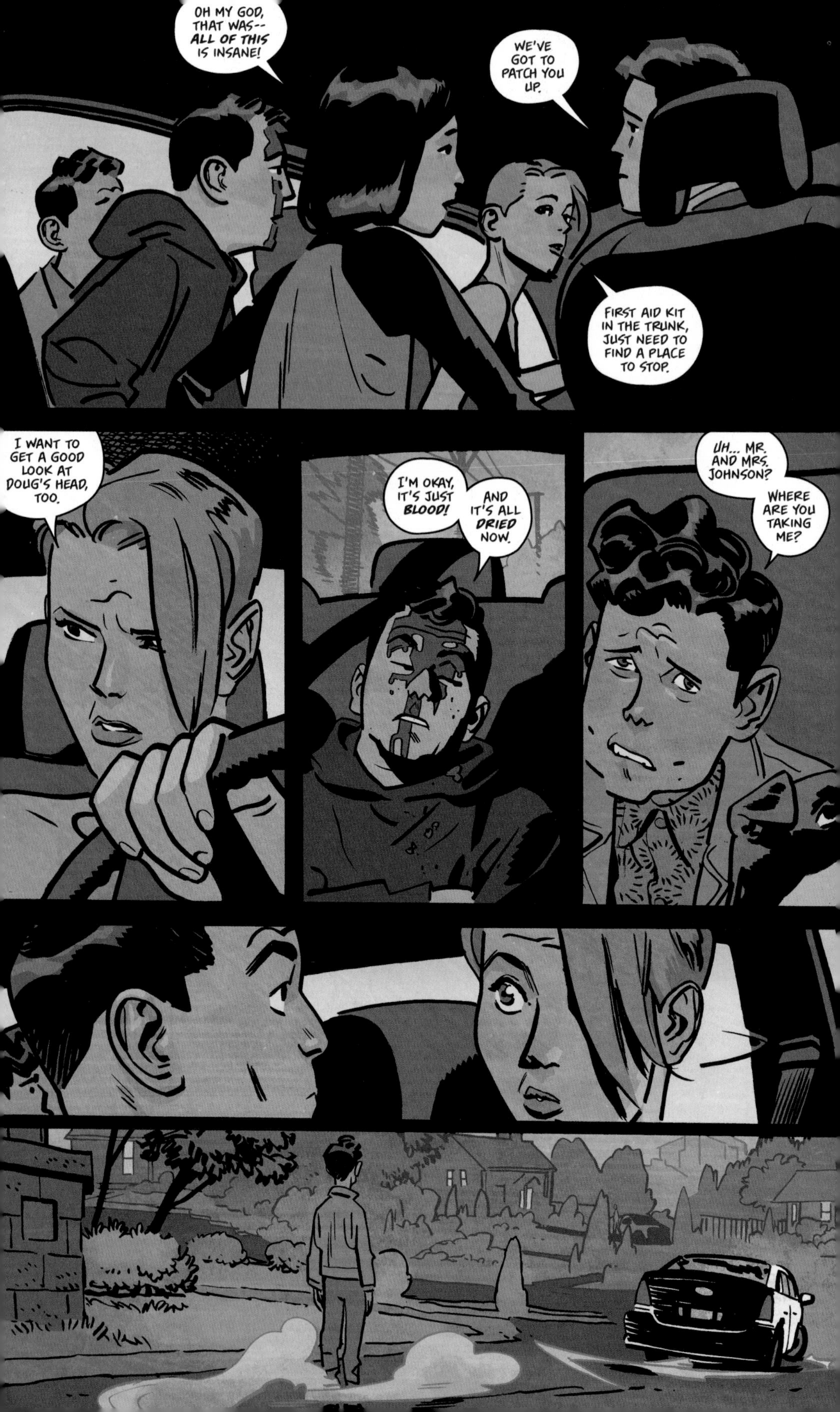
OH MY GOD, THAT WAS-- ALL OF THIS IS INSANE!
WE'VE GOT TO PATCH YOU UP.
FIRST AID KIT IN THE TRUNK, JUST NEED TO FIND A PLACE TO STOP.
I WANT TO GET A GOOD LOOK AT DOUG'S HEAD, TOO.
I'M OKAY, IT'S JUST BLOOD!
AND IT'S ALL DRIED NOW.
UH... MR. AND MRS. JOHNSON?
WHERE ARE YOU TAKING ME?

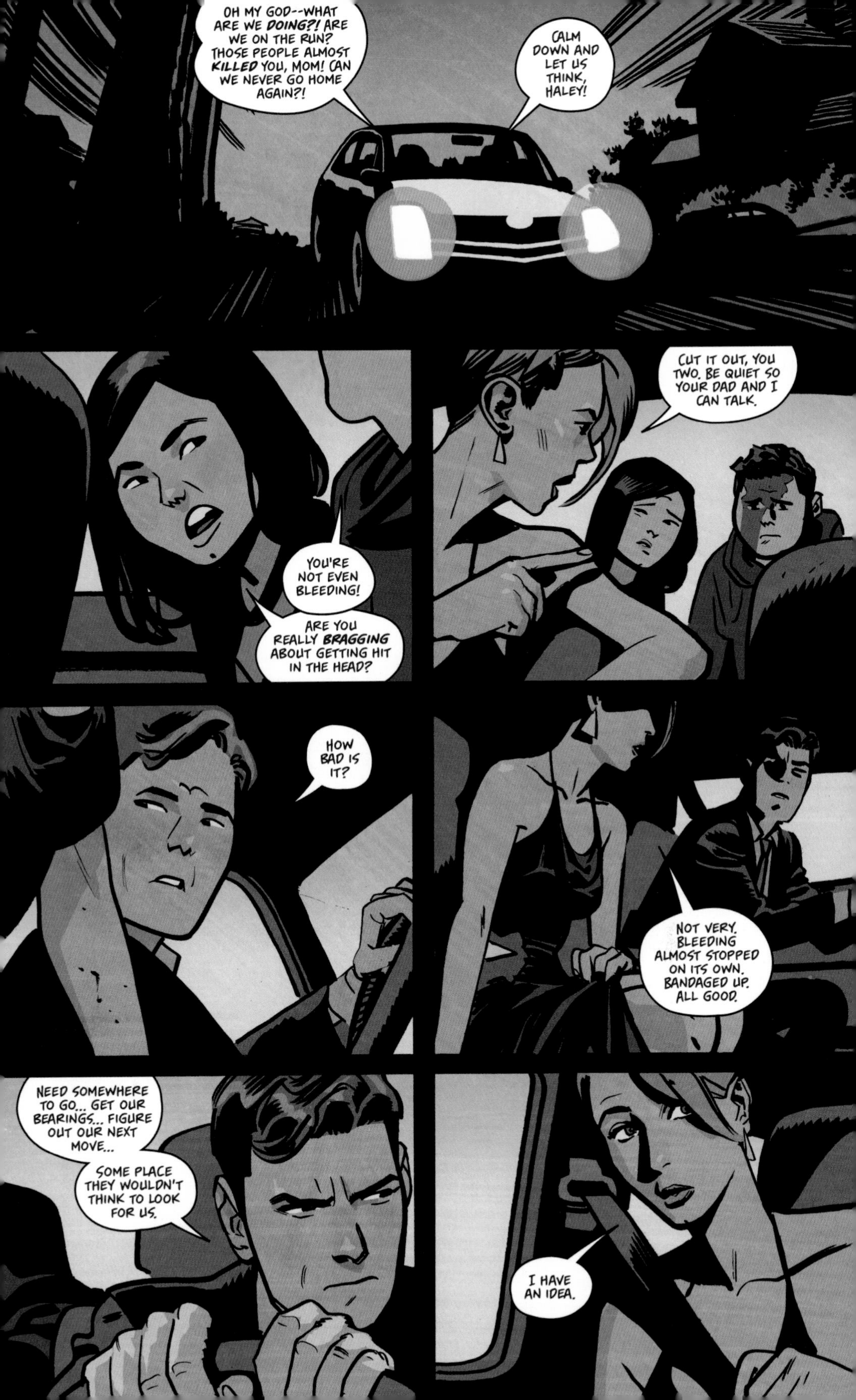
OH MY GOD--WHAT ARE WE DOING?! ARE WE ON THE RUN? THOSE PEOPLE ALMOST KILLED YOU, MOM! CAN WE NEVER GO HOME AGAIN?!
CALM DOWN AND LET US THINK, HALEY!
YOU'RE NOT EVEN BLEEDING!
ARE YOU REALLY BRAGGING ABOUT GETTING HIT IN THE HEAD?
CUT IT OUT, YOU TWO. BE QUIET SO YOUR DAD AND I CAN TALK.
HOW BAD IS IT?
NOT VERY. BLEEDING ALMOST STOPPED ON ITS OWN. BANDAGED UP. ALL GOOD.
NEED SOMEWHERE TO GO... GET OUR BEARINGS... FIGURE OUT OUR NEXT MOVE...
SOME PLACE THEY WOULDN'T THINK TO LOOK FOR US.
I HAVE AN IDEA.

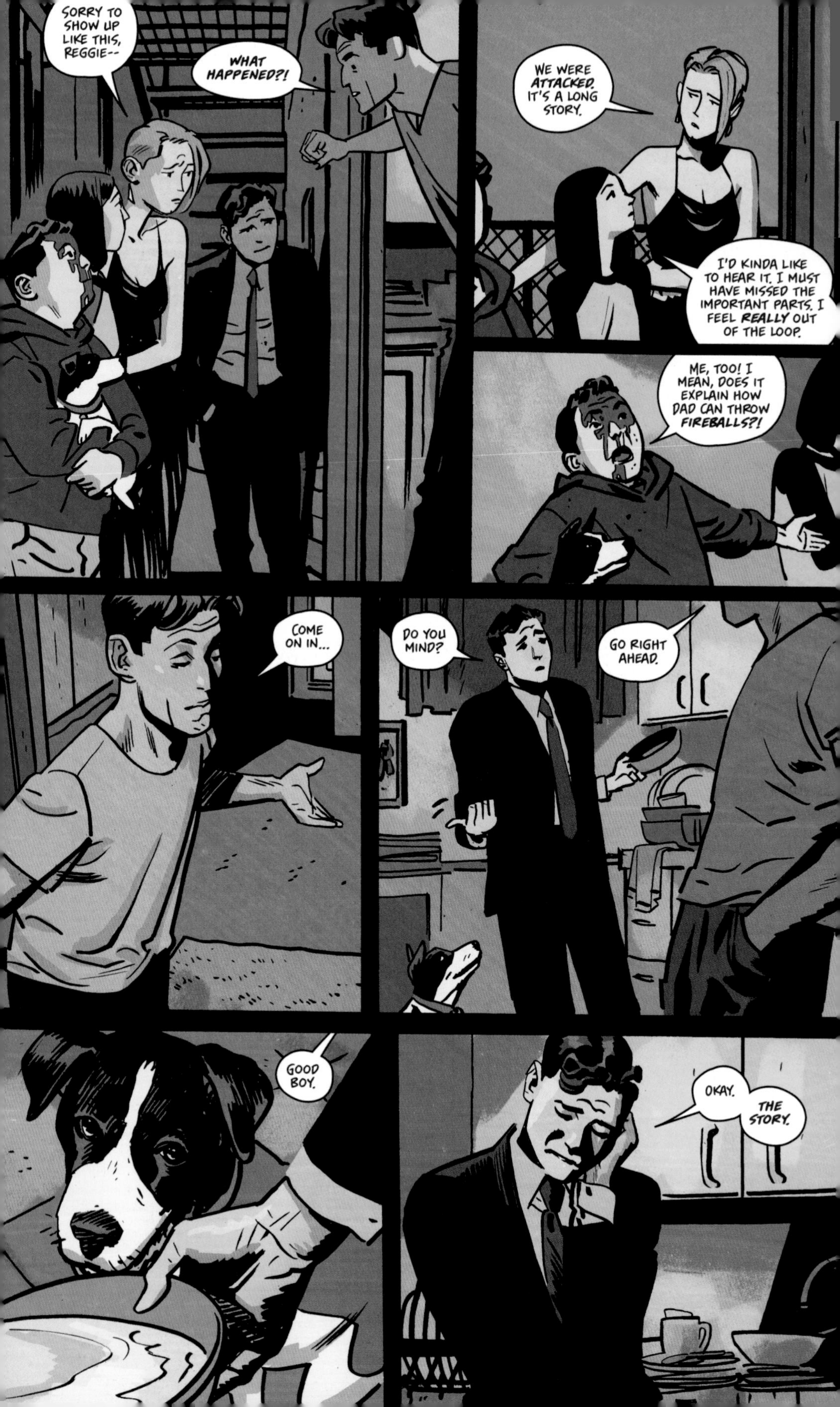
SORRY TO SHOW UP LIKE THIS, REGGIE--
WHAT HAPPENED?!
WE WERE ATTACKED. IT'S A LONG STORY.
I'D KINDA LIKE TO HEAR IT. I MUST HAVE MISSED THE IMPORTANT PARTS. I FEEL REALLY OUT OF THE LOOP.
ME, TOO! I MEAN, DOES IT EXPLAIN HOW DAD CAN THROW FIREBALLS?!
COME ON IN...
DO YOU MIND?
GO RIGHT AHEAD.
GOOD BOY.
OKAY.
THE STORY.

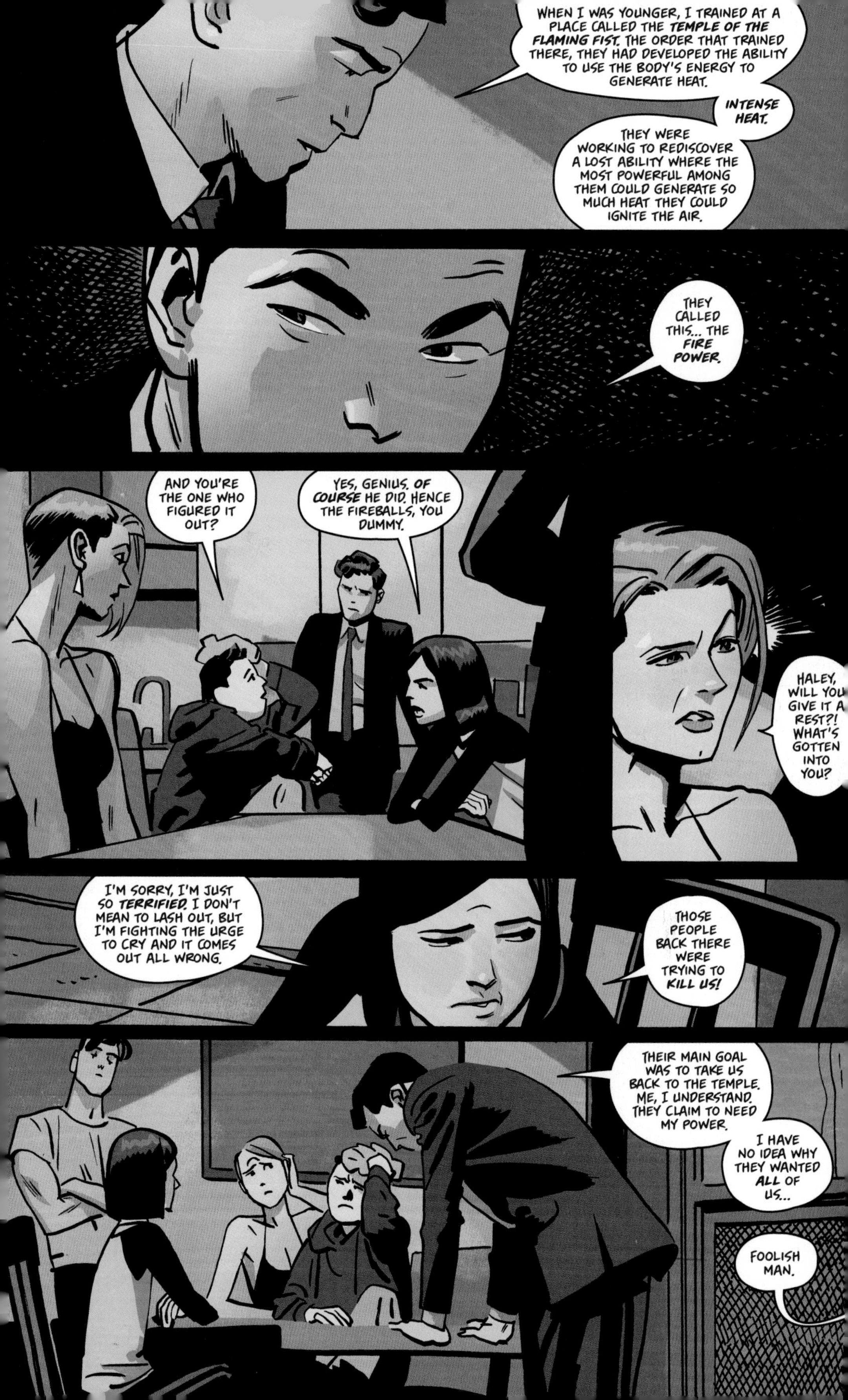
WHEN I WAS YOUNGER, I TRAINED AT A PLACE CALLED THE *TEMPLE OF THE FLAMING FIST.* THE ORDER THAT TRAINED THERE, THEY HAD DEVELOPED THE ABILITY TO USE THE BODY'S ENERGY TO GENERATE HEAT.
INTENSE HEAT.
THEY WERE WORKING TO REDISCOVER A LOST ABILITY WHERE THE MOST POWERFUL AMONG THEM COULD GENERATE SO MUCH HEAT THEY COULD IGNITE THE AIR.
THEY CALLED THIS... THE *FIRE POWER.*
AND YOU'RE THE ONE WHO FIGURED IT OUT?
YES, GENIUS. OF *COURSE* HE DID. HENCE THE FIREBALLS, YOU DUMMY.
HALEY, WILL YOU GIVE IT A REST?! WHAT'S GOTTEN INTO YOU?
I'M SORRY, I'M JUST SO *TERRIFIED.* I DON'T MEAN TO LASH OUT, BUT I'M FIGHTING THE URGE TO CRY AND IT COMES OUT ALL WRONG.
THOSE PEOPLE BACK THERE WERE TRYING TO *KILL US!*
THEIR MAIN GOAL WAS TO TAKE US BACK TO THE TEMPLE. ME, I UNDERSTAND. THEY CLAIM TO NEED MY POWER.
I HAVE NO IDEA WHY THEY WANTED *ALL* OF US...
FOOLISH MAN.

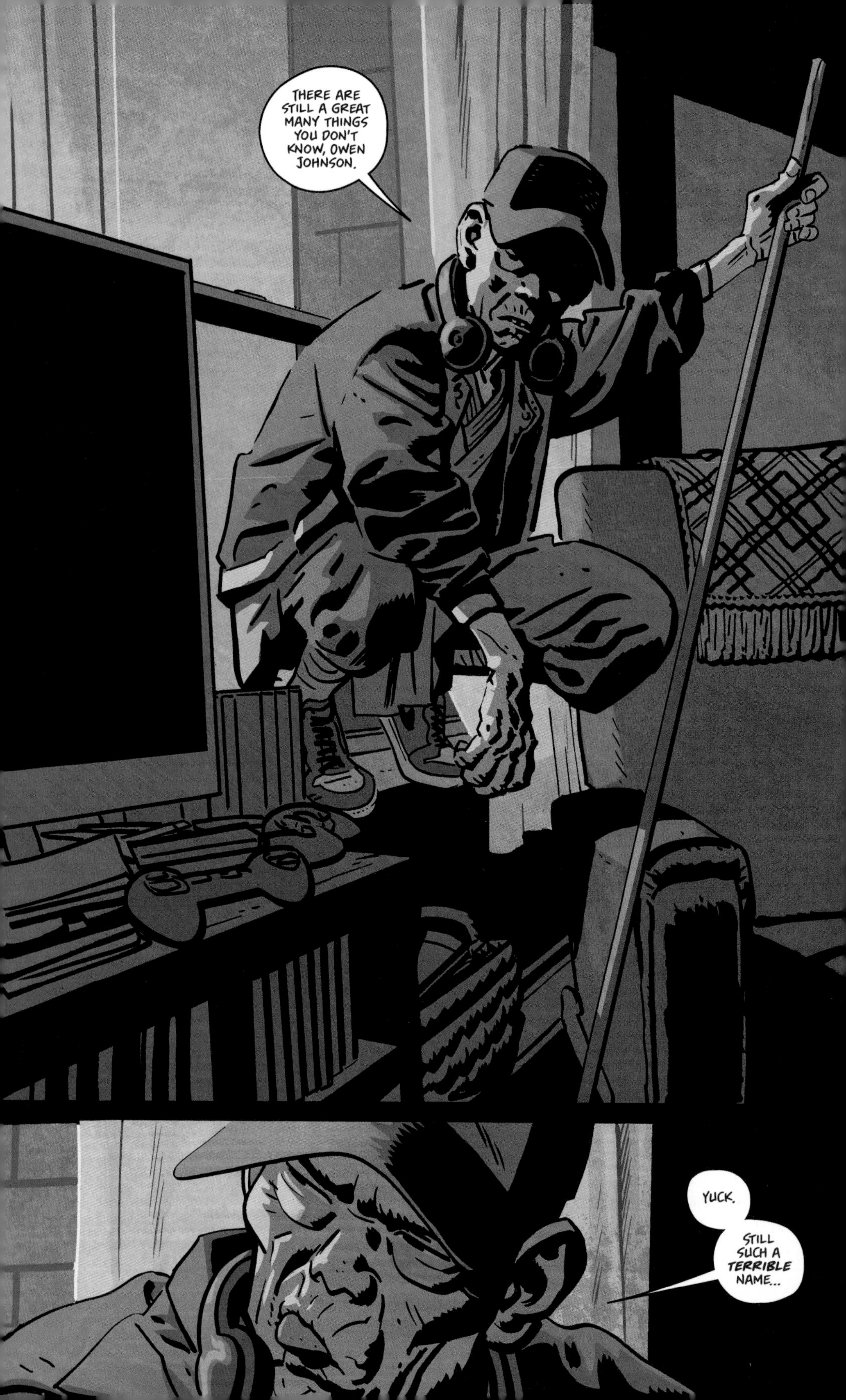
THERE ARE STILL A GREAT MANY THINGS YOU DON'T KNOW, OWEN JOHNSON.
YUCK.
STILL SUCH A TERRIBLE NAME...

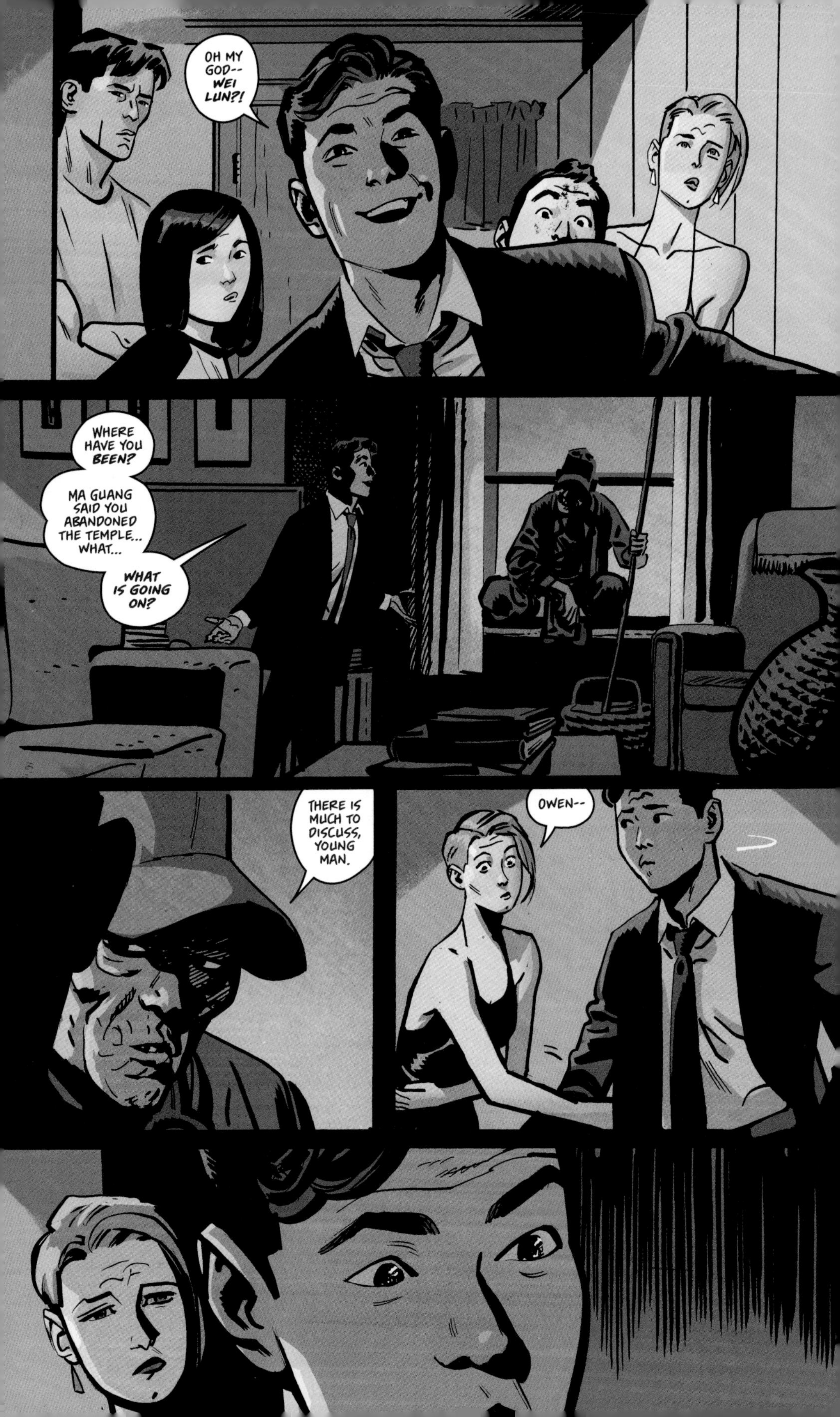
OH MY GOD-- WEI LUN?!
WHERE HAVE YOU BEEN?
MA GUANG SAID YOU ABANDONED THE TEMPLE... WHAT...
WHAT IS GOING ON?
THERE IS MUCH TO DISCUSS, YOUNG MAN.
OWEN--

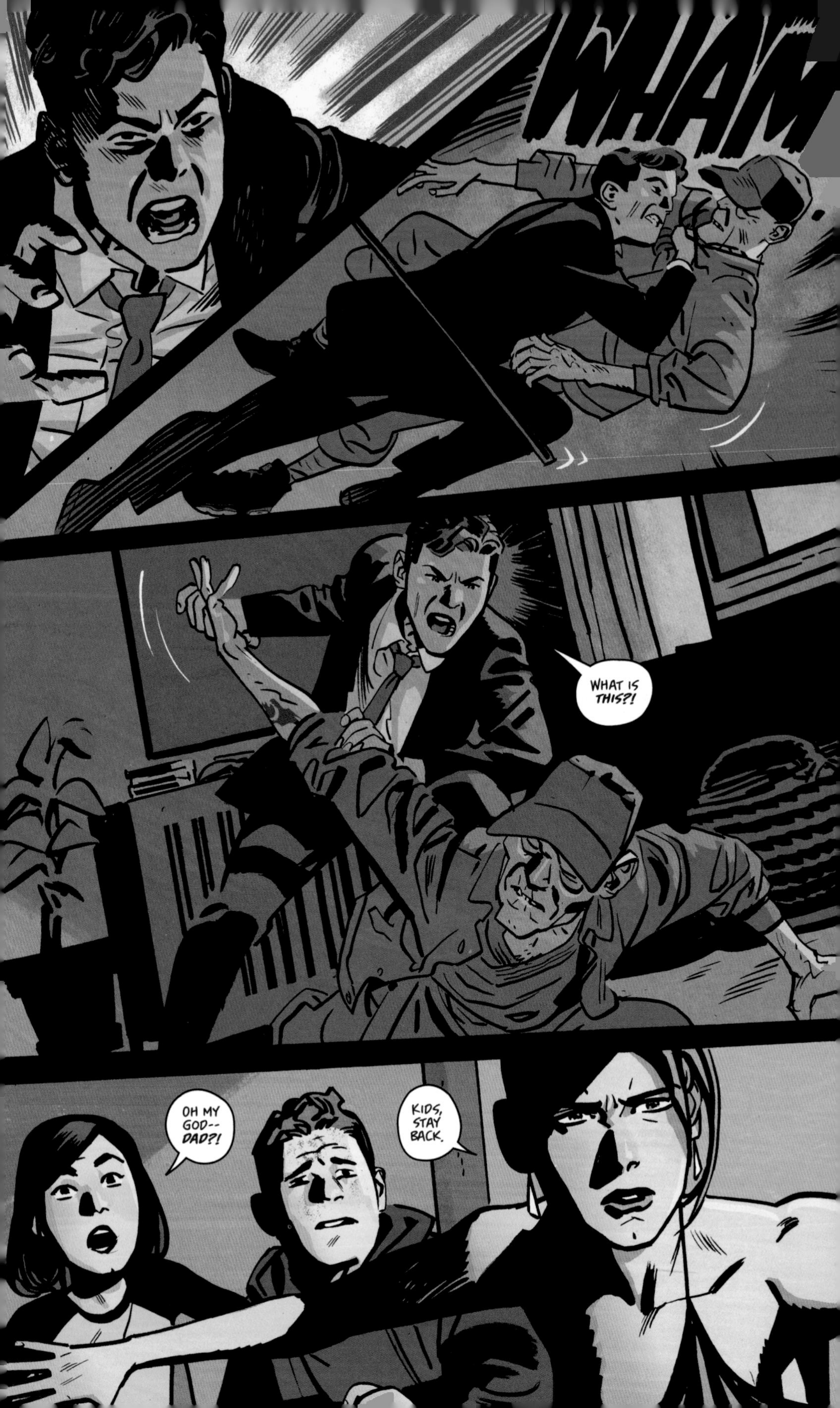
WHAM
WHAT IS THIS?!
OH MY GOD-- DAD?!
KIDS, STAY BACK.

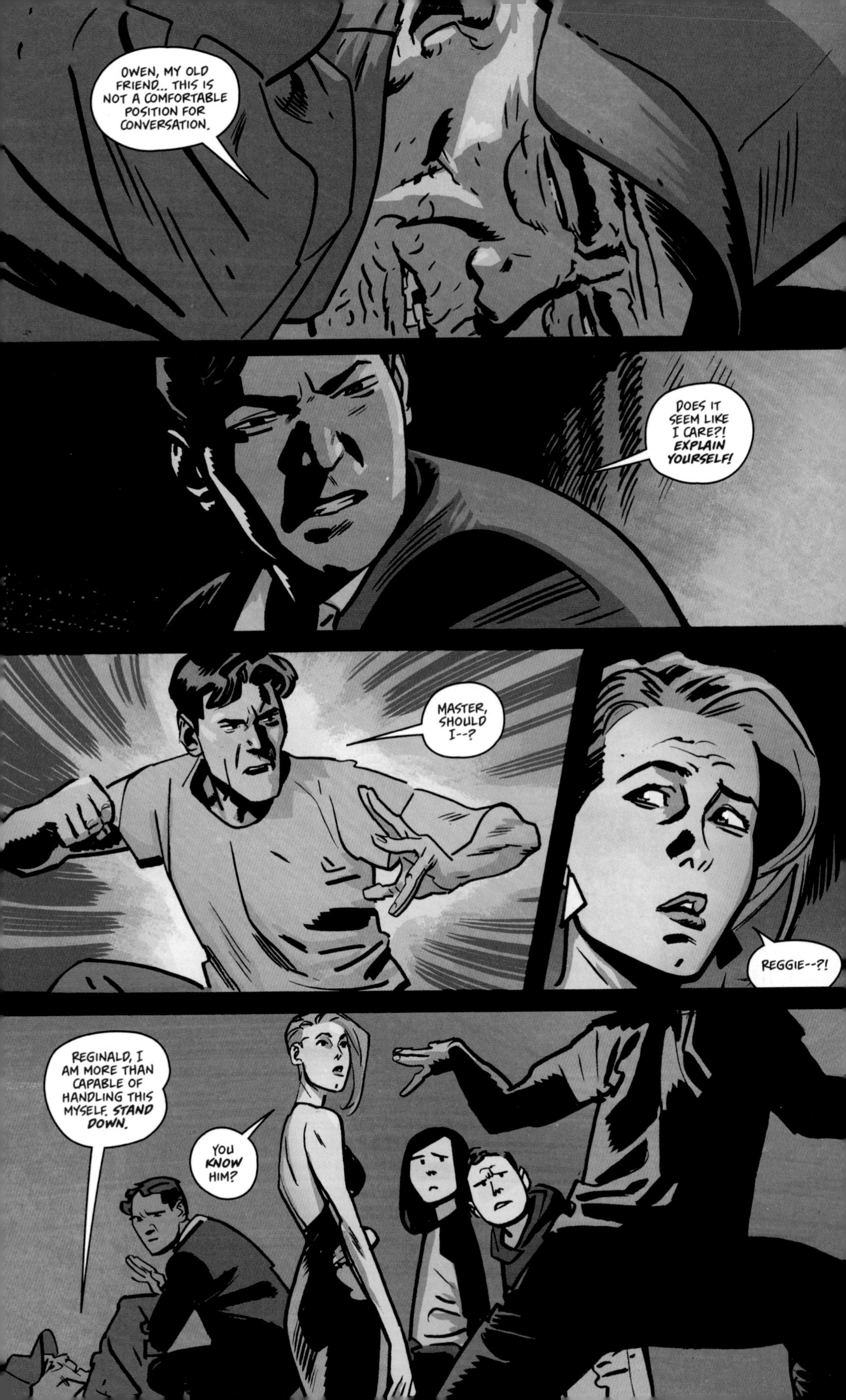
OWEN, MY OLD FRIEND... THIS IS NOT A COMFORTABLE POSITION FOR CONVERSATION.
DOES IT SEEM LIKE I CARE?! EXPLAIN YOURSELF!
MASTER, SHOULD I--?
REGGIE--?!
REGINALD, I AM MORE THAN CAPABLE OF HANDLING THIS MYSELF. STAND DOWN.
YOU KNOW HIM?

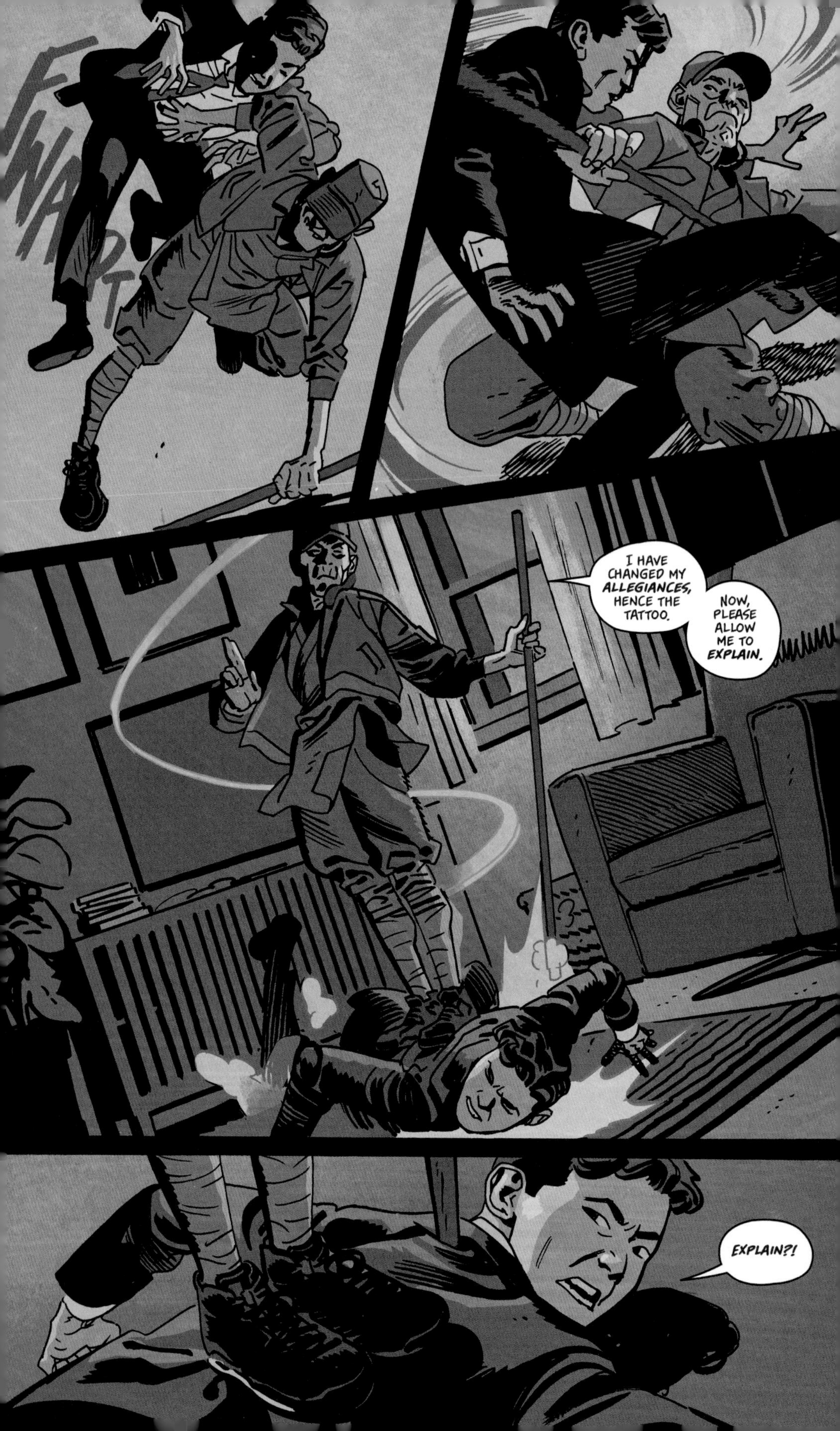
FWAPT
I HAVE CHANGED MY ALLEGIANCES, HENCE THE TATTOO.
NOW, PLEASE ALLOW ME TO EXPLAIN.
EXPLAIN?!

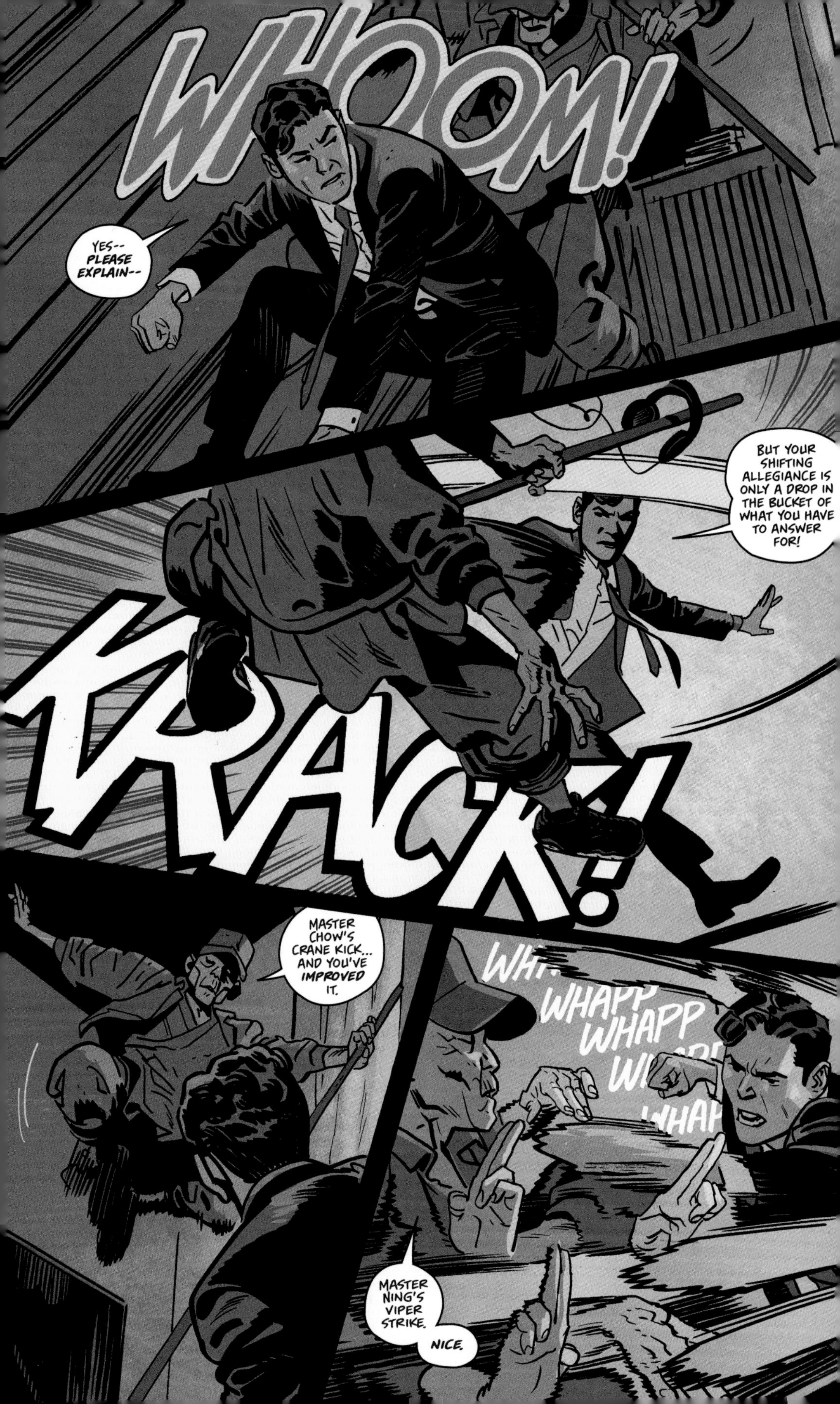
WHOOM!
YES-- PLEASE EXPLAIN--
BUT YOUR SHIFTING ALLEGIANCE IS ONLY A DROP IN THE BUCKET OF WHAT YOU HAVE TO ANSWER FOR!
KRACK!
MASTER CHOW'S CRANE KICK... AND YOU'VE IMPROVED IT.
WHAPP
WHAPP
MASTER NING'S VIPER STRIKE.
NICE.

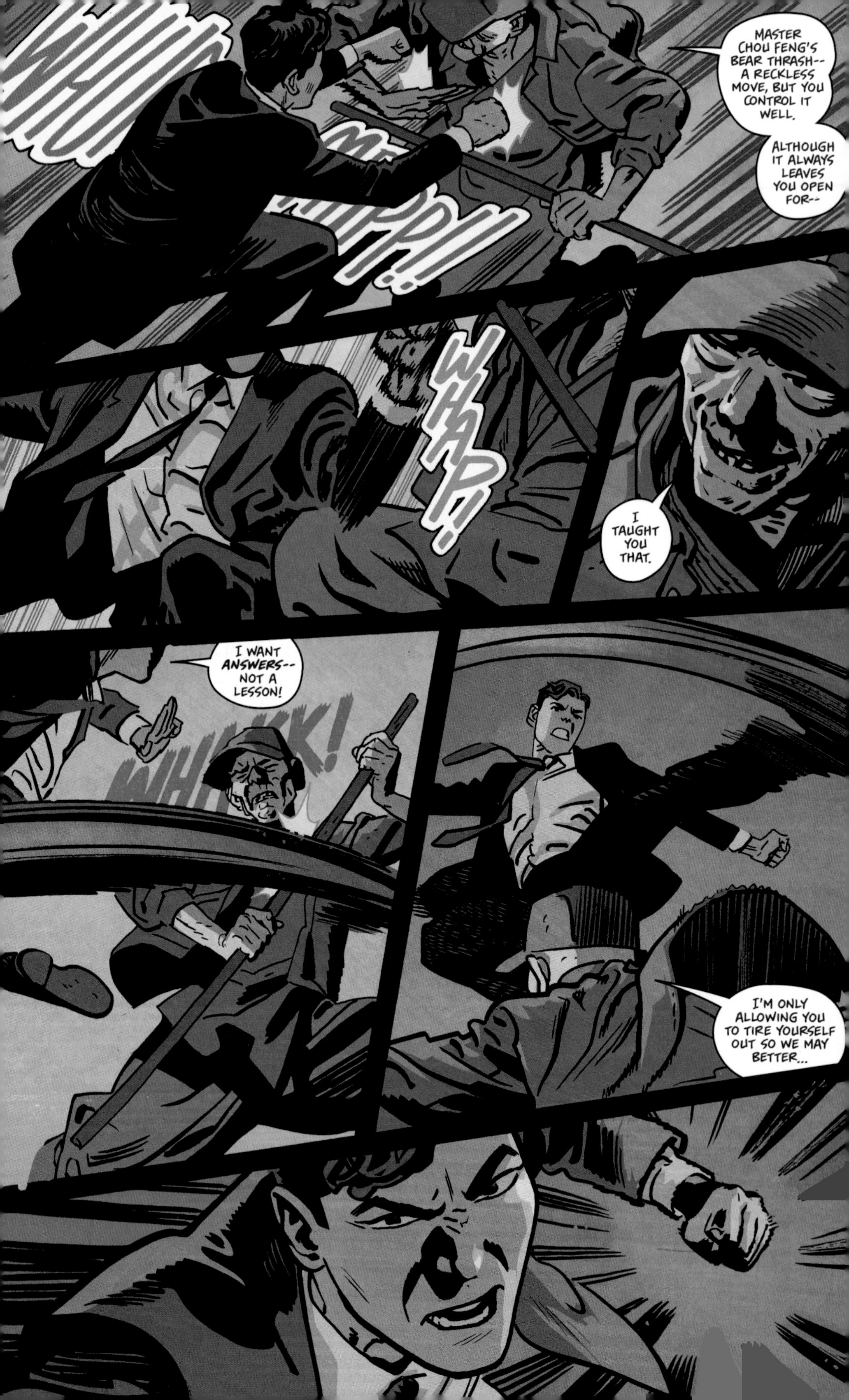
MASTER CHOU FENG'S BEAR THRASH-- A RECKLESS MOVE, BUT YOU CONTROL IT WELL.
ALTHOUGH IT ALWAYS LEAVES YOU OPEN FOR--
WHAP!!
I TAUGHT YOU THAT.
I WANT ANSWERS-- NOT A LESSON!
I'M ONLY ALLOWING YOU TO TIRE YOURSELF OUT SO WE MAY BETTER...

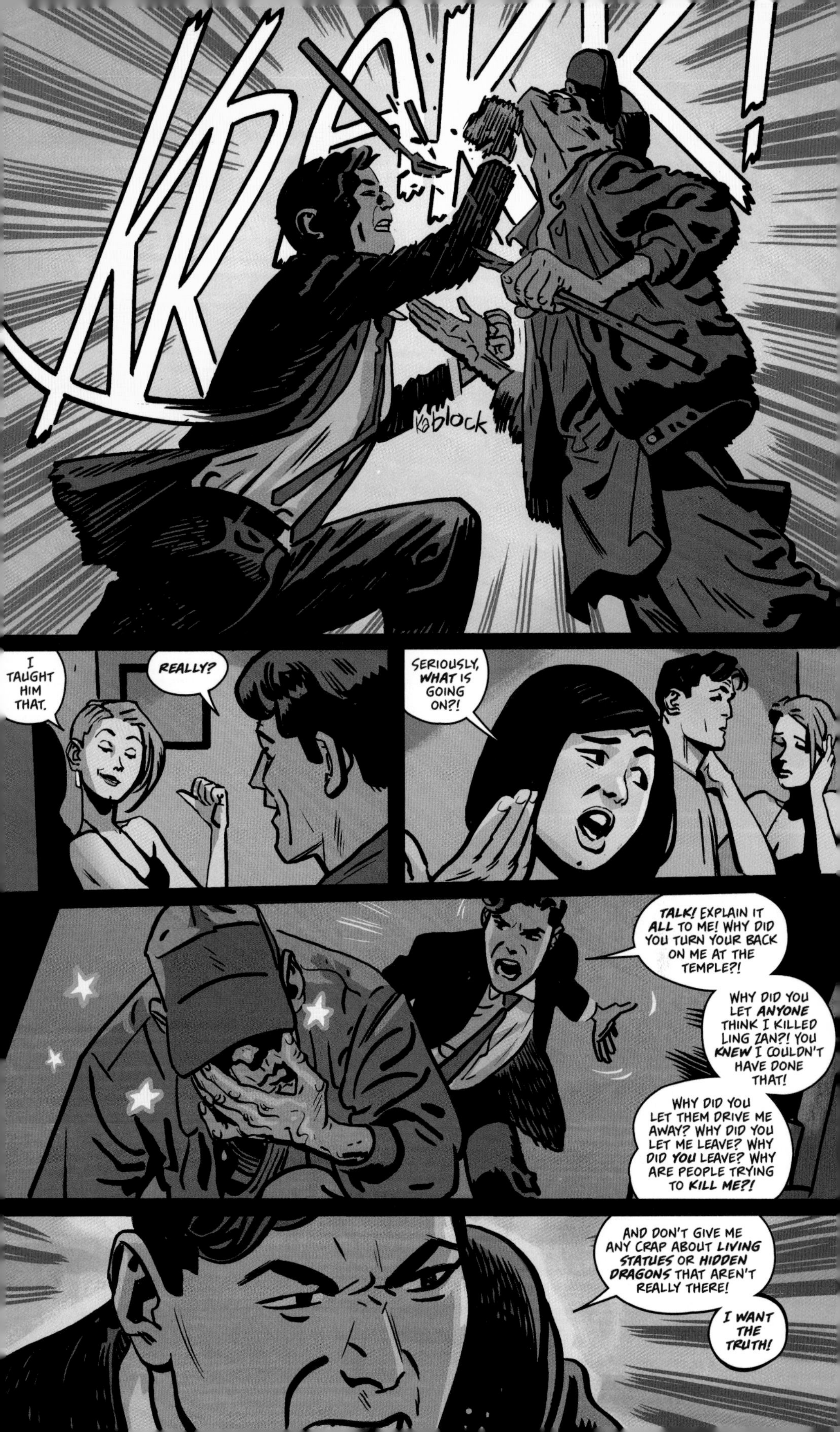
KRAKK!
kablock
I TAUGHT HIM THAT.
REALLY?
SERIOUSLY, WHAT IS GOING ON?!
TALK! EXPLAIN IT ALL TO ME! WHY DID YOU TURN YOUR BACK ON ME AT THE TEMPLE?!
WHY DID YOU LET ANYONE THINK I KILLED LING ZAN?! YOU KNEW I COULDN'T HAVE DONE THAT!
WHY DID YOU LET THEM DRIVE ME AWAY? WHY DID YOU LET ME LEAVE? WHY DID YOU LEAVE? WHY ARE PEOPLE TRYING TO KILL ME?!
AND DON'T GIVE ME ANY CRAP ABOUT LIVING STATUES OR HIDDEN DRAGONS THAT AREN'T REALLY THERE!
I WANT THE TRUTH!

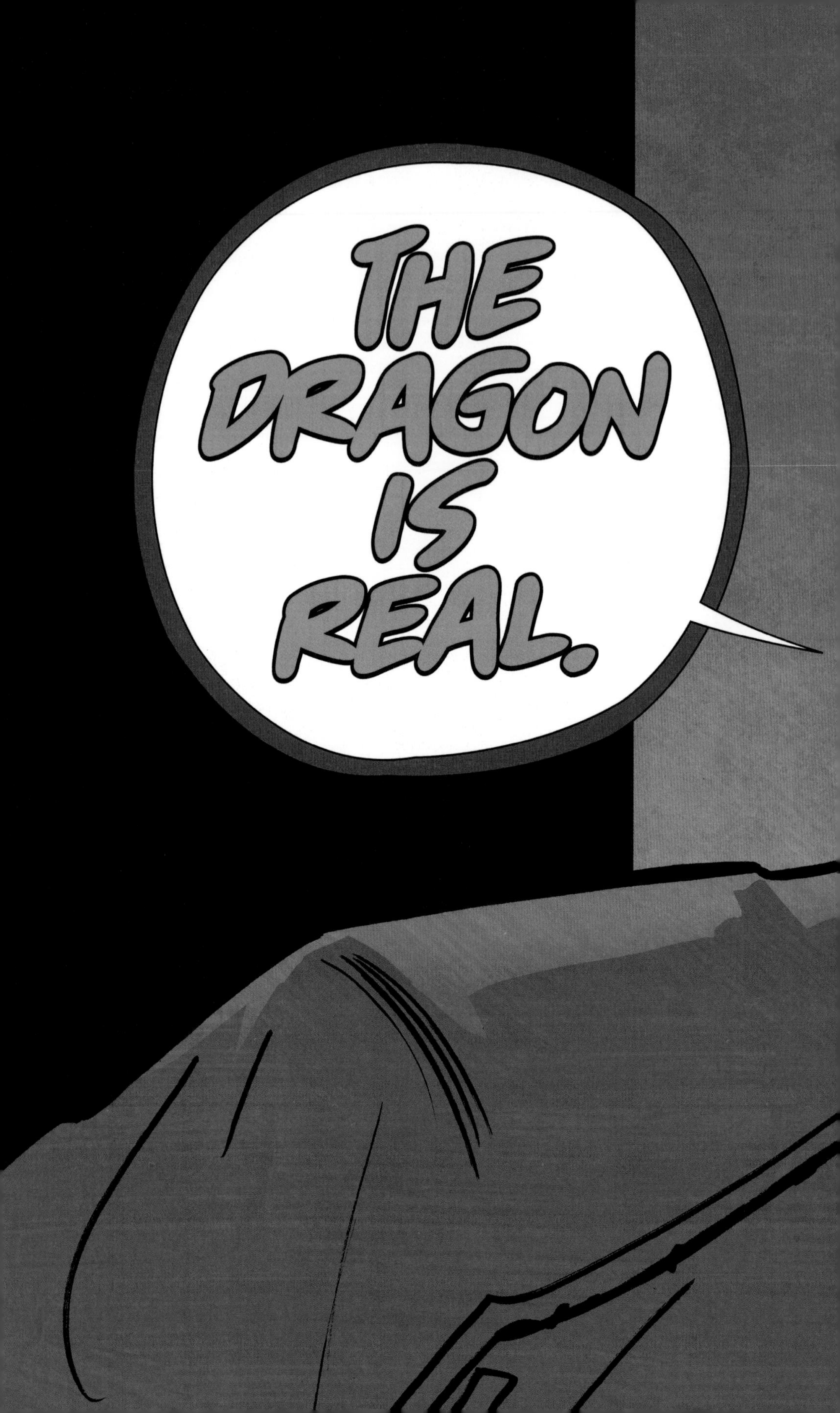
THE DRAGON IS REAL.

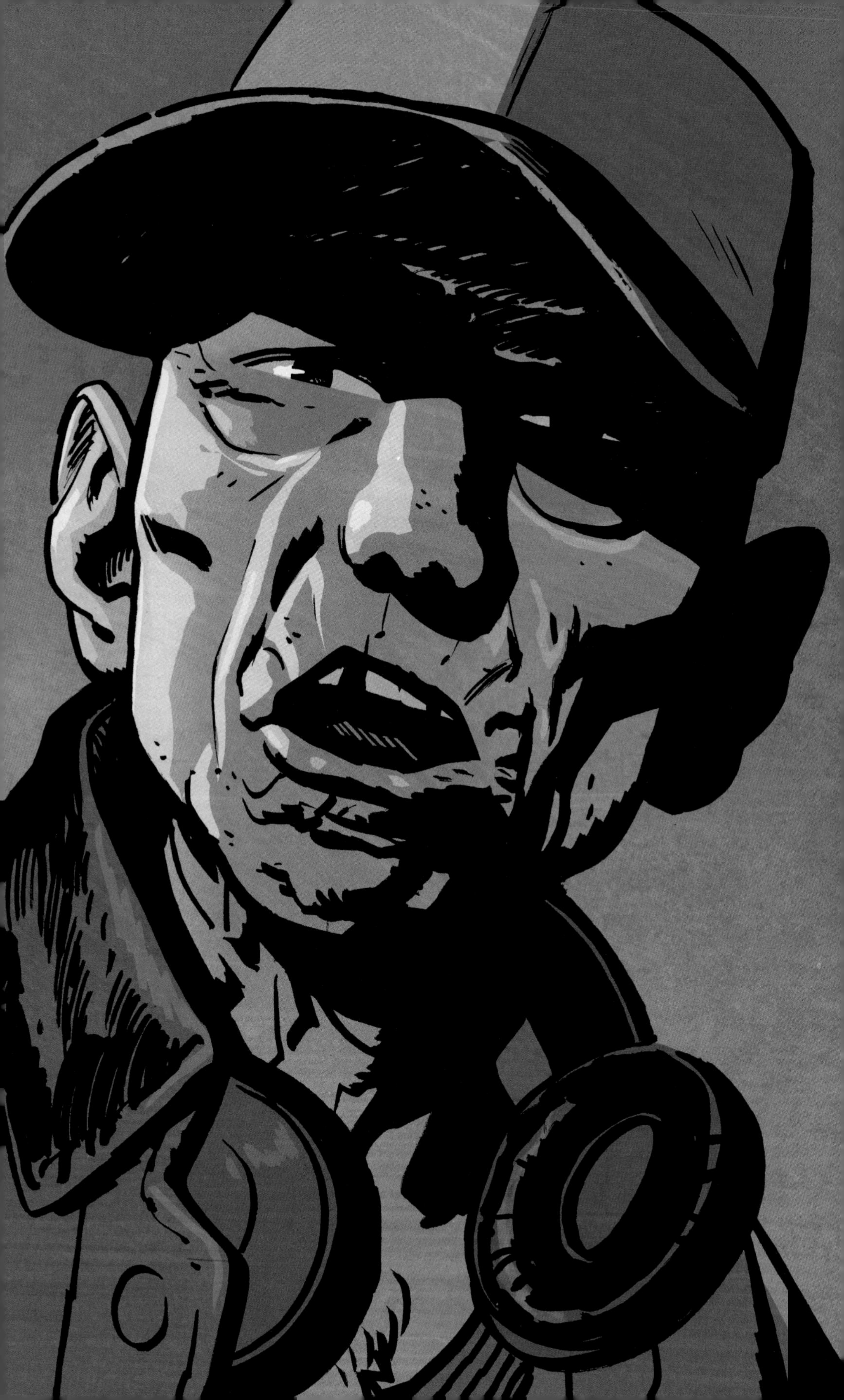

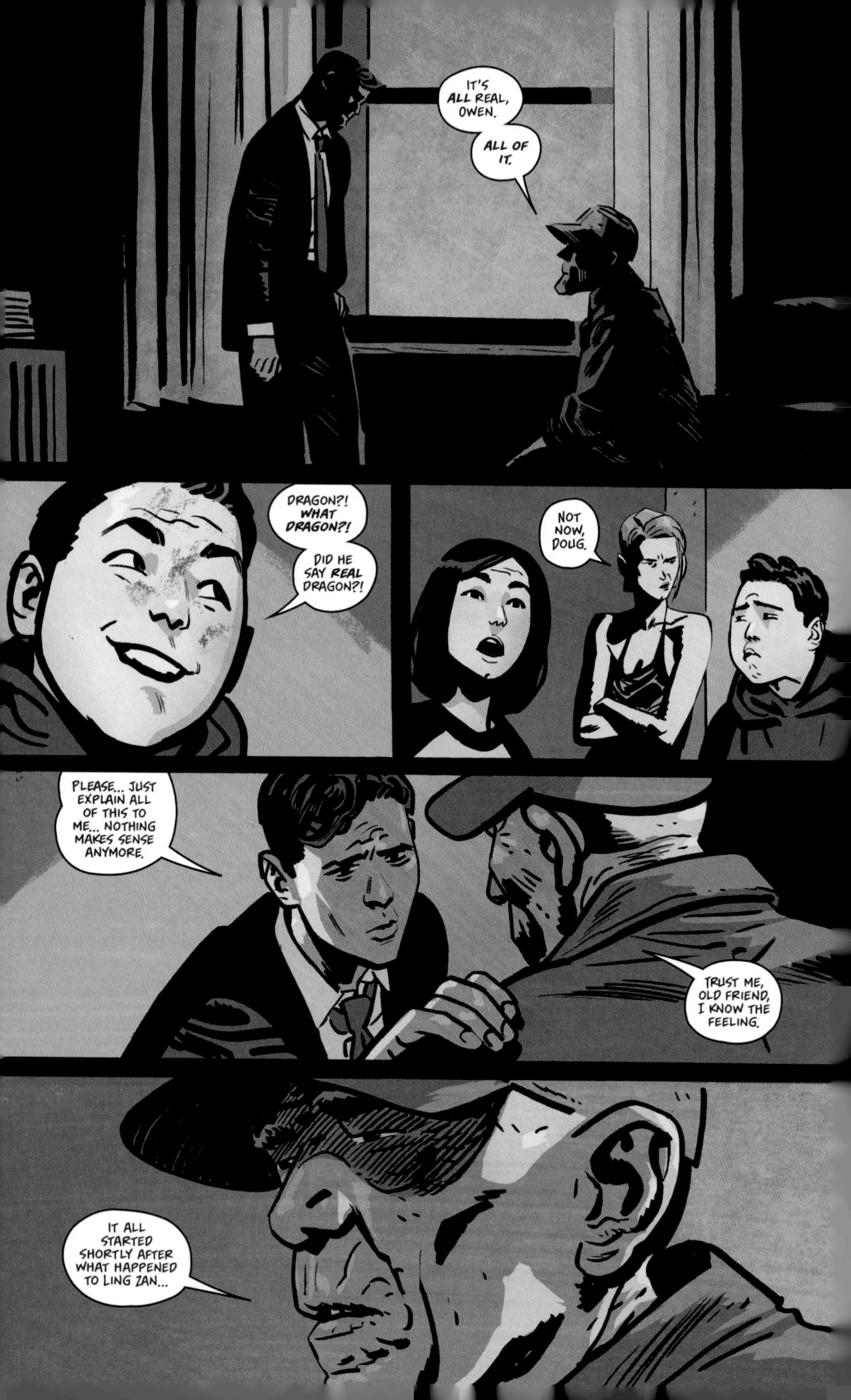
IT'S ALL REAL, OWEN.
ALL OF IT.
DRAGON?! WHAT DRAGON?!
DID HE SAY REAL DRAGON?!
NOT NOW, DOUG.
PLEASE... JUST EXPLAIN ALL OF THIS TO ME... NOTHING MAKES SENSE ANYMORE.
TRUST ME, OLD FRIEND, I KNOW THE FEELING.
IT ALL STARTED SHORTLY AFTER WHAT HAPPENED TO LING ZAN...

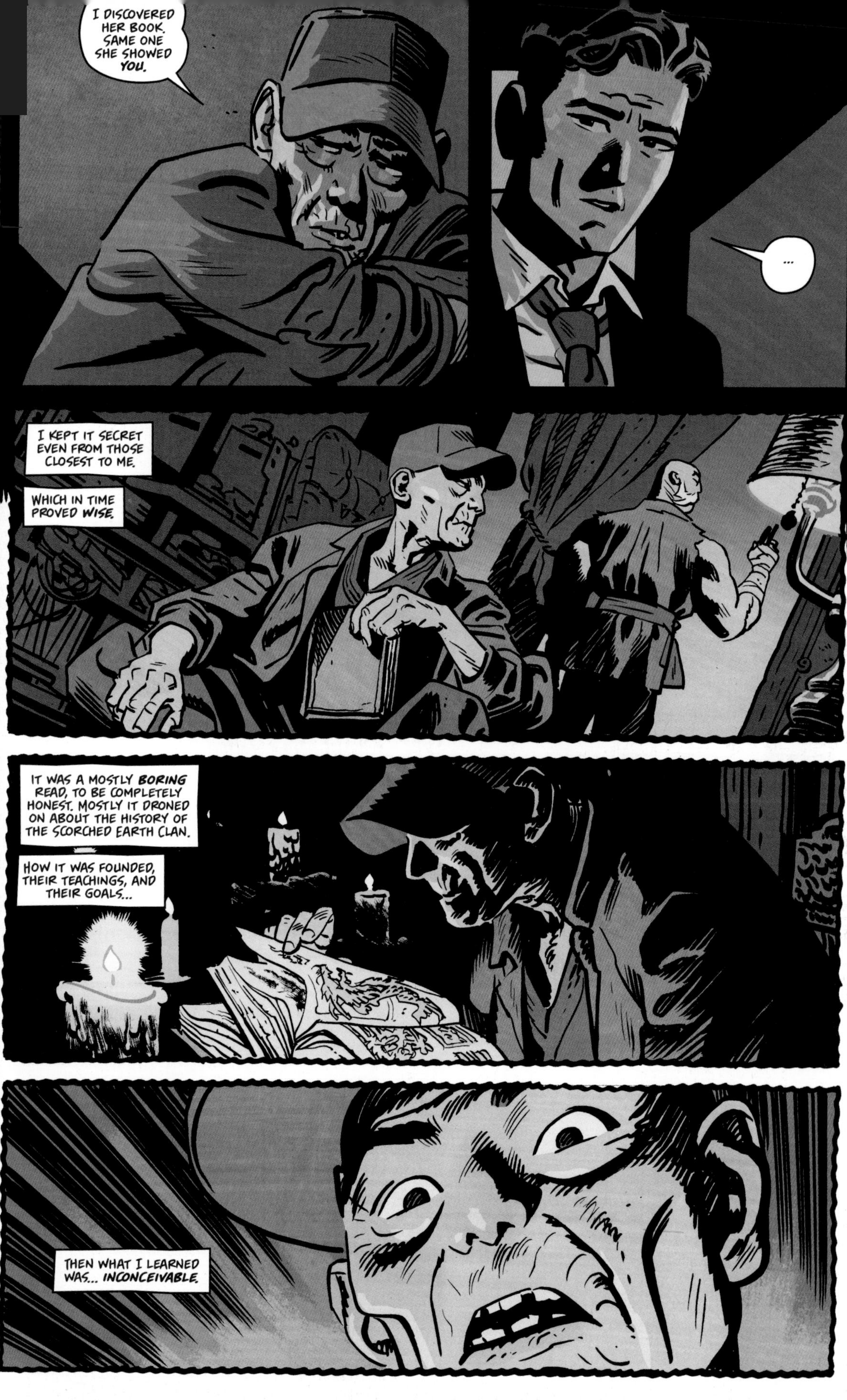
I DISCOVERED HER BOOK. SAME ONE SHE SHOWED YOU.
...
I KEPT IT SECRET EVEN FROM THOSE CLOSEST TO ME.
WHICH IN TIME PROVED WISE.
IT WAS A MOSTLY BORING READ, TO BE COMPLETELY HONEST. MOSTLY IT DRONED ON ABOUT THE HISTORY OF THE SCORCHED EARTH CLAN.
HOW IT WAS FOUNDED, THEIR TEACHINGS, AND THEIR GOALS...
THEN WHAT I LEARNED WAS... INCONCEIVABLE.

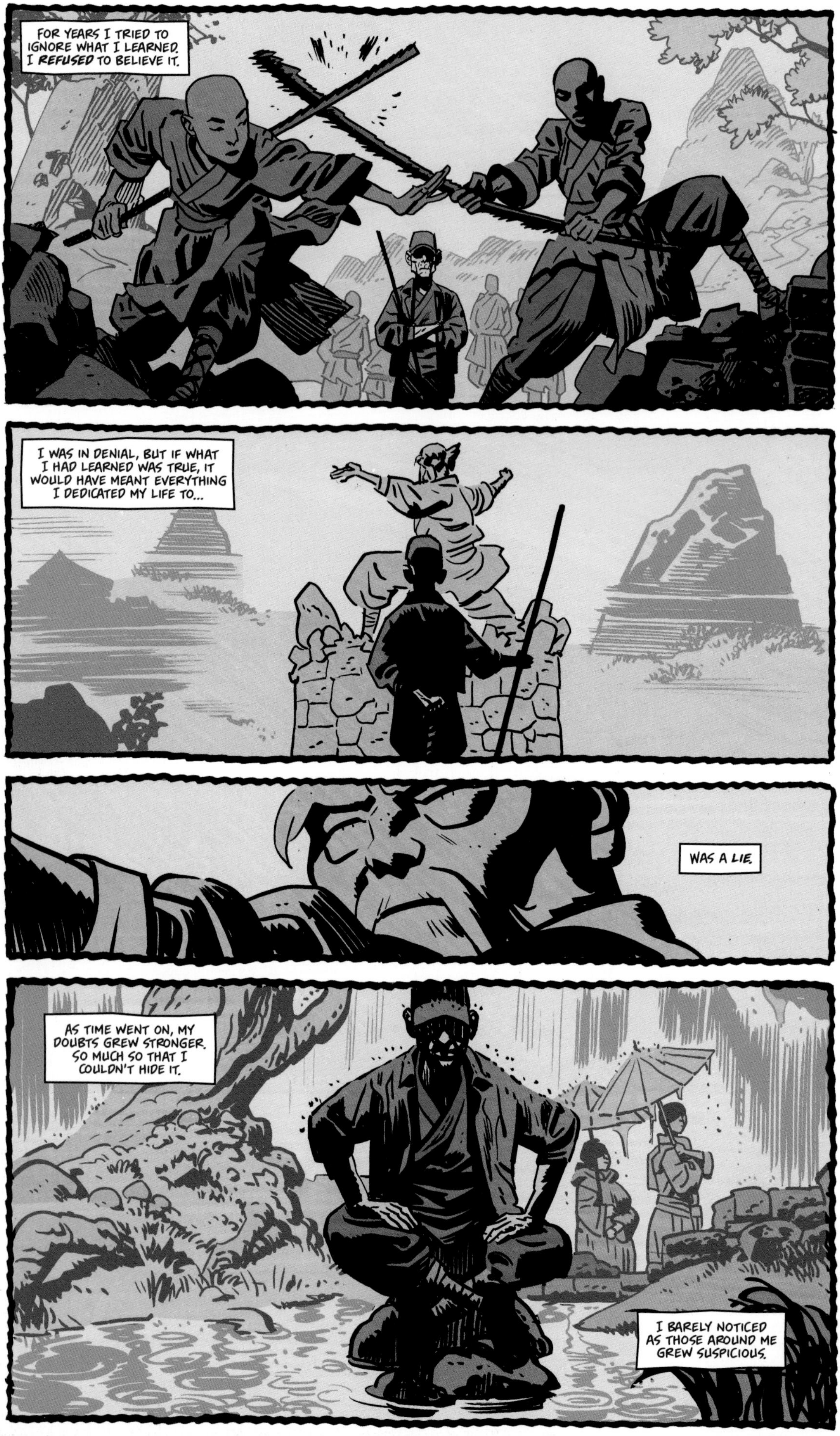
FOR YEARS I TRIED TO IGNORE WHAT I LEARNED. I REFUSED TO BELIEVE IT.
I WAS IN DENIAL, BUT IF WHAT I HAD LEARNED WAS TRUE, IT WOULD HAVE MEANT EVERYTHING I DEDICATED MY LIFE TO...
WAS A LIE.
AS TIME WENT ON, MY DOUBTS GREW STRONGER. SO MUCH SO THAT I COULDN'T HIDE IT.
I BARELY NOTICED AS THOSE AROUND ME GREW SUSPICIOUS.

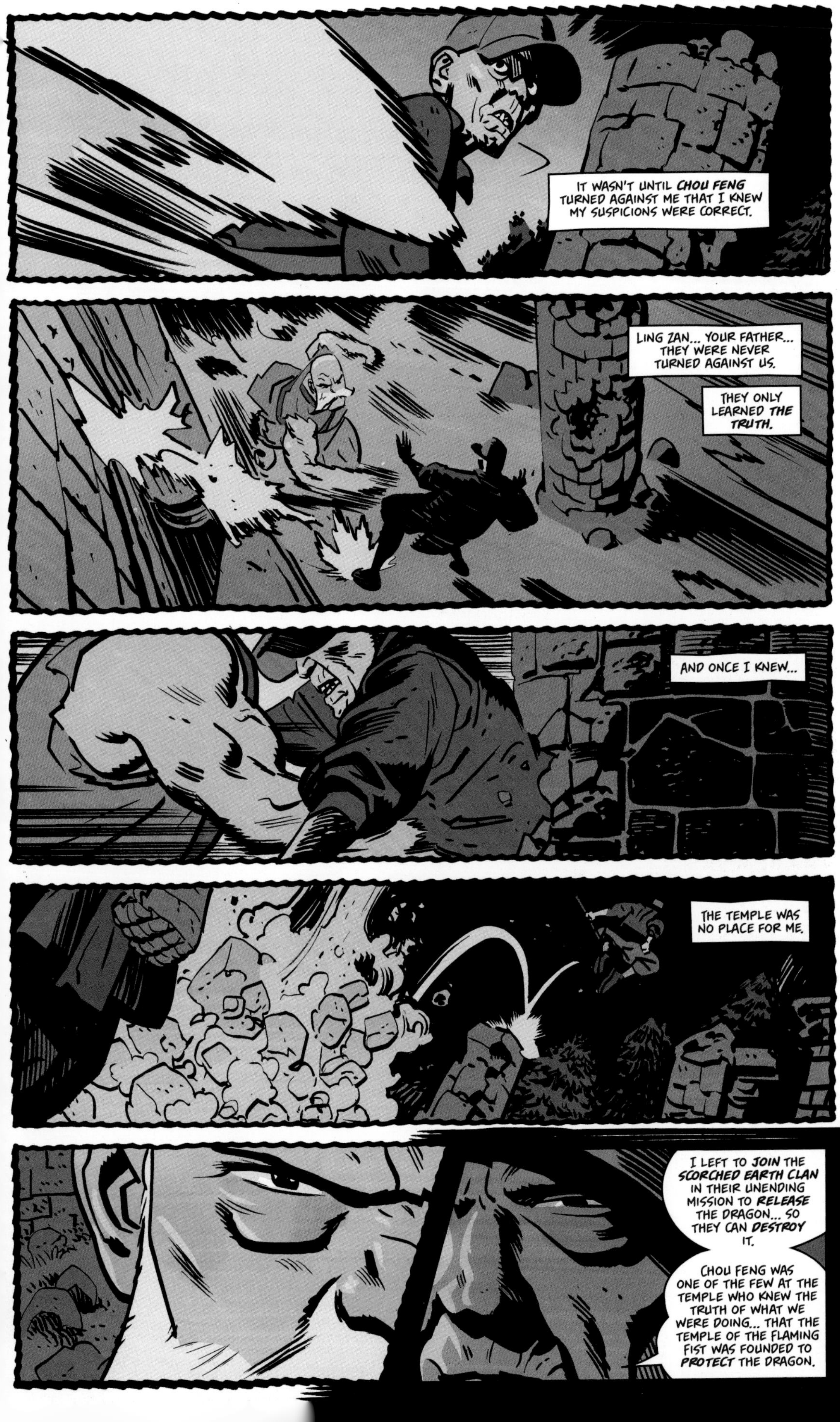
IT WASN'T UNTIL CHOU FENG TURNED AGAINST ME THAT I KNEW MY SUSPICIONS WERE CORRECT.
LING ZAN... YOUR FATHER... THEY WERE NEVER TURNED AGAINST US.
THEY ONLY LEARNED THE TRUTH.
AND ONCE I KNEW...
THE TEMPLE WAS NO PLACE FOR ME.
I LEFT TO JOIN THE SCORCHED EARTH CLAN IN THEIR UNENDING MISSION TO RELEASE THE DRAGON... SO THEY CAN DESTROY IT.
CHOU FENG WAS ONE OF THE FEW AT THE TEMPLE WHO KNEW THE TRUTH OF WHAT WE WERE DOING... THAT THE TEMPLE OF THE FLAMING FIST WAS FOUNDED TO PROTECT THE DRAGON.

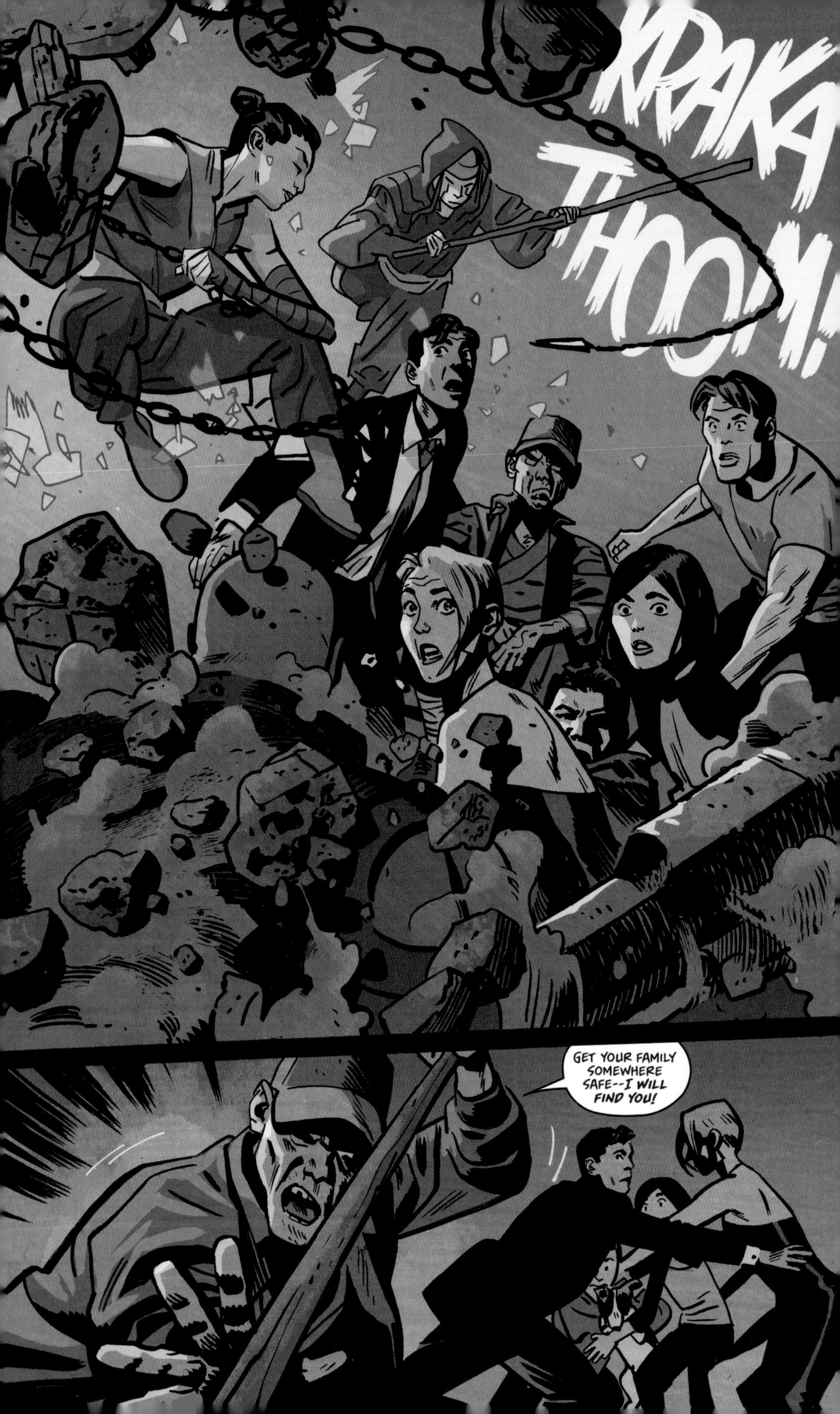
KRAKA THOOM!
GET YOUR FAMILY SOMEWHERE SAFE--I WILL FIND YOU!

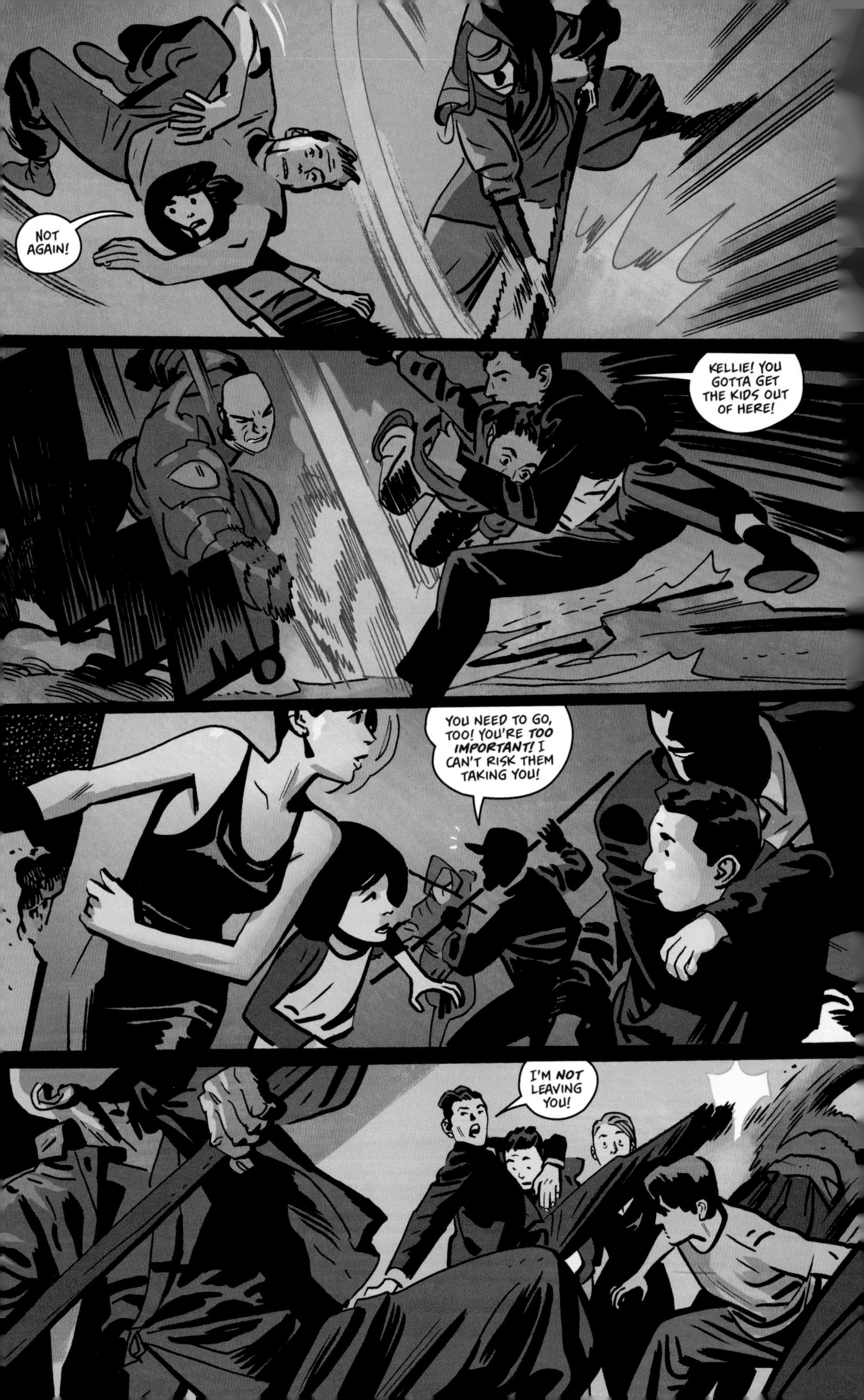
NOT AGAIN!
KELLIE! YOU GOTTA GET THE KIDS OUT OF HERE!
YOU NEED TO GO, TOO! YOU'RE TOO IMPORTANT! I CAN'T RISK THEM TAKING YOU!
I'M NOT LEAVING YOU!

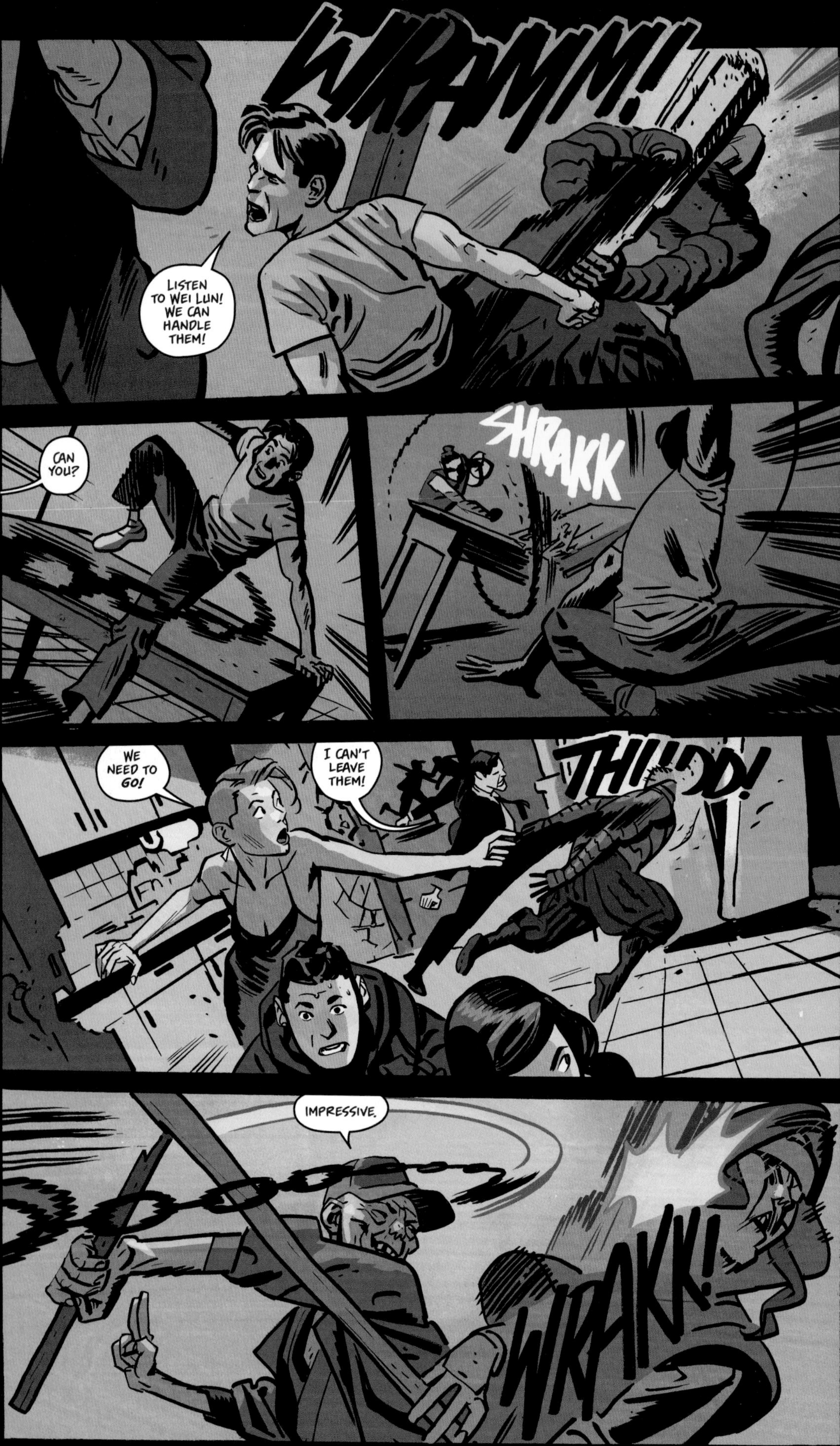
WHAMMM!
LISTEN TO WEI LUN! WE CAN HANDLE THEM!
CAN YOU?
SHRAKK
WE NEED TO GO!
I CAN'T LEAVE THEM!
THUDD!
IMPRESSIVE.
WRAKK!

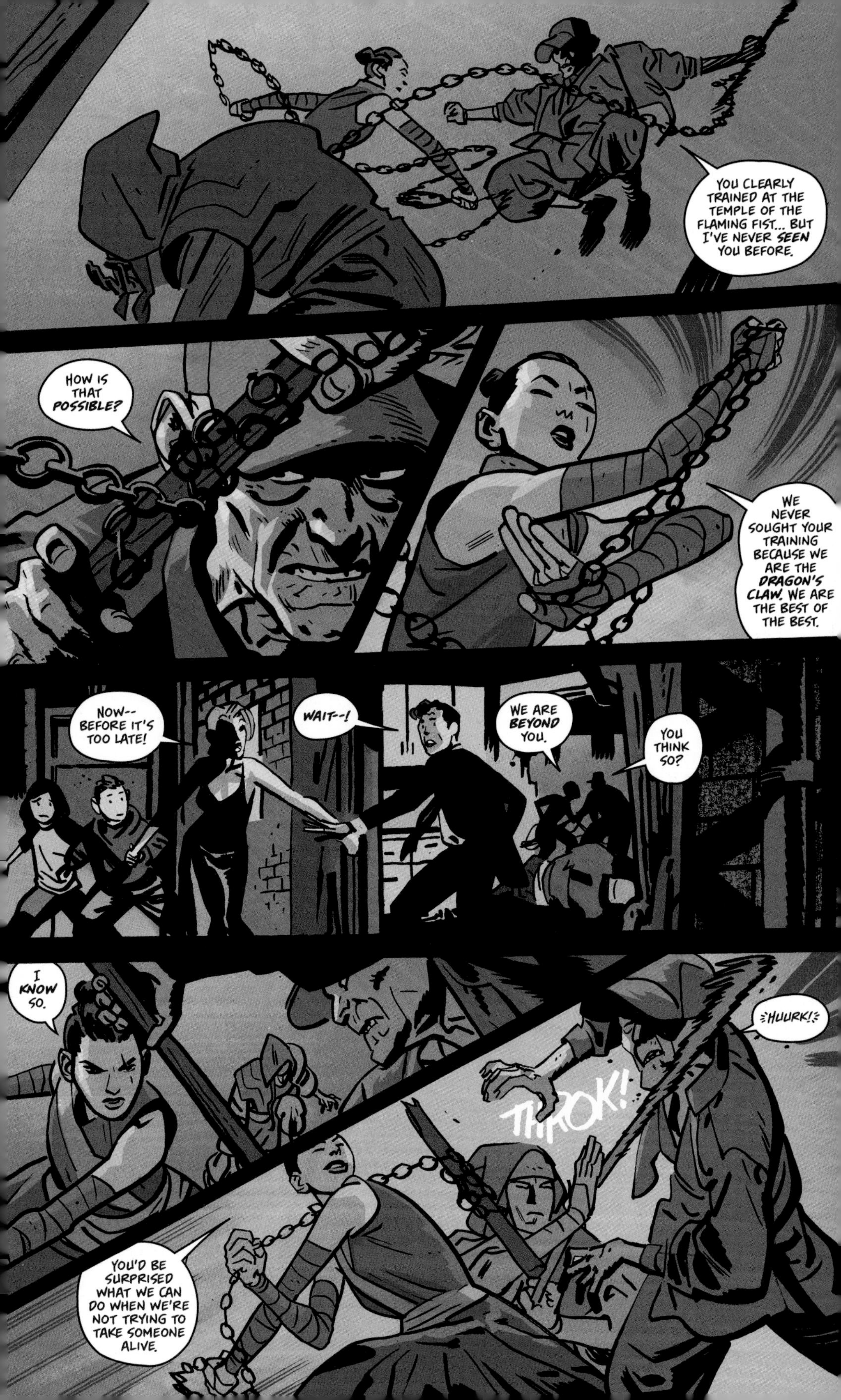
YOU CLEARLY TRAINED AT THE TEMPLE OF THE FLAMING FIST... BUT I'VE NEVER SEEN YOU BEFORE.
HOW IS THAT POSSIBLE?
WE NEVER SOUGHT YOUR TRAINING BECAUSE WE ARE THE DRAGON'S CLAW. WE ARE THE BEST OF THE BEST.
NOW-- BEFORE IT'S TOO LATE!
WAIT--!
WE ARE BEYOND YOU.
YOU THINK SO?
I KNOW SO.
HUURK!
THROK!
YOU'D BE SURPRISED WHAT WE CAN DO WHEN WE'RE NOT TRYING TO TAKE SOMEONE ALIVE.

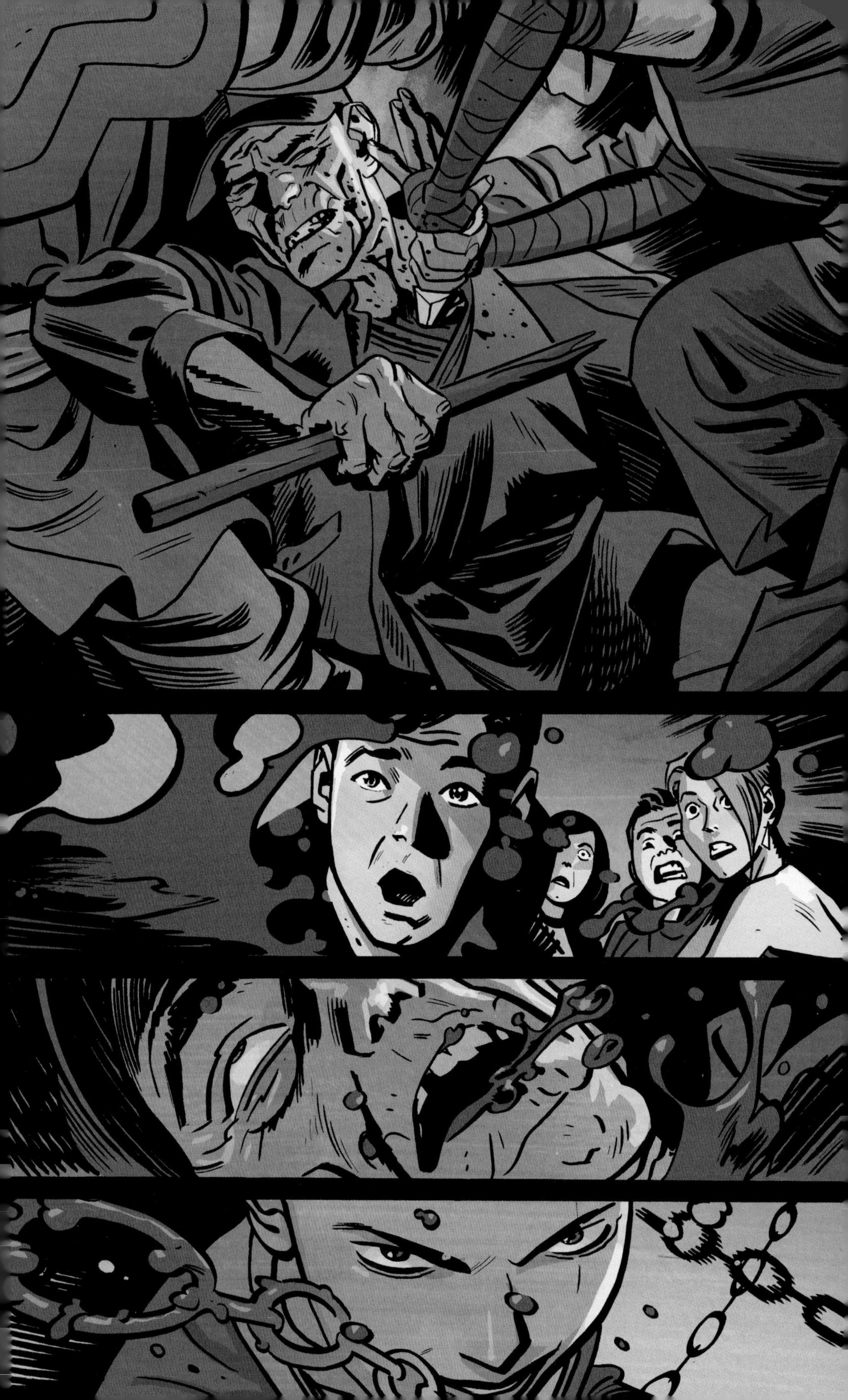

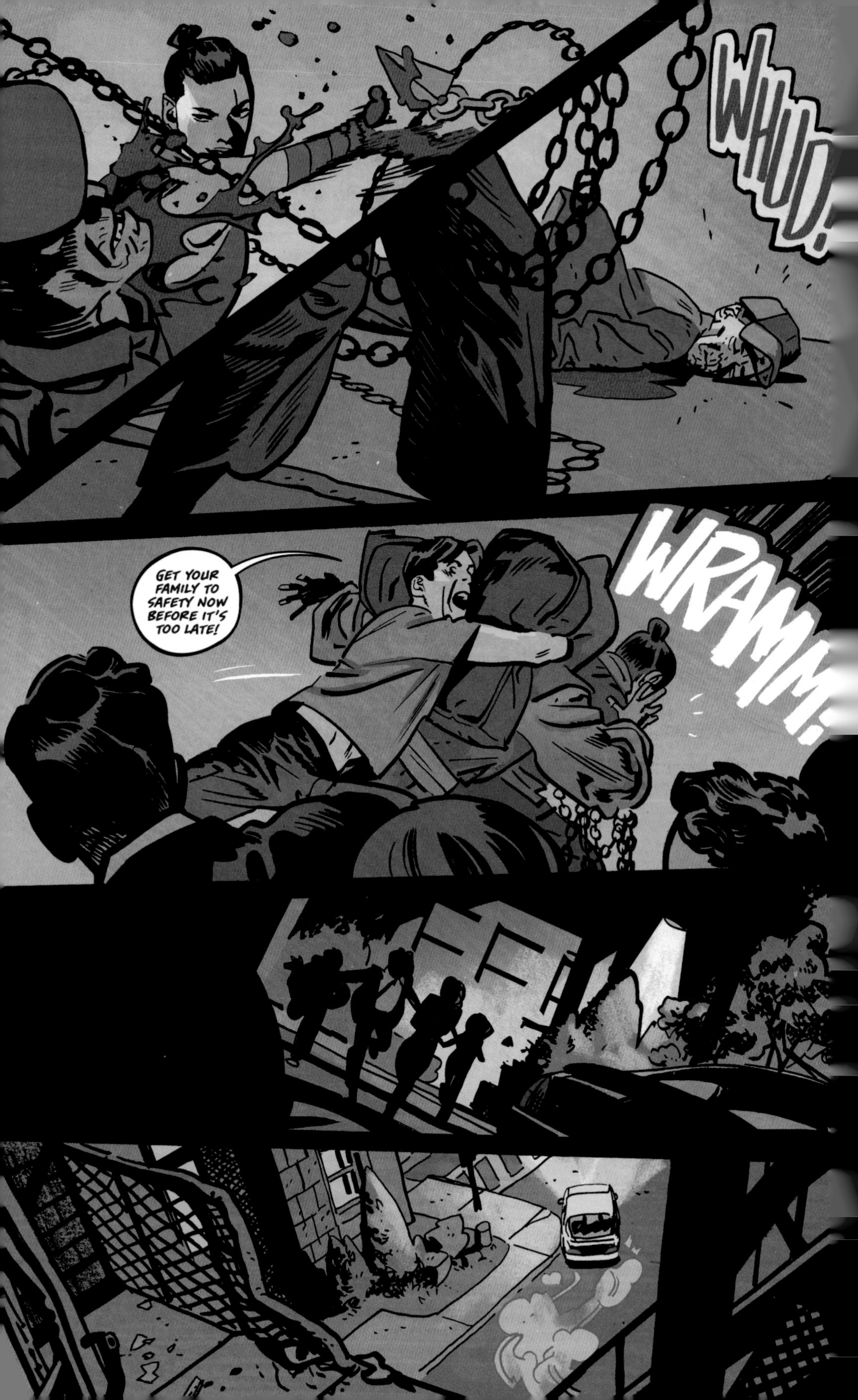
WHUD!
GET YOUR FAMILY TO SAFETY NOW BEFORE IT'S TOO LATE!
WRAMM!

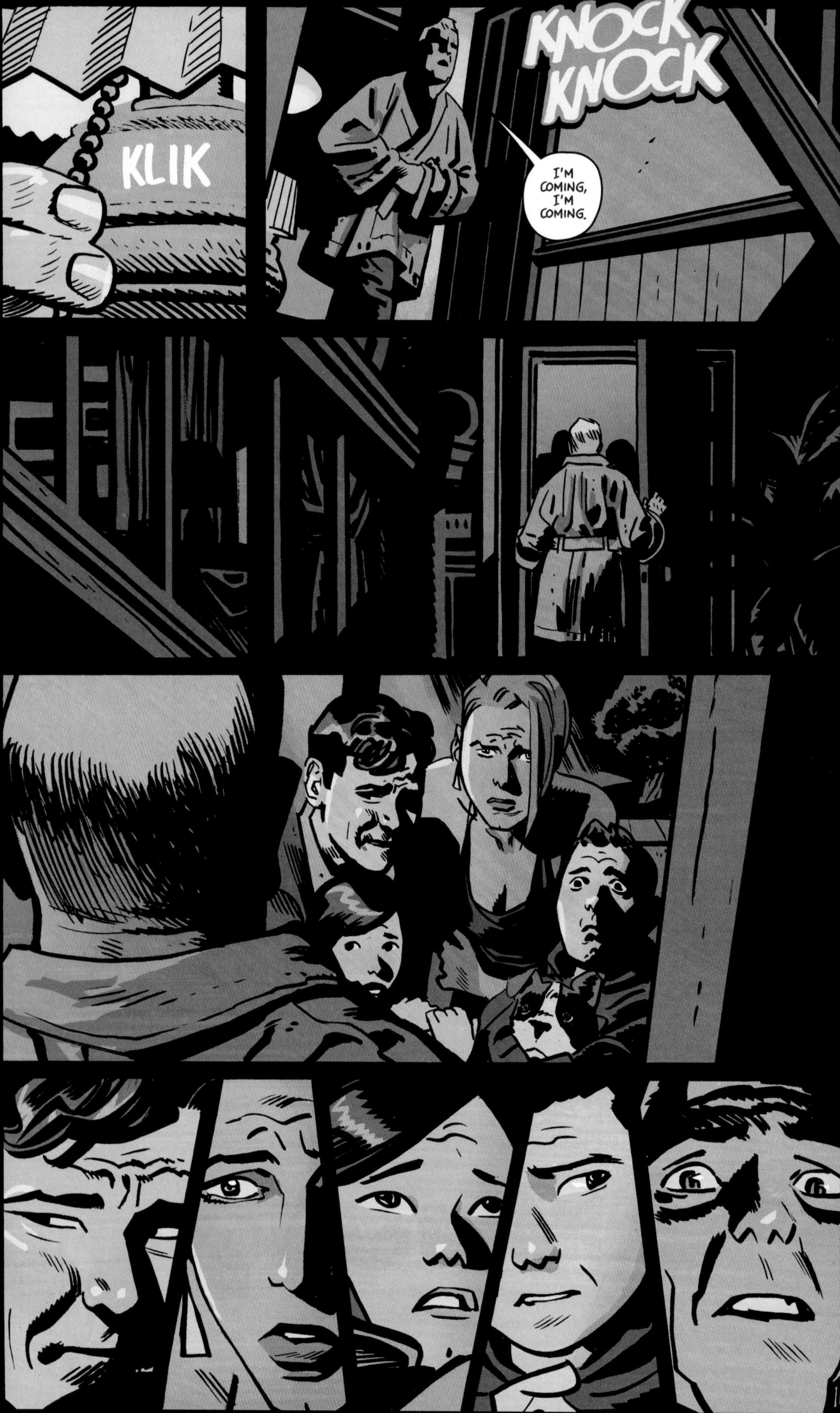
KLIK
KNOCK KNOCK
I'M COMING, I'M COMING.

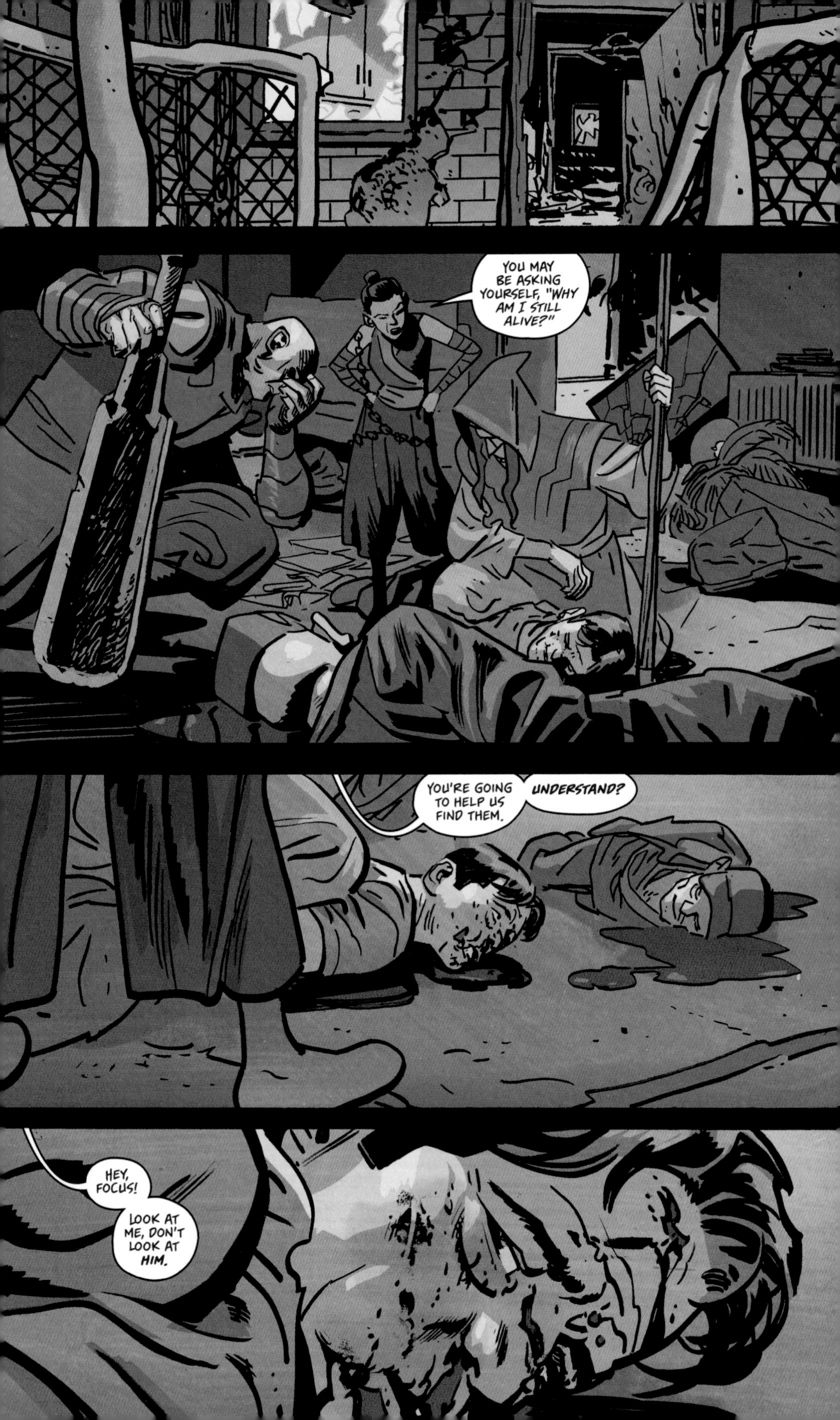
YOU MAY BE ASKING YOURSELF, "WHY AM I STILL ALIVE?"
YOU'RE GOING TO HELP US FIND THEM.
UNDERSTAND?
HEY, FOCUS!
LOOK AT ME, DON'T LOOK AT *HIM*.

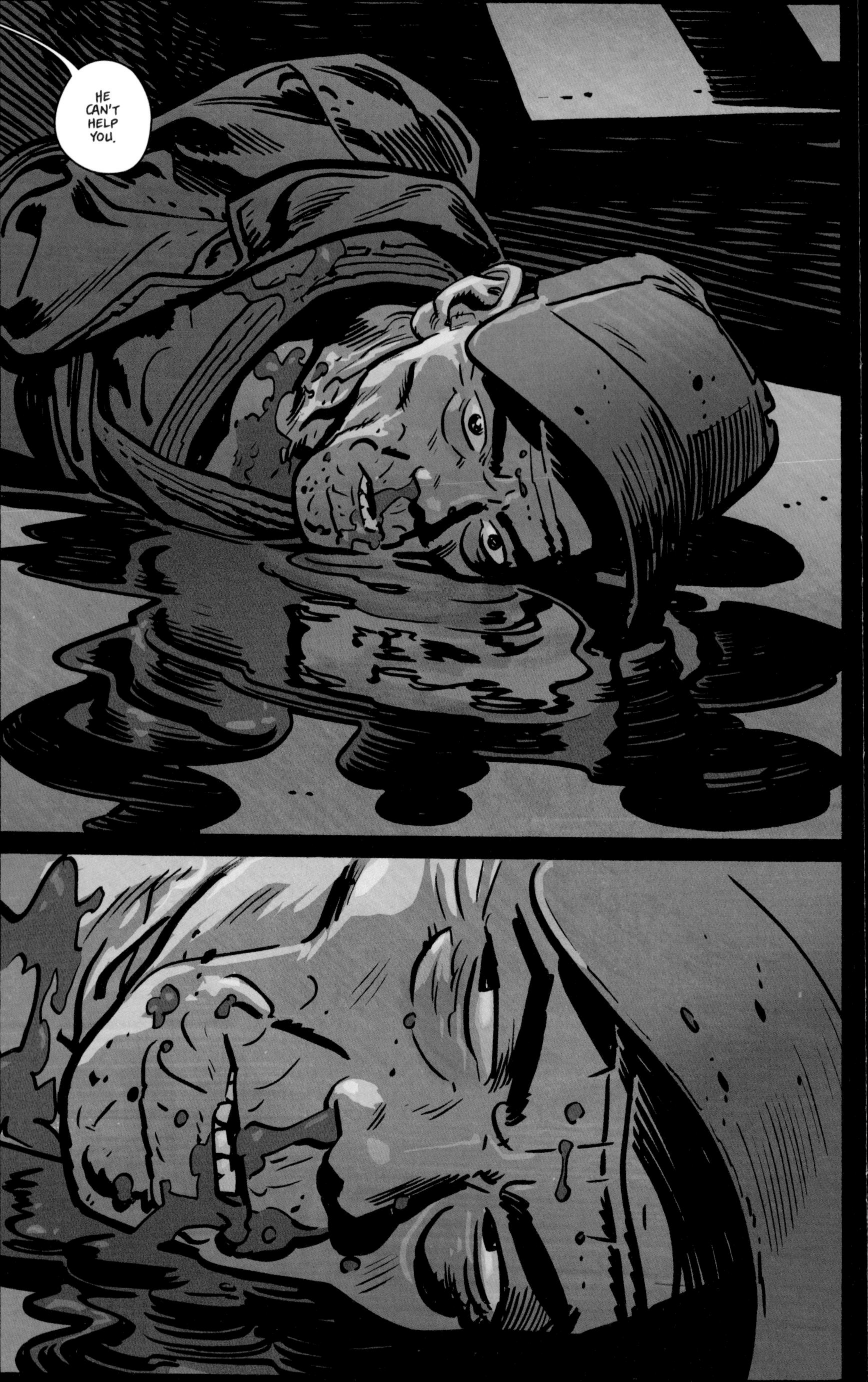
HE CAN'T HELP YOU.

TO BE CONTINUED

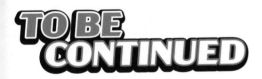

SKETCHBOOK GALLERY

ROBERT KIRKMAN: Holy smokes, working with Samnee on this book has been an amazing treat. Now you get to see all the glorious work he put into developing the characters for FIRE POWER!

CHRIS SAMNEE: My very first attempt at our guy Owen. I hadn't yet figured out how realistic I wanted to get or how far to push his features, and we ended up quite a ways off from this, but I've included it here for posterity's sake.

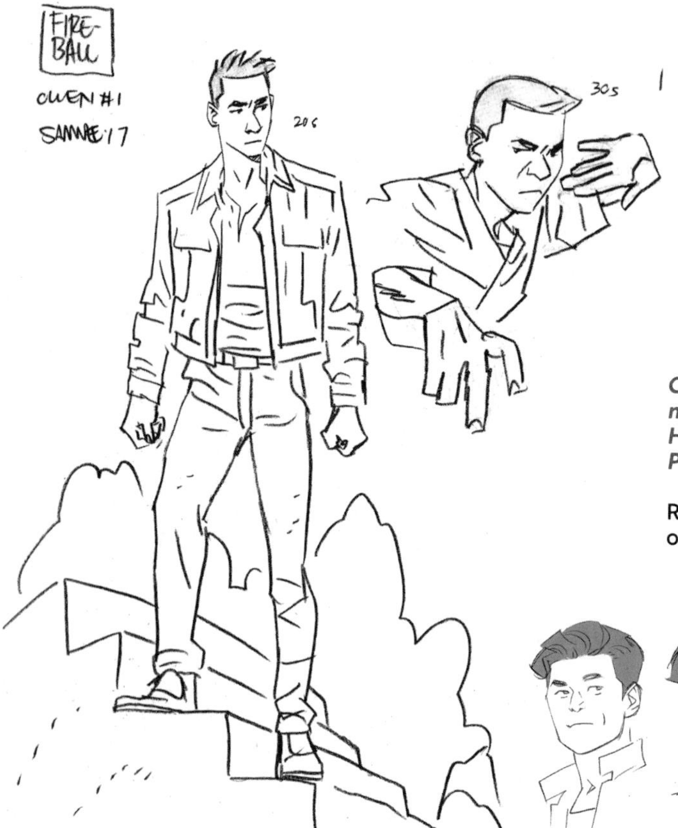

FIRE-BALL
OWEN #1
SAMNEE '17
20s
30s

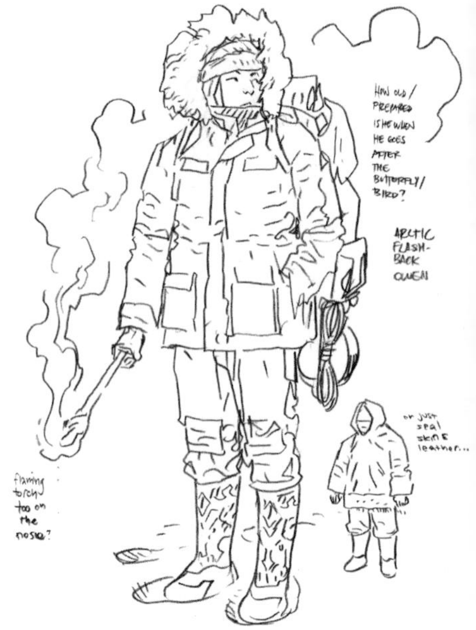

HOW OLD / PREPARED IS HE WHEN HE GOES AFTER THE BUTTERFLY / BIRD?
ARCTIC FLASH-BACK OWEN
flaming torch too on the nose?
or just seal skin & leather...

CHRIS: Arctic Flashback Owen sounds so much like a repainted '90s Batman toy— Hey, when are we making some FIRE POWER action figures?!

ROBERT: Let's not get too far ahead of ourselves!

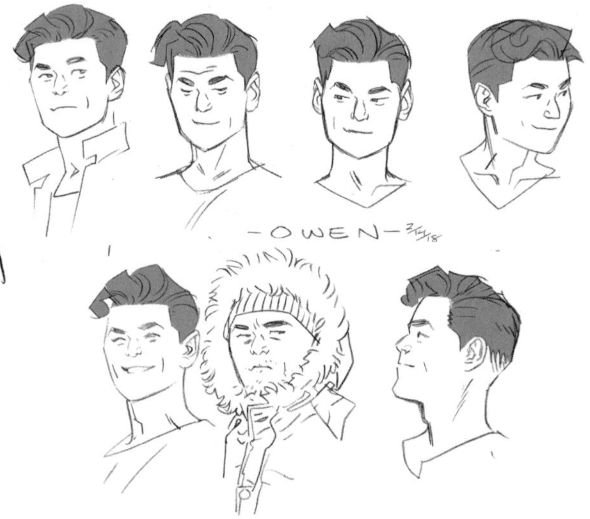

-OWEN-

CHRIS: The final turnaround that I printed out and pinned up on my bulletin board to keep Owen on model. These faces are what stared back at me the entire time I was working on the OGN.

ROBERT: All kinds of magic on this page. Haley was originally named Nancy until I realized Nate and Bonnie's daughter in DIE!DIE!DIE! (read that book, too) was also named Nancy, oops! What was the daughter in *Destroyer*'s name? I really don't have a deep bench when it comes to names.

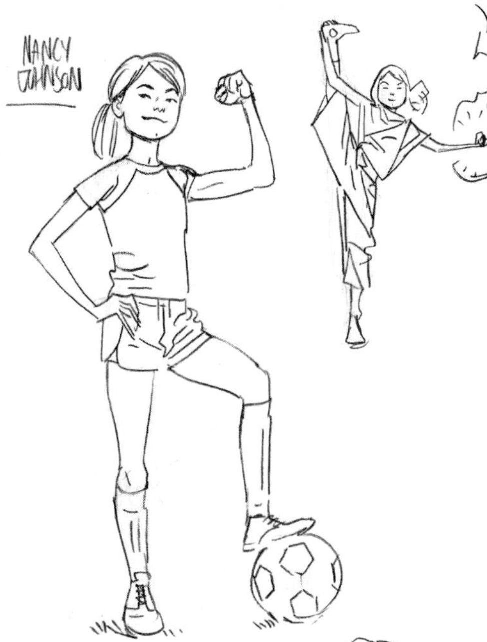
NANCY JOHNSON

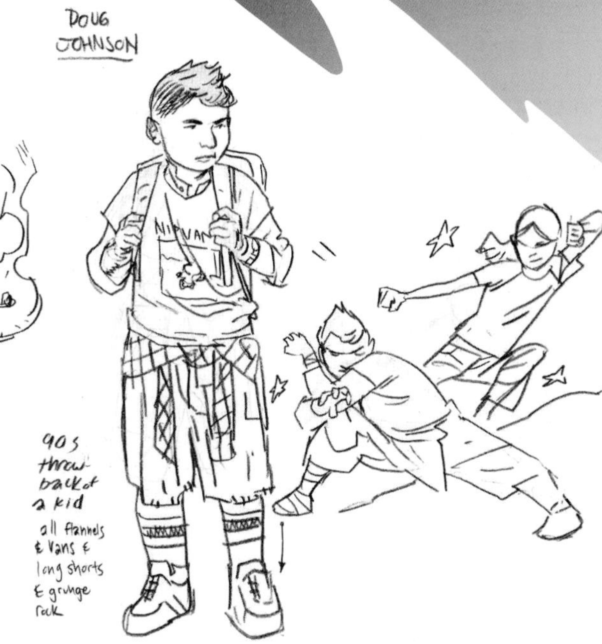
DOUG JOHNSON
90s throwback of a kid
all flannels & Vans & long shorts & grunge rock

ROBERT: The original designs for Owen's adoptive parents Bill and Pam Johnson were very cool, but a little quirky. I intended to make them Owen and Kellie's neighbors, but haven't really had much room to feature them in the series yet. Final Bill and Pam Johnson are just perfection. Peanut Butter was a slam dunk on Chris's first try. Holy heck is that guy good.

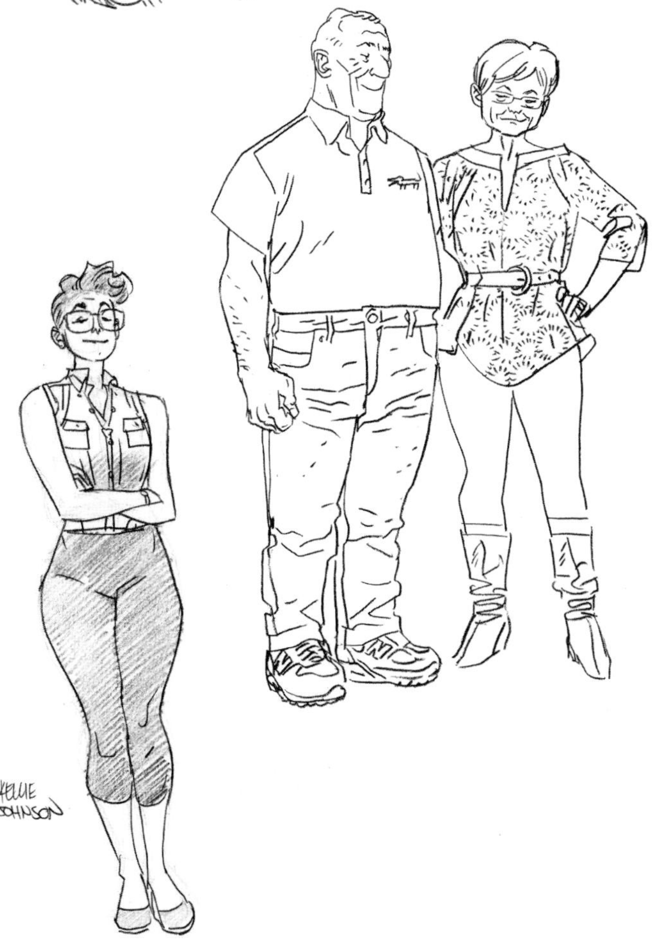
KELLIE JOHNSON

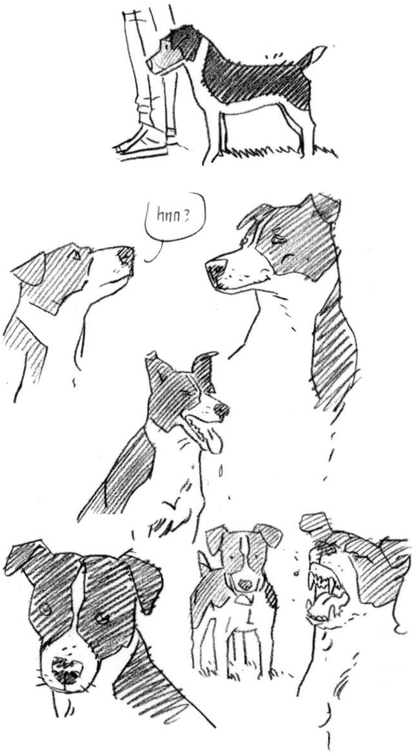
hmn?

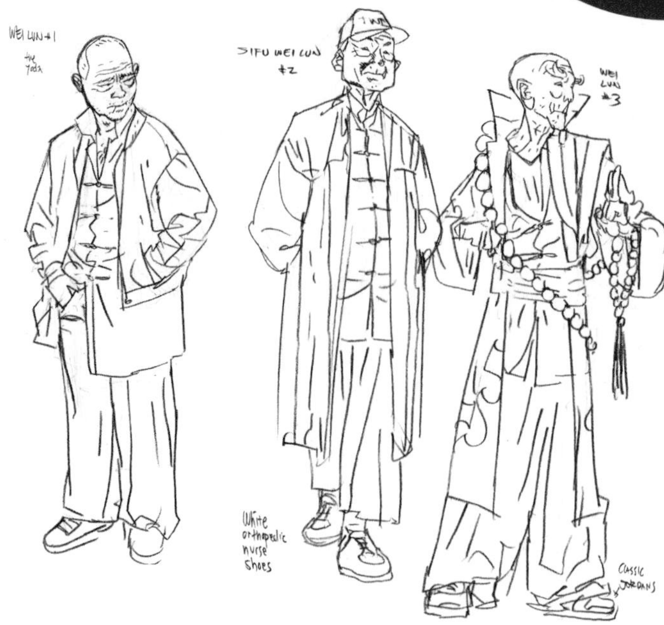
WEI LUN #1
SIFU WEI LUN #2
WEI LUN #3
White orthopedic nurse shoes
Classic JORDANS

CHRIS: So many different ways we could have gone with Wei Lun— gonna have to put these others to good use at some point down the line.

ROBERT: Oh, we will, don't you worry. I've already got plans for these alternate looks as different characters.

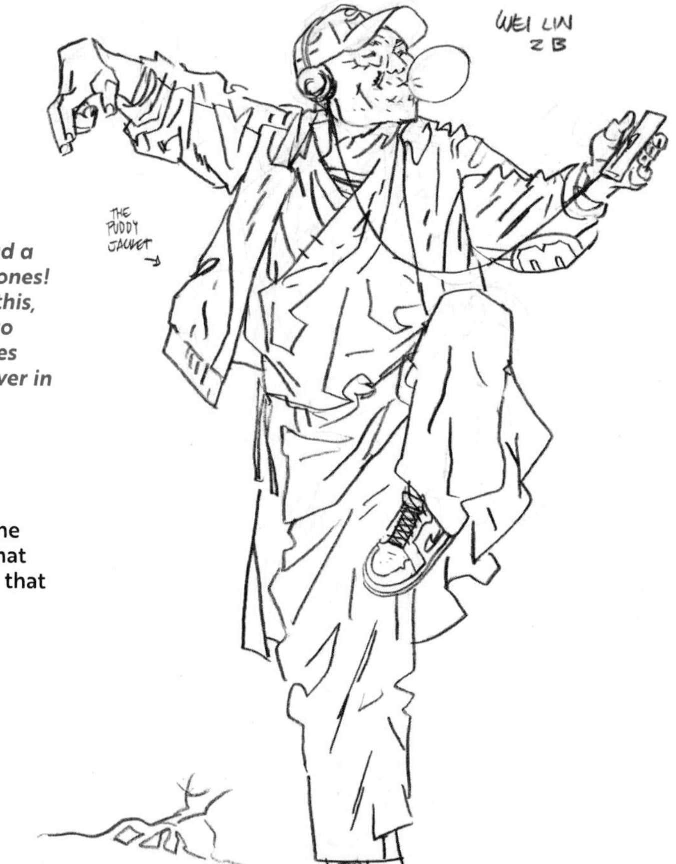
WEI LUN 2B
THE PUDDY JACKET

CHRIS: Oy, the shoes! UGH, the headphones!! For whatever reason, I had a mental block on the shoes and headphones! I'm sure Sean and Robert can attest to this, but I swear it took me literally months to patch in all of the headphones and shoes that my sleep-deprived brain glossed over in the final pages.

Everyone gets Converse All-Stars going forward, okay? :P

ROBERT: NEVER! Nike for life! For me, the most important thing about Wei Lun is that he looks friendly. It was important to me that he be more loveable than anything.

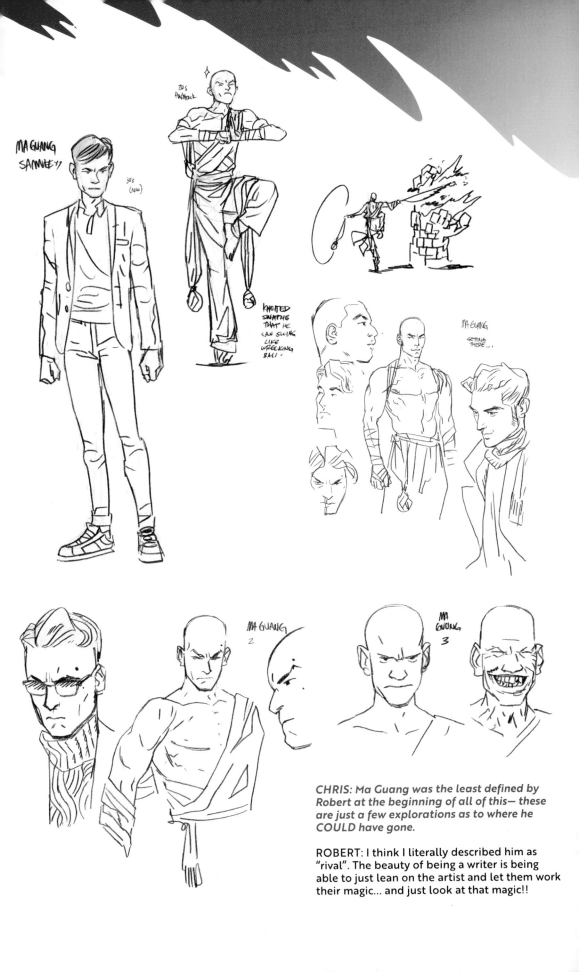

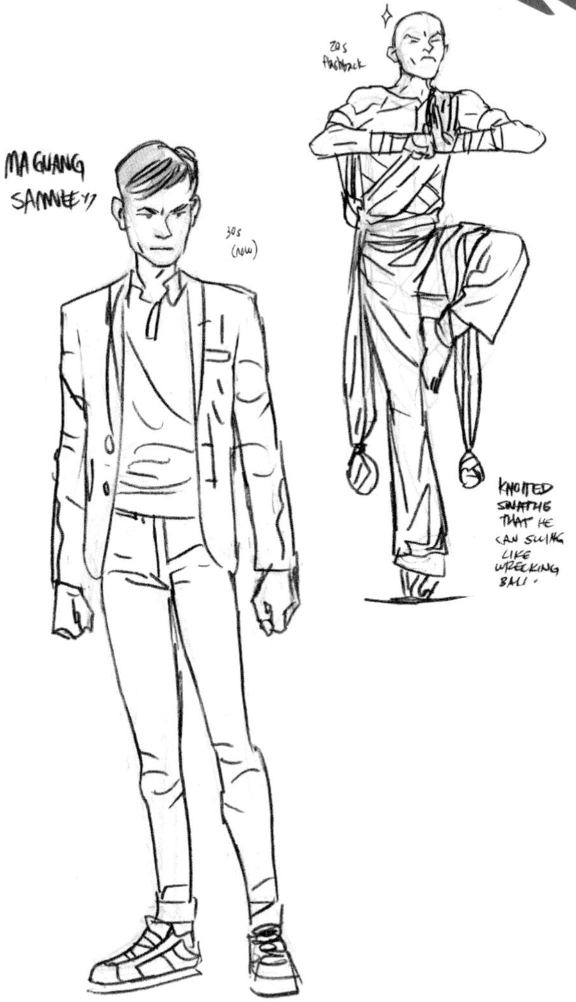
MA GUANG
SAMNEE '17
30s
(NW)
20s
flashback
KNOTTED SWATHE THAT HE CAN SWING LIKE WRECKING BALL.

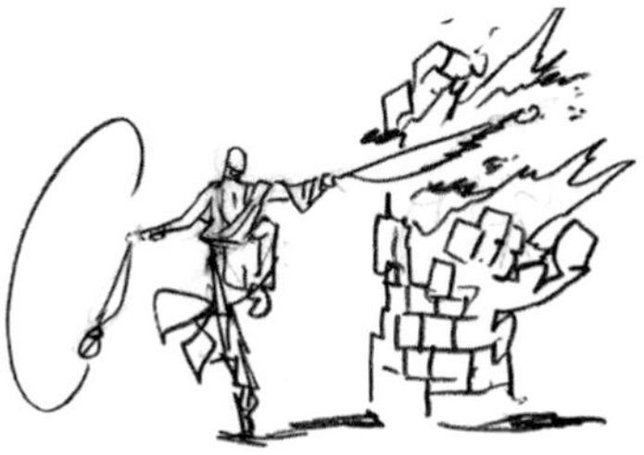

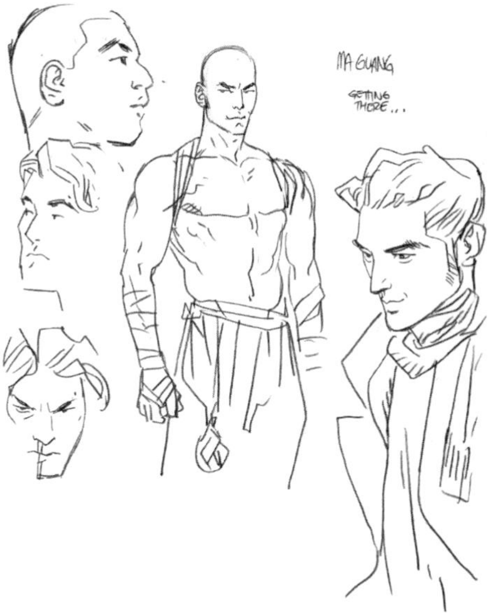
MA GUANG
GETTING THERE...

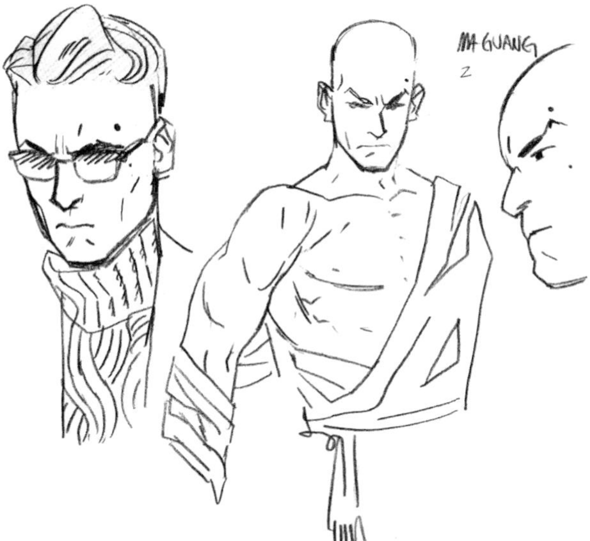
MA GUANG
2

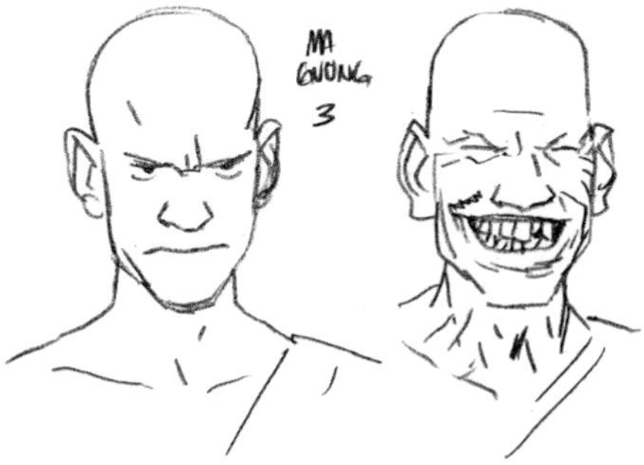
MA GUANG
3

CHRIS: Ma Guang was the least defined by Robert at the beginning of all of this— these are just a few explorations as to where he COULD have gone.

ROBERT: I think I literally described him as "rival". The beauty of being a writer is being able to just lean on the artist and let them work their magic... and just look at that magic!!

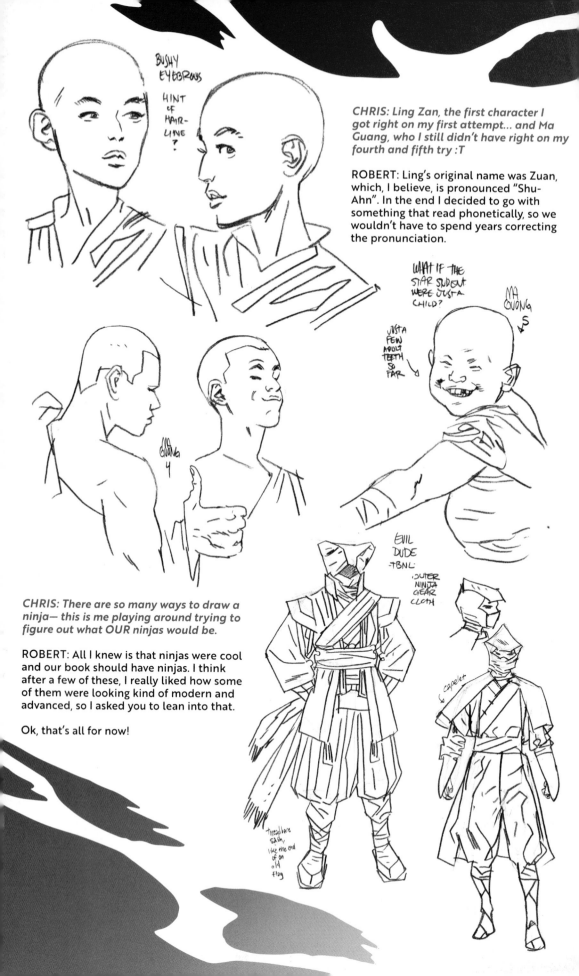

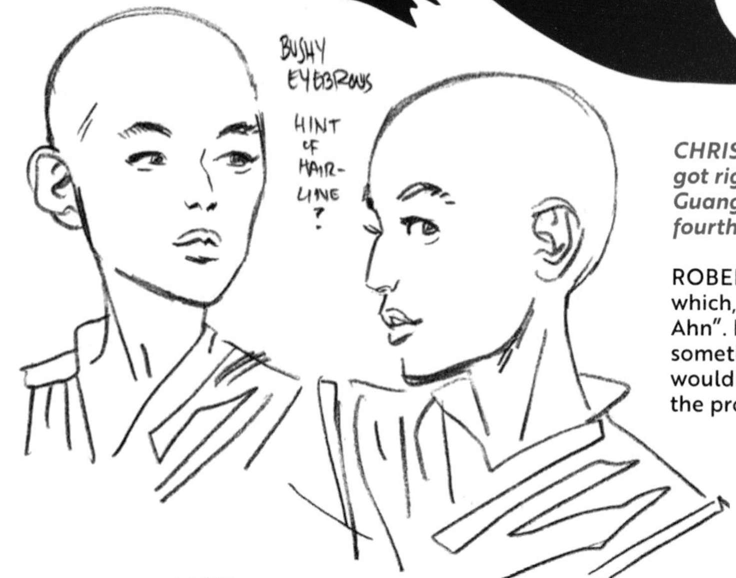
BUSHY EYEBROWS
HINT OF HAIR-LINE ?

CHRIS: Ling Zan, the first character I got right on my first attempt... and Ma Guang, who I still didn't have right on my fourth and fifth try :T

ROBERT: Ling's original name was Zuan, which, I believe, is pronounced "Shu-Ahn". In the end I decided to go with something that read phonetically, so we wouldn't have to spend years correcting the pronunciation.

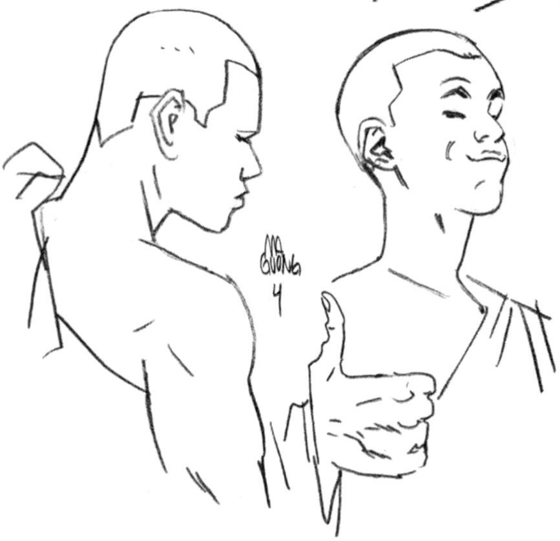
MA GUONG 4

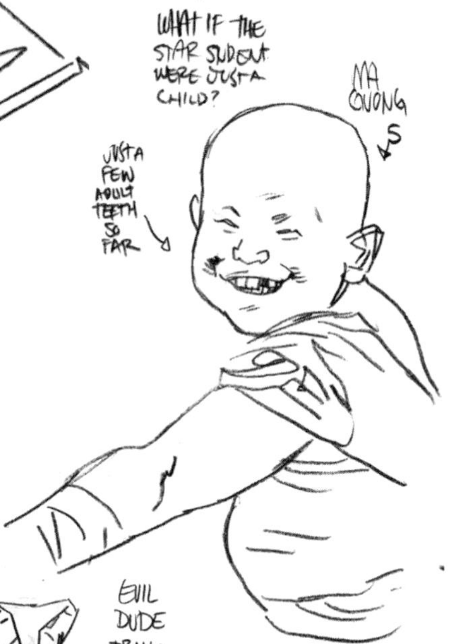
WHAT IF THE STAR STUDENT WERE JUST A CHILD?
MA GUONG 5
JUST A FEW ADULT TEETH SO FAR

CHRIS: There are so many ways to draw a ninja— this is me playing around trying to figure out what OUR ninjas would be.

ROBERT: All I knew is that ninjas were cool and our book should have ninjas. I think after a few of these, I really liked how some of them were looking kind of modern and advanced, so I asked you to lean into that.

Ok, that's all for now!

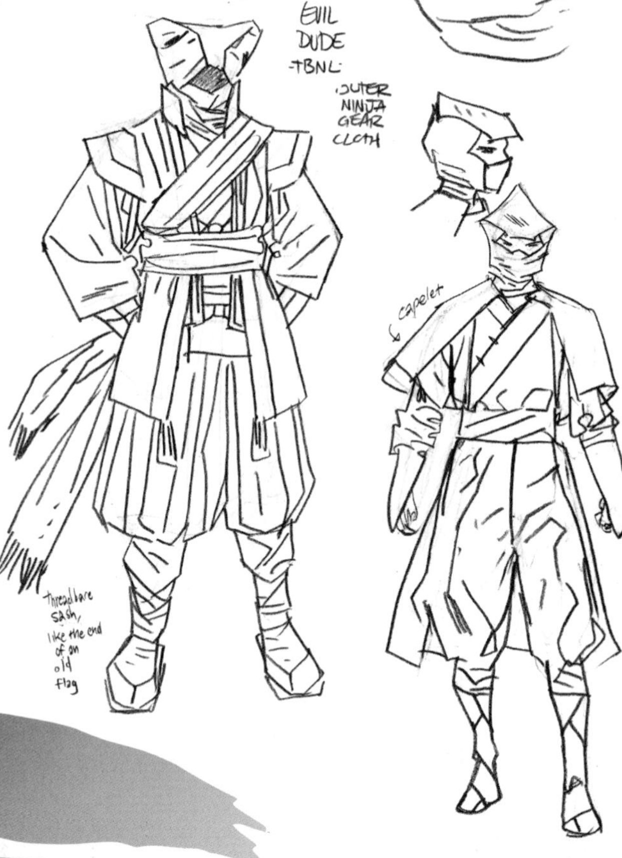
EVIL DUDE -TBNL
OUTER NINJA GEAR CLOTH
capelet
threadbare sash, like the end of an old flag